WESTWARD TO VINLAND

HELGE INGSTAD

WESTWARD TO VINLAND

The Discovery of Pre-Columbian
Norse House-sites in North America

Translated from the Norwegian by ERIK J. FRIIS

HARPER COLOPHON BOOKS
Harper & Row, Publishers, Inc.
New York, Evanston, San Francisco, London

TO ANNE STINE

Contents

List of Illustrations

ILLUSTRATIONS IN THE TEXT

Foreword

This book is meant to provide its readers with a popular account of my archaeological expeditions to North America that led to the discovery of a group of pre-Columbian house-sites of Norse origin in Newfoundland. The scientific treatise will be published at a later date.

It was around the year 1000 that Leif Eiriksson, according to the Icelandic sagas, discovered a new land in the west which must have been North America. He stayed for a time in an area that he called Vinland. Other Norsemen and women followed in his wake. The historical and geographical background for these voyages to Vinland must be sought in the Norse settlements in Greenland, founded in the year A.D. 986 by Eirik the Red and remaining in existence for almost five hundred years.

Where was the Vinland of the sagas? This question has occupied the thoughts of many outstanding scholars for about two hundred years. It has been commonly believed that Vinland had to be looked for quite far to the south on the North American continent – in the region of wild grapes.

Following my expedition of 1953 to the old Norse settlements in Greenland, I arrived at another conclusion. In my book *Land under the Pole Star* I gave my reasons for believing in a *northerly* Vinland, most probably situated in Newfoundland. I maintained at the same time that it ought to be possible to find traces of the Vinland voyagers, provided that a systematic investigation were carried out along the coasts of North America by boat and aeroplane.

I undertook such an investigation for the first time in 1960, and after a long search fortune at last smiled on me. At the northernmost tip of Newfoundland, in a place called L'Anse aux Meadows, I found traces of some very overgrown house-sites. I subsequently organized seven archaeological expeditions (1961–8) in which scientists from five countries participated. Eight house-sites were excavated, and interesting finds were made. In the ruins of the largest house-site, the 1968 expedition found a bronze ring-headed pin of the late Viking type, commonly used as a cloak fastening. They also located and examined a group of four boat sheds lying in a row above the shoreline, to the north-west of the main site. A scholarly interpretation of the entire material can hardly lead to any other conclusion than that the sites are of Norse origin and date from the period around A.D. 1000, that is, the time when Leif Eiriksson and other Norsemen sailed to Vinland – to North America. The main participants in the various expeditions were as follows: From Norway: besides the author, his wife *mag. art.* Anne Stine Ingstad (who was in charge of the archaeological work), and his daughter Benedicte, State Geologist Kari Henningsmoen, Dr Odd Martens, Paul Sørnes, and the photographers Erling Brunborg, Hans Hvide Bang and Nicolay Eckhoff. From Iceland: Dr Kristján Eldjárn, Professor Thórhallur Vilmundarson, and Gísli Gestson. From Sweden: *phil. cand.* Rolf Petré. From Canada: Dr William Taylor, Dr Ian Whitaker, and Tony Beardsley. From the United States: Dr Henry Collins, Dr Junius Bird, *phil. cand.* Birgitta Wallace (a Swedish-born and Swedish-educated archaeologist), and the archaeologists Charles Bareis and John Winston.

The expeditions received aid and assistance from many quarters. They were to a great extent financed from Norway, but I also received valuable aid from the Government of Newfoundland, the National Historic Park Branch, Ottawa, the Royal Canadian Air Force, the Royal Canadian Navy, the Grenfell Mission, the Early Sites Foundation, New Hampshire, and Dr Terris Moore through the Arctic Institute of North America.

For its major contribution to three expeditions, I am indebted to the National Geographic Society, Washington, D.C., not only for its financial help, but also because the Society gave the expedition valuable scientific and practical aid.

In Norway the expeditions received help from the following: A/S O. Andersen & Co.'s Eftf., A. O. Andersens Shipping Company A/S, Askim Gummivarefabrik A/S, ship-owner Nils Astrup, A/S Auto Supply Co., Johan H. Bentzon, A/S, Bergens Mekaniske Verksteder A/S, Bergens Privatbank, ship-owner Sig Bergesen d. y., the shipping company Harry Borthen & Co., A/S Christiania Portland Cementfabrik, Christiania Spigerverk, the Norwegian Foreign Department, the shipping company Ditlev-Simonsen, Elektrokemisk A/S, Fiskereidskap P/L, Framhuset, A/S Freia, G. R. Fuglesangs Sønner, W. G. Giertsen A/S, Gyldendal Norsk Forlag, the shipping company Sigurd Herlofsen & Co., A/S, Yngvar Husebye, the shipping company Kristian Jebsen A/S, the Kon-Tiki fund, ship-owner Ludvig Lorentzen, ship-owner Øivind Lorentzen, Mandals Reperbane, director F. H. Münster, the Nansen fund, A/S Nestlé, Norges Almenvitenskapelige Forskningsråd, Norsk Braendselolje A/S, Norsk Polarinstitutt, A/S Norske Esso, Norske Meieriers Salgsentral, the shipping company Oddfjell A/S, the ship-owners Thomas Olsen and Fred Olsen, the shipping company Olsen & Ugelstad, A/S Rieber & Co., director Gunnar Schjelderup, ship-owner Peder Smedvig, Smith-Corona Inc., Stabburet A/S, director Otto Staib, Steen & Strøm A/S, A/S

Sydvaranger, J. L. Tiedemanns Tobaksfabrik, ship-owner Nordahl Wallem, the shipping company Wallem Steckmest & Co. A/S, ship-owner Niels Werring.

It should be mentioned that the ship-owners Niels Werring and Thomas Olsen, besides giving aid to the 'Vinland expeditions', financed my former expedition to Greenland which was in preparation for the later ones.

With regard to the transport of materials, etc., across the Atlantic, valuable aid was received from the Norwegian American Line A/S, Braathens S.A.F.E., A/S Loftleidir Icelandic Airlines, the shipping company Olsen & Ugelstad and the Scandinavian Airlines System.

Among the many other Norwegians or people of Norwegian descent who have rendered assistance in different ways I may mention Dr Thor Heyerdahl, Director Alexander Holst, Ambassador Kaare Ingstad, ship-owner Karl Karlsen (Halifax), Director Svein Molaug, Dr Hallvard Magerøy, press officer Sven Oftdeal, press officer Odd Medbøe, and magister Søren Richter.

In other countries I also owe thanks to many: The Icelandic Government; in Sweden, Professor Hans W:son Ahlmann, archivist Sverker Jansson, Professor Holger Arbman and Professor Mårten Stenberger. In Canada, the Premier of Newfoundland, Mr Joseph Smallwood, Director-general J. G. Channing, the Grenfell and the Moravian Missions, Dr Gordon Thomas, Dr W. A. Paddon, Miss Pamela Sweet, Miss Louise Greenfield, Hon. J. W. Pickerskill, Deputy Minister E. A. Coté, Professor R. A. MacKay, Secretary Graham Rowley and his wife.

The inhabitants of L'Anse aux Meadows will always be remembered for the helpfulness and friendliness they showed us during the excavations. It is with great sadness that we also recall the cheerful help and companionship of our good friend the late George Decker.

We collaborated with the Collection of Antiquities, Oslo University, and the great interest and helpfulness shown us by Professor Bjørn Hougen aided us greatly in furthering our work.

Last but not least, I owe thanks to my splendid co-workers, all of whom have a share in the final result. But my most heartfelt thanks go to my wife, Anne Stine.

HELGE INGSTAD

Chapter One

The Way to the West

About a thousand years ago a remarkable fleet of twenty-five ocean-going Viking ships set sail and departed from north-west Iceland. They carried a motley cargo of men, women, and children—perhaps five hundred persons in all—as well as cattle, sheep, and horses, in addition to provisions, hay, and weapons and tools commonly used in the Viking Age.

Standing silently beneath the billowing sails, the voyagers saw their homeland slowly disappear below the horizon; mixed feelings of sadness and hope must have prevailed among one and all—for these were emigrants who were leaving Iceland for good and were heading for a completely new country. The country had already been named Greenland.

This expedition set out in the year 986 (or possibly 985), and its leader was Eirik the Red. He had originally come to Iceland from Norway but had been declared an outlaw in his new country, whereupon he had sailed his ship westward across the open ocean in order to seek a land which other sailors had barely glimpsed. He became the actual discoverer of Greenland, and he spent three whole years exploring its south-western coasts. Following his return to Iceland he took the initiative in organizing this large expedition and assumed leadership of the pioneers who were to colonize the new land. He must indeed have been a remarkable man.

The voyage was a hazardous one, through the drift-ice and the stormy seas along the coasts of Greenland. Fourteen ships arrived at last in the south-western part of the island; the rest were either shipwrecked or forced to turn back. The newcomers settled along strips of land in the shadow of the great inland glacier and prepared for a new life. They constructed their dwellings from stones and turf; the men fished, and hunted caribou and seals with bows and arrows or with harpoons, while the women tended the cattle and kept busy with spinning and weaving and other household chores.

Two separate settlements came into being: the so-called Eastern Settlement (Eystribyggð) on the south-west coast of Greenland, and the Western Settlement (Vestribyggð) somewhat farther north. A community emerged, an independent republic was set up, and the population increased. This Greenlandic society existed for almost five hundred years – then the people completely vanished. Their fate has remained a mystery to this day.

Eirik the Red had selected for himself one of the most beautiful and fertile areas in the Eastern Settlement. It was situated at the head of Eiriksfjord, now known as Tunugdliarfik, and here he built his chieftain's manor and called it Brattahlid ('Steep Hillside'). It was from here that his son Leif and other Norsemen set out to search for new lands in the west – and to discover large areas of the North American continent. These events took place around the year 1000.

In the summer of 1953, my wife Anne Stine and I, together with an experienced seaman by the name of Harald Botten, had been sailing along the west coast of Greenland in a small motor-boat. The purpose of the trip had been to investigate the old Norse ruins in Greenland, to learn more about the conditions that had actually prevailed in the Greenlandic settlements of long ago, and to find out how the medieval Norsemen had lived. Each of several hundred ruins investigated had told us something about life on this Arctic island a long time ago. We came upon ruins of large farm buildings, great halls and many out-buildings, but also ruins of smaller cottages, most probably the dwellings of people of low birth. Most of the ruins were situated near the shore, but quite a few were a long distance inland, even at the very edge of the great ice-cap and in places where it is hard to imagine that human beings were able to exist.

It had been an absorbing experience, in a strange country, along whose coasts drift-ice and bluish-white icebergs move slowly northward, where green fields are bright spots in an otherwise rocky and treeless landscape, and towering peaks seem to be striding eastward, towards the gleaming white shield that is the great inland glacier.

We arrived at Brattahlid, the ancient chieftain's manor where Eirik the Red and his son Leif Eiriksson had lived. Green slopes, red sandstone rocks and a glittering brook lay bathed in the bright light of the sun. We got the immediate impression that Brattahlid must have been a large farm, since all around we noticed ruins of many different kinds, such as remains of byres, out-houses, stone fences, storehouses, a smithy, and a church. Brattahlid manor used to lie on the high ground behind the smaller houses, its front facing the fjord; from the main building there must have been a splendid view of the fjord and the mighty mountains surrounding it. The archaeologists Poul Nørlund and Mårten Stenberger[1] have excavated the main building and have unearthed a great hall and five connecting rooms, and beneath these traces of an older building.

This was the place where the voyages to Vinland originated, the starting-point for the Norse expeditions to North America. Around the long fire hardy sailors had at one time assembled and had talked into the late hours about the

Plate 1. Manuscript page of *Hauksbók*, about A.D. 1330. A part of Eirik the Red's Saga, this page is written on parchment and tells of the Norsemen's encounter with the Skraelings. (Photograph: Arnamagnaean Collection, Copenhagen.)

Plate 2 (*over*). The head of a Viking, carved in wood. It adorned a cart found in the Oseberg ship (see Plate 8). The cart was part of the equipment that a high-born woman took with her on the voyage to the realm of the dead. (Photograph: Collection of Antiquities, University of Oslo.)

new and strange country that had been sighted by Bjarni Herjolfsson when his ship had been driven off course by wind and weather, a land on which no one as yet had set foot. What was the new country like? they had wondered. Would it be a difficult undertaking to sail so far and return safely? Was it a good and fertile land, a place where perhaps one could settle down and live permanently?

Nothing could be more inspiring to these men who were pioneers to the core and had adventure in their blood.

It was Eirik's son Leif who decided to make the voyage. His ship was fitted out, the women busying themselves with the large woollen square-sail, mending and strengthening it, while the men and eager youngsters carried provisions and equipment on board, including dried fish, smoked meat, butter, cheese, and water for the large barrels. They also brought axes, tongs and a sledge-hammer for a smithy, various kinds of gear for hunting and fishing, weapons, and many other things. It was rather sparse equipment for a long voyage into the unknown, but these people knew how to live off the land. A large hide, sewn together from many smaller skins, was stretched over the equipment and then lashed securely. The square-sail was hoisted, and the ship stood out in Eiriksfjord, while from rocks and crags the people of Brattahlid watched it depart. There were thirty-five persons on board.

The next autumn a weatherbeaten, storm-tossed ship entered Eiriksfjord, and everyone recognized it immediately. Yes, the new land in the west had been found; it was a big and strange country, with riches of many kinds, pastures for cattle, forests, game, seals, walrus, and fish. Leif had built large houses in the new country, and he had called it Vinland. By the long fire in the great hall at Brattahlid everyone discussed Leif's voyage—and before long other men set out towards the new land.

I was standing amid the ruins of the ancient farm, looking out across Eiriksfjord, absorbed in thoughts about these events of long ago. What part of the North American continent did Leif Eiriksson actually discover? Just where along the coast had he built his houses?

Down through the years many outstanding scholars had attempted to solve this problem, but not even one single indisputable trace of the Norsemen had been found in the whole of North America. There might have been many reasons for this; it is certainly no simple matter to discover traces of thousand-year-old houses along this enormously long coastline. Then again, was it so certain that the accepted view was correct, that is, that the Vinland of the sagas had to be sought far to the south, in a region abounding in wild grapes?

Once again I turned over in my mind the many reasons which in my estimation indicated a different approach and other conclusions. And as I stood among the old ruins of Leif Eiriksson's home after having familiarized myself with the living conditions in the old settlements, these reasons of mine seemed even more compelling. The voyagers to Vinland must have settled in an area much farther to the north than has been previously thought, and there is much to indicate that it must have been Newfoundland.*

In the summer of 1960, I was standing on the north coast of Newfoundland, on a grassy plain known as L'Anse aux Meadows. From there one has an extraordinarily fine view towards the north, of the islands, the ocean, and the blue coastline of Labrador. I had come here after an investigation lasting many months along far-flung coasts, searching for traces of Leif Eiriksson or of other Norsemen who had sailed in his wake to North America. There had been many disappointments – until now. In the grass covering an old marine terrace adjacent to a river-mouth, I detected the faint, at times hardly visible, contours of old house-sites.

Archaeological investigations and excavations during seven expeditions in the years 1961 to 1968 were to show that these dwellings were Norse and that they dated from about the year 1000 – the time when Leif Eiriksson and, later on, others sailed from Greenland to Vinland, the new land in the west. This was about five hundred years before Columbus discovered America.

In order to be able to see the discovery of Greenland and North America in a clearer light, we must take a closer look at the men behind the deeds: Eirik the Red and his family. Eirik must have been a forceful personality, proud and impressive in many ways – a type of leader not found very often. In the saga it says very appropriately that everyone in Greenland bent to his will.

He was born in the south-western part of Norway (the district of Jæren), from where so many Vikings set out, and the year of his birth may have been about 950. His father's name was Thorvald, and his family was a prominent one in the district. Thorvald had to flee the country for having committed manslaughter, and he sailed to Iceland with his wife and children. The earliest settlers in Iceland, most of whom had come from Norway, had already appropriated the best land, and he had to go on to the more remote area in the north-west. He settled at Drangar by the shores of the Hornstrandir.

Thorvald died. Eirik married Thjodhild and moved south to Haukadal where he built his homestead at Eirikstadir. But he got into a quarrel and killed two men and was banished from his home. He went west to the district around Breidafjord and built his new home at Oxney. But once again he got into

* Detailed arguments to support my theory have been presented in the book which I wrote following my Greenland expedition, *Landet under Leidarstjernen* (Gyldendal Norsk Forlag, Oslo, 1959). It has been translated into English by Naomi Walford and published by Jonathan Cape Ltd, London, and St Martin's Press, New York, under the title *Land under the Pole Star* (1966).

disputes and fights with Icelandic families, and this resulted in his being made an outlaw at the Thorsnes *Thing* — in other words, he was chased out of Iceland.

Then it was, as mentioned before, that he sailed westward, discovered and explored the south-west coast of Greenland (982–5) and thereupon organized and led the great immigrant expedition to that country.

Eirik had four children: Leif, Thorstein, Thorvald, and Freydis, the last-named having been born out of wedlock. It is related in the Greenlanders' Saga that all four set out on voyages for Vinland, and Thorstein was the only one who did not reach his destination.

We do not know much about Leif Eiriksson except what the saga tells us about his voyage. It has this to say about him: 'Leif was big and strong, the most excellent man to look at, and in addition wise and moderate in everything as well as highly respected.' In the sagas he is given the nickname '*hinn heppni*' ('the lucky').

We know nothing about where and when he was born or died. He may have been born in Iceland or on board ship during one of his father's voyages; there are many instances of wives being taken on distant voyages. At any rate, it is most probable that Eirik did not leave his wife behind when he sailed for Greenland as an outlaw and remained there for three years. If Leif was born in Greenland, he would have been nearly twenty years old when he made his Vinland voyage — the age of a man at that time. His place of birth is of minor importance; what is of significance is the fact that he grew up in Greenland, and the strenuous life in an Arctic country put its stamp upon him. It was a country where good seamanship was a matter of course and where voyages of discovery were part of the family tradition. It is true that his father Eirik the Red had come from Norway, but the settlements in Greenland constituted an independent state in every respect, and Leif was a Greenlander.[2]

In the sources[3] we find an interesting piece of information to the effect that Leif sailed for Norway fourteen years after Eirik the Red had set out to settle in Greenland. In Trondheim he met the king, Olaf Tryggvason, who received him with much honour and assigned to him the task of converting the Greenlanders to Christianity. The next summer, probably in the year 1000, Leif sailed back to Greenland; his mother Thjodhild* espoused the new faith, but Eirik remained loyal to the pagan gods.

Leif must have died before A.D. 1025, since the Icelandic Fosterbrothers' Saga[4] relates that when Thormod Kolbrunarskald arrived in Greenland on a voyage of vengeance Leif's son Thorkel was the chieftain at Eiriksfjord and

---

* According to Eirik the Red's Saga, Thjodhild had her own church built at Brattahlid, not too close to the farm. The ruins of this church, very probably the first ever built in Greenland, together with the cemetery and many skeletons, were discovered in 1961. The site is now being excavated by Danish archaeologists.

lived at Brattahlid. This is the last time we hear about this renowned family — it completely disappears from the pages of history.

Since the Norse voyages to North America originated in the Greenland settlements, I shall dwell on a few aspects of that ancient society. A knowledge of those times is of importance in the evaluation not only of the voyages made around the year 1000 but also of others that occurred later on.

When Eirik the Red and his followers had settled permanently in Greenland, it seems that the population increased at a comparatively high rate through immigration from Iceland and Norway. The Arctic land made great demands on the settlers, and they were hardened by the struggle for existence. But many aspects of their life were a continuation of ancient traditions in the home countries — such as long sea voyages, the construction of houses from stones and turf, the clearing of rocks and stones from patches of meadow, the hunting of whales, seal, and wild reindeer, as well as fishing.

Subsistence was based on the raising of livestock as well as hunting and fishing. It was not possible to grow grain, but the sparse vegetation was nutritious and enabled them to keep many cows, sheep, and horses. They also made butter and cheese.

The most important implements and weapons were: axes, knives, scythes, sledge-hammers, blacksmith's tongs, harpoons and fishing gear, bows and arrows, and spears. Excavations revealing smithies and slag indicate that the Greenlanders produced iron from bog-iron. Spindle-whorls made from soapstone tell about women's activities — they used to spin thread and weave cloth besides doing their usual work on the farm.

When the first pioneers arrived in Greenland there must have been many, possibly stunted, birch trees growing on the slopes and hillsides. Along the shores there must have been heaps of driftwood, brought by the currents across the Arctic Ocean from the large rivers of Siberia. The birch trees could be used as fuel and for other limited purposes, but the driftwood was the only material available for the building of boats and ships. For this reason these had to be made smaller than before. The demand for wood must always have been very great, and the supply of this material was in time greatly diminished by the wasteful cutting down of the forests, as well as the keen competition to secure driftwood. The solution to this problem, however, was near at hand: namely, the importation of timber from the extensive forests in the new lands — Labrador and Newfoundland.

Hunting was always of great importance, for besides food it provided the people of Greenland with objects of barter and exchange which at times fetched a high price in European markets. Hunting activities were not limited to the settled and neighbouring areas; every summer expeditions were fitted out and departed for the far northern coasts of Greenland, the so-called Nordrsetur.

We know for certain that the Greenlanders went at least as far north as Kingigtorssuaq Island (latitude 72° 58′ N.). On that island have been found three tumbledown cairns, and in one of them there was a rune-stone on which were carved the names of three Norsemen together with some magic runes. Besides this evidence, historical sources indicate that the Greenlanders sailed as far as about 76° North. During these voyages it must have happened from time to time that, while crossing the narrow Davis Strait, the sailors glimpsed the lofty, snow-covered mountains of Baffin Island.

The articles exported from Greenland were of various kinds: walrus and narwhal teeth, walrus and seal skins, caribou and polar bear hides, white and blue fox furs, dried fish, down, white falcons, live polar bears, as well as the woollen cloth called wadmal, and butter and cheese. Ever since the earliest years of the settlement ships would sail direct from Greenland to Norway; in the latter country it was the city of Bergen which became the centre for the Greenland trade.

The god Thor's hammer carved on a piece of soapstone. Found at Brattahlid in Greenland.

When Eirik the Red colonized Greenland, the people were, as previously mentioned, still heathens, Thor being the most powerful among their gods. After Leif Eiriksson and others had introduced Christianity, a number of churches were built in the settlements. In 1124 King Sigurd Jorsalfare[5] gave the Greenlanders their own bishop, partly perhaps as a consequence of receiving a live polar bear as a gift. A large bishop's mansion and a cathedral were built on the plain at Gardar (the present-day Igaliko). In 1153 the Church of Greenland was placed under the Archbishop of Nidaros (Trondheim).

The Norse Greenlanders created a free state with its own laws and its own parliament; juridically it was not dependent in any way on Iceland or Norway. But in 1261 the Greenlanders voluntarily placed their country under the suzerainty of King Håkon Håkonsson.[6] Greenland became a part of the Norwegian kingdom.

We know very little about the spiritual and intellectual life of the medieval Greenlanders. Not a single document originating in that Arctic island has been preserved—but it is not impossible that some time in the future a yellowed parchment may be found in the frozen earth. Several runic inscriptions have been discovered, but they do not yield much information. From other sources we get glimpses of information revealing that the Norse Greenlanders created their own poetry, as well as sagas, but in general it must be admitted that whatever engaged the minds of the people in the course of almost five centuries has vanished in the mist of ages. A realm of mind and spirit disappeared when the people died out. We shall never know what the weatherbeaten old man related by the long fire, with wide-eyed youngsters sitting round him on the earthen floor. Nor shall we ever know what song a Greenland girl would have sung when the cattle were grazing in the meadow and the blue mountains were bathed in the sunlight.

When Eirik the Red arrived in Greenland he did not see any Eskimoes, but he did find traces of them. It was not until some time in the thirteenth century that the Eskimoes (the so-called Thule Eskimoes) slowly trickled southward along the west coast and at last settled in the areas in which the Norsemen lived. The sources indicate that the Norsemen, by and large, got along well with them, and it would indeed have been rather strange if they had not taken full advantage of this unique opportunity to carry on a lucrative trade.

The Greenlandic society probably reached its zenith in the course of the thirteenth century; its high point coincides with the greatest expansion of the Norwegian kingdom, which under Håkon Håkonsson included the Shetlands, the Orkneys, the Hebrides, the Isle of Man, the Faroes, Iceland and Greenland. In Greenland have been found ruins of nearly three hundred farms, seventeen churches, one episcopal mansion, a nunnery, and a monastery. In the times of greatest prosperity, the population probably numbered between four and five thousand.

We do not have any source-material informing us how the people lived through the centuries. We do know, however, that in time a marked decline set in. In the end the last of the Greenlanders disappeared, supposedly around the year 1500. At any rate, there must have been Norse people living in Greenland at the end of the fifteenth century. The astonishing find made by Poul Nørlund[7] of hooded capes and caps in the old churchyard belonging to the great farm at Herjolfsnes attests that fact, since some of these garments are cut according to the fashions prevalent in Paris and Burgundy in the late fifteenth century.

What, then, was the reason for the disappearance of the people? Some scholars believe that the Eskimoes killed the Greenlanders, but this explanation is not very plausible. As mentioned above, the sources create the impression that, on the whole, relations between the two groups were harmonious, and certain heroic legends among the Eskimoes dating from as late as the nineteenth century which might indicate the contrary are of no significance in this respect. Did the Norsemen mix with the Eskimoes, adopting their way of life? To this question it may be replied that anthropological investigations of skeletons from the cemeteries have shown that the Norse race remained pure. If a mixture of the races had taken place, we should at least have found some indications to that effect. Did the people die out as a consequence of a process of degeneration? This has been a common belief, based on the results arrived at by the Danish anthropologist Fr C. C. Hansen[8] after he had investigated some skeletons from Herjolfsnes. But later anthropologists[9] have established that Hansen's conclusions are not tenable and that better preserved Norse skeletons indicate that the people were healthy and vigorous. Can it have been the plague, then, that struck the people down, as was the case in Norway and Iceland? About that we know nothing.

None of the above theories provides a satisfactory explanation. There is much to indicate that the disappearance of the people was caused by the confluence of a number of factors down through the centuries. We shall list some that may have been significant in this respect. Important export articles, such as walrus tusks, may have sunk in value, the result being that it became less profitable for merchants to set out on the long and arduous voyage across the ocean. Excessive cutting down of birch trees and the consequent elimination of any protection against wind and flying sand may have damaged pastures and meadows. The keen competition for driftwood may have impeded the construction of ships. Cold summers may have been the cause of the cod disappearing from the fjords. The Black Death, which descended on Norway in 1349–50, may have made it difficult to maintain ship connections with Greenland. The attacks of German pirates on the important harbour and city of Bergen in 1393 and again in 1428–9, when many of the citizens were killed and the town itself was burned down, may also have had considerable influence on the maintenance of communications between Norway and Greenland.

The final and decisive blow must have hit the Greenlanders later on, and it is quite probable that it was dealt them by pirates.[10] During the fifteenth and sixteenth centuries they continually harried the northern countries, and faraway places like the Faroes and Iceland suffered greatly from their attacks and their plundering. A few sources strongly indicate that pirates burned and pillaged the central Norse area in Greenland, and archaeological investigations have brought out the fact that several churches were burned. Such attacks may have been repeated and would have been catastrophic to the small Greenlandic community. Life in Greenland would no longer be possible.

When the Norwegian pastor Hans Egede sailed in 1721 as a missionary to

Map showing the sea-routes of the Norsemen in the Viking Age, including the so-called 'Western Way' from Norway to Iceland and the Norse settlements in Greenland and then on to North America — Helluland, Markland, and Vinland.

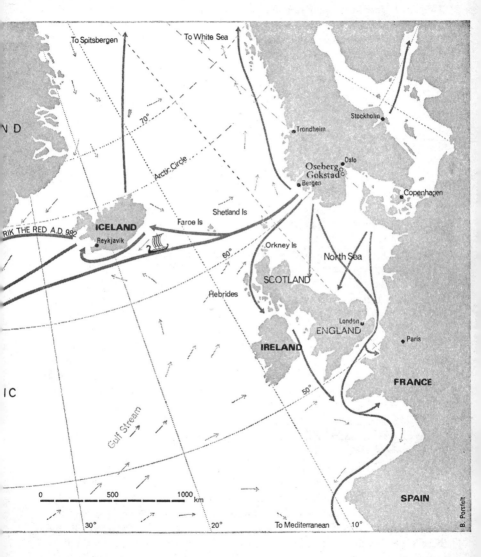

To Spitsbergen

To White Sea

N D

70°

Stockholm

Trondheim

Arctic Circle

Oseberg Oslo
Gokstad
Bergen

Copenhagen

Shetland Is

Faroe Is

RIK THE RED A.D. 982

ICELAND

Reykjavik

60°

Orkney Is

North Sea

SCOTLAND

Hebrides

London
ENGLAND

Paris

IC

IRELAND

FRANCE

50°

Gulf Stream

0   500   1000 km

SPAIN

B. Porsfelt

30°

20°

To Mediterranean

10°

Greenland in order to preach the gospel to his countrymen, in the belief that they were still living there, he did not find a single Norseman. Only ruins testified to what once had been.

Where then had the people gone? Some of them probably found their way to the European continent, but it is also possible that at least some of them emigrated to North America, to a land which they and their forebears over the centuries must have grown to know well.

The discovery of Greenland and North America is due to the bold achievements of certain individuals, but it must be looked at within a wider historical framework. This brings into the picture Norse seamen who down through the centuries, with a curious kind of stubbornness, pressed ever westward across the great ocean, as if they could sense that there was new land to be found out there.

The background is the Viking Age, which erupted throughout the North with an explosive force around the year 800. Young men hoisted sail and made for foreign shores; they were an adventurous breed, and many of them, who led a rather difficult existence at home, sought new land and homes for their families.

The Viking Age began with small-scale forays along the coasts of England and Scotland; then came larger warlike expeditions, the purpose of which was conquest and settlement in foreign lands. It was a time of fighting, brutal in many ways. But it is often forgotten that the Viking Age was also a time of bold voyages of discovery and exploration as well as peaceful colonization, where hard work, rather than battle and plunder, was the order of the day.

The expeditions launched by Swedish Vikings were usually destined for the countries to the east, up the Baltic to Russia. The Danes would usually sail to England, France, and the countries farther south. New states, under Viking rule, were established in the conquered areas. The Norwegians too followed a favourite route southward, along the west coast of Scotland and England to Ireland, France, and on to the countries of the Mediterranean. Norwegian Vikings settled in and established their rule in the Shetlands, the Orkneys, the Hebrides, in the Isle of Man and on the English mainland, in Ireland, and in Normandy.

But there was one overseas route which the Norwegians largely had all to themselves, because of the geographical situation of their homeland, namely, the route westward across the North Atlantic Ocean. Norway's far-flung coasts faced the Atlantic, and it became the great highway of the people living there. The maritime experience of many generations would enable them to construct a type of ship especially suitable for voyages on the high seas.

In the course of time these seamen ventured farther and farther west, and settled island after island. First they went to the Shetlands, the Orkneys, the Hebrides, and the Isle of Man, then on to the Faroe Islands, until they reached Iceland about the middle of the ninth century. But the longest and most dangerous voyage was still to be made, the voyage to Greenland. Here Eirik the Red was to lead the way. Finally, Leif Eiriksson was to put behind him the last remaining miles and to set foot on the North American continent. The 'Way to the West' had been followed to its very end.

Chapter Two

Old Manuscripts tell of Vinland the Good

When parts of south-west Greenland had been colonized by Eirik the Red the North American continent became a neighbouring country to the lands of the Norsemen. Only Davis Strait lies between; at its narrowest it is only about two hundred nautical miles wide. We know from historical sources,[1] which may be assumed to be reliable, that the Norsemen in Greenland undertook extensive trips along the west coast of the island, hunting walrus, seal and caribou, and looking for driftwood—very probably as far north as the homes of the Polar Eskimoes. It might easily have happened in the course of time that the ships of the Greenlanders came close to the shores of North America, or at least got within sight of the high mountains of Baffin Island. Furthermore, the coast of America in the far north would have pointed the way to more southerly parts of the continent.

The crossing of Davis Strait would have been an easy cruise for seamen who maintained permanent communications across the North Atlantic between Greenland and Norway—a distance of about fifteen hundred nautical miles across the open ocean.

If we bear in mind, then, that the Norsemen lived in Greenland for almost five hundred years, it would seem that these seafarers could hardly have avoided discovering North America. This would be a valid assumption even if there was no written evidence in support of their discoveries.

We are, however, in the fortunate position of actually possessing evidence from various sources containing information about Norse voyages from Greenland to the unknown land in the west. Some of the documents are brief, but they are often of particular value inasmuch as they were written for another purpose than that of providing information about the Vinland voyages. Then there are the Icelandic sagas, written down a few hundred years after the Norse discoveries, which give direct and comparatively detailed accounts of the voyages to the new lands.

We shall first note some of the more important miscellaneous sources and then discuss the sagas as source-material.

The earliest mention of the Vinland voyages was made by the German, Adam of Bremen,[2] in about A.D. 1070. He had obtained his knowledge of the

Norse discoveries during a stay in Denmark, probably at the court of King Svein Estridsson. Adam writes about an island which had been discovered in the great ocean and which had been called Vinland because wild grapes growing there produced the best of wines; he adds that there was corn growing wild there. This source, which in many respects gives rise to certain doubts, will be more fully dealt with later (see pp. 74ff).

The earliest Icelandic account of Vinland is to be found in *Íslendingabók*[3] (the Book of the Icelanders), written by the famous scholar Ari Thorgilsson, the learned (born 1067). He lived at a time close to the events and in a milieu in which he could gain more reliable knowledge about the lands in the west than could most people. He had obtained much of his information from his uncle Thorkel Gellison, who had probably made a journey to Greenland. Ari tells first about the discovery and colonization by Eirik the Red, and then continues: 'Both east and west in the country [i.e. in both the Eastern and the Western Settlements] they found the habitations of men, fragments of boats, and stone implements, which made them realize that the same sort of people had lived there as in Vinland, those whom the Greenlanders called Skraelings.'

This source provides us with the interesting piece of information that at the time of Eirik the Red there were probably no natives living in these areas of Greenland settled by the Norsemen. Further, we observe that Ari, in order to be able to explain what kind of people had been living at these sites, had to make use of his knowledge of people in another country, namely, the natives of Vinland. Clearly he is convinced that his brief explanation will be easily understood by his contemporaries. It presupposes, indeed, current knowledge of Vinland. The uniqueness of this extract makes it an especially valuable one.

The Icelandic *Landnámabók*[4] (Book of Land-taking), which is supposed to have been written down in the eleventh century but exists in later versions, tells about Ari Marsson who was driven by wind and weather to Hvitmannaland, called by some people Ireland the Great. 'It lies west in the ocean near Vinland the Good. To sail thither takes six days.' The Norwegian historian Gustav Storm[5] has decisively shown that this is a purely legendary account that has nothing to do with Vinland, but this quotation is of some interest because it is the first time that the phrase 'Vinland the Good' is used.

Landnámabók also contains another significant piece of information; in the middle of a genealogical listing we find: 'Thord Horsehead, father of Karlsefni, who found Vinland the Good.'

In the *Kristni Saga*[6] (which was written down in the thirteenth century) there is a brief account of Leif Eiriksson's discovery of Vinland, and a similar account is to be found in Snorri Sturluson's *Heimskringla*, or History of the Kings of Norway, in the Saga of Olaf Tryggvason, and also in *Hauksbók* (Hauk's Book). The *Kristni Saga* says: 'That summer King Olaf [Tryggvason]

sailed from Norway south to Vendland. At that time he also sent Leif Eiriksson to Greenland in order to introduce the Christian faith. Then Leif found
Vinland the Good. He also found men shipwrecked at sea. For that reason he
was called Leif the Lucky.'

The *Kristni Saga* is a brief account of the introduction of Christianity in
Iceland and the mention of Leif's discovery must be seen in the light of this
circumstance, a point which will be discussed in greater detail later.

The *Eyrbyggja Saga*[7] (written down about A.D. 1250) states that Snorri
Thorbrandsson sailed to Vinland the Good together with Thorfinn Karlsefni,
and that his son Thorbrand Snorreson was killed in a battle with the Skraelings.

In *Gretti's Saga*[8] (dating from about 1300), Thorhall Gamlason is called
'Vindlending' and 'Vidlending'.

In the Icelandic Annals,[9] consisting of manuscripts written down in the
1300s, a curious piece of information has been put down for the year 1121 (23):
'Eirik bishop of Greenland set out in search of Vinland.'

There is something mysterious about this man and his life. The Annals say
that he came to Greenland in 1112, and he was presumably the first bishop to
reside in the country. His position, however, can hardly have been as official
as the appointment of the cleric Arnald by King Sigurd Jorsalfare in 1124;
Arnald selected Gardar in the Eastern Settlement as his bishop's seat. There is
much to indicate that Bishop Eirik lived at Sandnes in the Western Settlement,
at the farm which had belonged earlier to the Vinland voyager Thorfinn
Karlsefni. Apart from the short note appearing on the now famous Vinland
Map published in 1965, we have no other information about him.

What purpose, then, might this bishop have had in mind when he undertook his voyage to Vinland? It is usually assumed that it was a missionary
voyage, to convert the natives, but it does not seem very likely that a Norseman in his day, without knowing more about the country, would plunge into
such a dangerous situation and assignment among the numerous tribes of
Eskimoes and Indians of North America. We cannot discount the possibility
that the purpose of Eirik's voyage was to preach among Norse people still
living in Vinland at that time.

For the year 1347 the Icelandic Annals have recorded the following information, which clearly shows that parts of North America were well known at
that time:

> There came also a ship from Greenland that was smaller than the small
> Icelandic vessels. She put in at Ytre Straumsfjord. She had no anchor.
> There were seventeen (some say eighteen) men aboard; they had sailed
> to Markland, but were afterwards driven hither by storms.

Several of the geographical descriptions to be found in the manuscripts of the fifteenth century[10] are also of interest in this connection. In one of the manuscripts, which was probably the work of the widely travelled abbot Nicholas of Munka-Thverá (died 1159), it says:

> From Bjarmeland there is uninhabited country running northward to where Greenland begins. South of Greenland lies Helluland, and next to that Markland, whence it is not far to Vinland the Good which some hold to be continuous with Africa. If this be so, the Outer Ocean must run in between Vinland and Markland.

The author tried to make it clear that the discoveries in the New World encompassed three lands, and it is of interest to note that the sources stress the fact that it is not very far from Markland to Vinland.

These cosmographical descriptions are also of interest in another respect: they make the newly discovered lands fit into the Norse geographical concept of the world. First there is a continuous Arctic land area, reaching from Bjarmeland (the White Sea) to Greenland. Trolls and related beings inhabited these parts. Farthest west and towards the south lay Helluland, Markland, and Vinland. The Outer Ocean encircled the entire world, but between Markland and Vinland there was a channel, and this narrow opening into Mare Oceanum was called Ginnungagap.

In Norway there was a remarkable potential source of evidence – the so-called Hønen rune-stone. This large stone, more than four feet tall, was found in the district of Ringerike in the early nineteenth century. The stone has since disappeared, but a transcription of the runic writing has been preserved. The well-known runologist Sophus Bugge[11] thinks that the name Vinland occurs in the text and that the stone was erected in memory of a man from Ringerike who perished in the pack-ice somewhere in the direction of Vinland. Magnus Olsen, on the other hand, does not believe that the word Vinland is mentioned in the text; he thinks that the stone was erected in memory of Finn Fegin, a relative of Saint Olav, who lost his life off the coast of eastern Greenland. It is impossible, however, to arrive at a definitive interpretation of the text until the Hønen rune-stone has been recovered.

We shall finally mention three old maps, one made by Sigurður Stéfansson in 1590, another by Hans Poulsen Resen in 1605, and a third map which I have found in Hungary (see Plate 5). On all these maps Helluland, Markland, and Vinland are clearly marked, the name Vinland being placed on a peninsula which may correspond to the northern point of Newfoundland. Furthermore there is the so-called 'Vinland Map' which according to some experts is supposed to date from about 1440 (see pp. 87–90). I shall discuss these maps further in another chapter in this book.

*

We have now mentioned the most important of the widely scattered sources that have a bearing on the Vinland voyages. In addition, there are the sagas. Their accounts of Vinland were put down for the specific purpose of giving information about the voyages to the new lands in the west. There are two sagas that concern us here, namely, the Greenlanders' Saga and Eirik the Red's Saga. They are both based on older manuscripts whose age it is impossible to determine with any degree of certainty.

The Greenlanders' Saga[12] has been preserved as three interpolations inserted in the 'Large' Saga of Olaf Tryggvason and included in the famous codex *Flateyjarbók*, the greater part of which was written down by the Icelandic priest Jón Thórdarson at the end of the fourteenth century.

Eirik the Red's Saga[13] has been preserved in two different manuscript versions. One of these is part of a large codex entitled *Hauksbók,* which Hauk Erlendsson put down on parchment some time before 1334. He was born about 1265 and settled in Bergen, where he became a lawman, knight, and member of the Norwegian Council of the Realm. He was descended from Thorfinn Karlsefni and seems to have been quite proud of that fact. This circumstance ought perhaps to be kept in mind when one attempts to evaluate this saga.

The other manuscript is called *Skálholtsbók* and was written down during the second half of the fifteenth century. It contains the same accounts as *Hauksbók*, but there are divergences in several places in the way they are set down and also in regard to facts. The Swedish scholar Sven B. F. Jansson[14] has shown conclusively that the differences have arisen because Hauk Erlendsson made a number of improvements in his own copy. *Skálholtsbók* must therefore be regarded as the more trustworthy of the two sources.

The two sagas are different in several respects. The Greenlanders' Saga seems particularly concerned with the family of Eirik the Red and whatever might be of interest to the people of Greenland; it seems probable that this saga is based in the main on material originating in Greenland, as G. M. Gathorne-Hardy has pointed out.[15] It tells about several independent voyages to the new land in the west. First we hear about Bjarni, whose ship was driven westward by storms, and the sighting of new and strange shores. Then the saga deals with the voyage of Leif Eiriksson—a carefully planned expedition, the objective of which was to reach the land that Bjarni had already seen. Subsequently, Leif's brothers, Thorvald and Thorstein, as well as his sister Freydis, set out on expeditions of their own. Thorvald and Freydis actually reached Vinland and lived for some time in the houses that Leif had put up. This saga also contains an account of the expedition led by Thorfinn Karlsefni.

Eirik the Red's Saga is focused more on Thorfinn Karlsefni and dwells to a greater extent on whatever might be of interest to the Icelanders of that time.

Plate 3. View from Brattahlid in western Greenland, where the home of Eirik the Red and Leif Eiriksson stood, about A.D. 1000. In the foreground, the ruins of a church belonging to a somewhat later time. (Photograph: Helge Ingstad.)

Plate 4. This rune-stone was found in what had been a cairn on the island of Kingigtorssuaq off the west coast of Greenland (72° 57′ N.). It says: 'Erling Sigvatsson, Bjarni Thordsson and Eindride Oddsson erected these cairns on the Saturday before Procession Day and runed them well … ' (Photograph: National Museum of Copenhagen.)

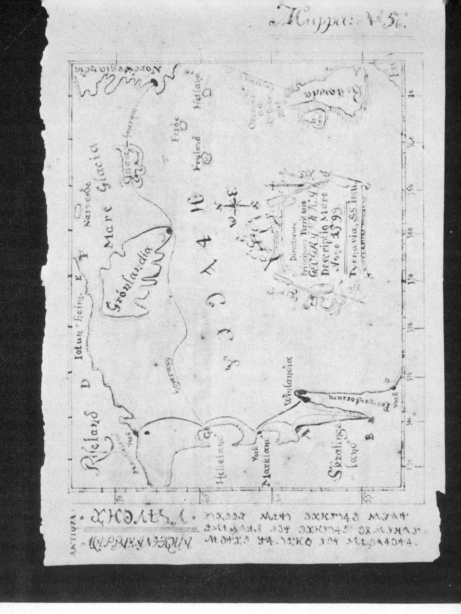

Plate 5. This map was discovered by the author in Hungary in the private collection of former archivist Géza Szepessy. It was reproduced in print for the first time in the original Norwegian edition of this book. It has many features in common with the Icelandic Skálholt map, but in addition shows the route all the way to *Winlandia*, which is shaded in black. The text is in part in Hungarian runes. The map is $11\frac{3}{4}$ inches by $8\frac{1}{2}$ inches.

The discovery made by Leif Eiriksson is noted in only a few lines; the saga writer makes the discovery of Vinland a part of the story of the voyage Leif made from Olaf Tryggvason's court in Trondheim to Greenland, when he was given the task of introducing Christianity in his homeland. The sober account of Bjarni's voyage is not included. The account of Thorstein's unsuccessful voyage has been included in this saga, but in a somewhat different version. The independent Vinland voyages of Thorvald and Freydis are not mentioned; on the contrary, both appear as participants of the Karlsefni expedition.

The discrepancies between the two sagas may, to some extent, have derived from a rivalry between two great families as to which had the honour of having fostered the discoverer of Vinland. Such a situation is not unknown in connection with important discoveries and explorations in the past. It seems that Karlsefni's family in Iceland enjoyed a great advantage, for in the course of time there was to belong to it a number of influential men, including Icelandic bishops; moreover, Iceland was the land where the sagas were written down. The family of the Greenlander Leif Eiriksson, on the other hand, disappears from history with the death of his son. It may be that, in the course of centuries, the Icelanders centred their accounts of the Vinland voyages on their great hero and countryman Thorfinn Karlsefni, and as time passed the distant Greenlanders and their achievements were felt to be of less interest. In an oral tradition, influenced by family and national feelings, the accounts of the Greenland voyages could have become incorporated into the saga of Thorfinn Karlsefni, with Leif Eiriksson's accomplishments relegated to a subsidiary place in the narrative. This does not necessarily mean that a conscious effort was made to falsify or alter the facts. It is very hard to prove that this kind of modification of the saga text may have taken place in the course of time, but one is tempted to ask: When Hauk Erlendsson, who very strongly emphasized his relationship with Thorfinn Karlsefni, took the liberty of improving on the saga as late as the fourteenth century, what may not his powerful family in Iceland have done in this respect during previous centuries?

There has been a great deal of discussion as to whether Eirik the Red's Saga or the Greenlanders' Saga is the more reliable. Recent research has arrived at the conclusion that each one offers valuable information, all of which must be properly evaluated and taken into consideration. Their significance does not lie in their differences and in a number of obscure passages, but in the remarkable fact that in important respects they provide us with reliable information about events that occurred a thousand years ago.

To sum up, we have no hesitation in saying that the various scattered sources in conjunction with the sagas constitute historical evidence removing any doubt that the Vinland voyages actually took place—that Norsemen sailed to North America about five hundred years before Columbus.

But it is one thing to know that this is a fact, it is quite another to determine which areas of the New World they visited and where they built their houses. Where then is the Vinland of the sagas to be found?

It is true that the sagas contain valuable information touching on sailing and navigation, geography, astronomy, ethnography, zoology, and botany, but to give everything a correct interpretation is nevertheless quite difficult. And not least because we must attempt to understand the mentality of the Vinland voyagers and their descendants; we are here concerned with popular traditions and not with scholarly dissertations. The traditions were based on accounts and reports made by young seamen and were retold through the centuries from generation to generation, in houses made of turf and stone, to people sitting on an earthen floor by an open fire.

Chapter Three

Ships and the Sea

The necessary prerequisite for the great seafaring expeditions across the ocean was a tradition of seamanship, its roots extending far back in time. As part of this tradition, a shipbuilding technique of a high standard had developed. Winston Churchill has written: 'The soul of the Vikings lay in the long-ship.'

The magnificent Gokstad ship, excavated from a burial mound in south-east Norway and dating back to the Viking Age, is a marvel to behold, with its tall and graceful stem and supple clinker-built hull of oak. Its length is 77 feet, its greatest width 17 feet, its height from keel to gunwale amidships 6.4 feet. In the water, it would have a draught of only 2.8 feet, permitting sailing in shallow waters. It had been rigged with a square-sail and a side rudder.

The seaworthiness of this ship was amply demonstrated in 1893 when the Norwegian Magnus Andersen sailed across the Atlantic in the *Viking*, a replica of the Gokstad ship. The ship maintained an amazingly high speed and handled well in rough weather. It made between five and six knots on the average, at times even more. Magnus Andersen has written about one of the experiences they had on the way: 'It was a splendid voyage. In the twilight the Northern Lights threw their fantastic, pale light across the ocean, while the *Viking* glided over the waves like a seagull. With much admiration we watched the graceful motion of the ship, and with great pride we noted its speed, which from time to time was as high as eleven knots.'

In this way the Norse Greenlanders sailed forth time and again, but the voyage could turn out quite differently when storms tossed the open vessel and huge waves roared in over the gunwales, while chilled and weary men baled and baled.

In the early days of the settlement of Greenland, the most powerful men owned large ships — ships that had been built in Norway and sailed across the ocean. We do not have any certain knowledge about their construction, but they were probably a kind of cargo-carrying merchant ship, perhaps the so-called *knarr* — its basic design was probably the same as that of the Gokstad ship.

The compass was not known in Scandinavia at the time of the Vinland voyages; it was not introduced in that part of the world until the early thirteenth century. The Norse sailors got their bearings from the sun and the stars, and they would select a course straight along a certain latitude wherever that was possible; they might also follow a coastline for a fair space of time and make use of landmarks in their navigation. But they would keep a safe distance away from the shore when sailing past strange coasts.

The ships of the Viking Age could stand rough weather, but they were not very well suited to ride out a storm; when it got rough they would prefer to stay away from the storm and for that reason would often get well off course, as Bjarni did when he drifted in the direction of the North American coast.

There is little doubt that the Norse Greenlanders paid close attention to the ocean currents; these may even have been a decisive factor in their choosing a route to North America. It is worthy of note that on their way to Vinland they almost always sailed in the same direction as the currents. At first they followed the strong current which sweeps from the Arctic Ocean down along the east coast of Greenland, round the southern tip of the island, and then northward along the west coast; from there they would follow the Labrador Current southward to Vinland.

Ice conditions also constituted a problem of great importance to these far wanderers. The currents carry huge masses of ice along with them, and along the Greenland coast as well as the coast of Labrador these ice masses can completely block any navigation far into the summer. If conditions were similar to those of our day, the Vinland voyagers would be forced to get off to a late start, probably not until some time in late July or August.

The reports as to how long the various voyages lasted are among the most important information about the Vinland expeditions supplied by the sagas. The term used is *døgr*; used in connection with this kind of transoceanic voyage it must have meant a day and a night, a full twenty-four hours. The average speed of an ocean-going Viking ship must be estimated to have been about six knots, so that it would travel about 150 nautical miles* every twenty-four hours. On this basis it is possible in several cases to calculate approximately the distances of the various voyages mentioned in the sagas.

According to the sagas, few *døgr* were needed for the Vinland voyage. Historians have been wont to disregard the numbers given, chiefly because of the attendant account of the finding of grapes. It would be impossible, it was thought, to reach the land of wild grapes if the number of days given in the sagas is right. Finnur Jónsson was of the opinion that a copying error had been made in the saga manuscripts, but we must take note of the fact that the number of days spent on the voyages was written down as a numeral and it is a small one, both in the Greenlanders' Saga and in Eirik the Red's Saga.

There is reason to believe that the sailing directions and times given in the

* One nautical mile equals 2,026⅔ yards.

sagas are approximately the true ones. If there was anything that a seafaring people would make an essentially correct part of their tradition, it would be the facts and circumstances related to ships and the sea.

A very characteristic seafaring milieu must have been created fairly quickly in Greenland. Men got together—skippers, seamen, farmers—and discussed their experiences and adventures on distant voyages. They could exchange much useful information concerning the wind and the weather, currents and ice conditions, far-away oceans and distant coasts. Bits and pieces of other knowledge and information were fused into a solid whole—a maritime tradition was being created.

In this tradition the accounts of the voyages to the new lands in the west must have stood out as milestones in the history of the people. They have been handed down orally from generation to generation—to youngsters in the Greenlandic settlements they must have been part of the process of growing up.

Before we render the sagas and discuss the various Vinland voyages, we shall summarize the two accounts appearing in the Greenlanders' Saga and Eirik the Red's Saga.

The Greenlanders' Saga	*Eirik the Red's Saga*
1. Bjarni Herjolfsson sails from Iceland for Greenland; he is blown off course and glimpses the coast of North America. Chapter 2.	
2. The planned expedition of Leif Eiriksson. He discovers Helluland, Markland and Vinland, where he builds 'large houses' and remains for a year. He rescues a ship's crew on the voyage home. Chapters 3–4.	1. Leif Eiriksson sails from Norway for Greenland, and finds a new land across the ocean. He returns to Greenland the same year. He rescues a ship's crew. Chapter 5.
3. The Vinland voyage of Thorvald Eiriksson. He stays at Leifsbudir. He fights the natives, and is killed. The expedition remains in Vinland two years. Chapter 5.	
4. The unsuccessful expedition of Thorstein Eiriksson. Chapter 6.	2. The unsuccessful expedition of Thorstein Eiriksson. Chapter 5.
5. The Thorfinn Karlsefni expedition, with women and cattle, the objective of which was settling in Vinland. He settles at Leifsbudir.	3. The Thorfinn Karlsefni expedition, with women and cattle, to Helluland, Markland and Vinland. He settles at Straumfjord. He

37

<table>
<tr><td>*The Greenlanders' Saga*</td><td>*Eirik the Red's Saga*</td></tr>
</table>

The Greenlanders' Saga	*Eirik the Red's Saga*
He trades and fights with the natives. He remains two years in Vinland. Chapter 7.	explores the country to the south (Hop). He trades and fights with the natives. He remains three years in Vinland. Chapters 8–14.

6. The expedition of Freydis, which includes men and women. She settles at Leifsbudir. Internal quarrels and manslaughter. She remains in Vinland one year. Chapters 8–9.

The following two chapters contain English translations of those parts of the Greenlanders' Saga and Eirik the Red's Saga which are pertinent to the Vinland voyages and the Norse discovery of America.

Chapter Four

The Greenlanders' Saga

Bjarni Herjolfsson Sights a New Land

Herjolf was the son of Bard Herjolfsson. He was a kinsman of Ingolf, the first settler of Iceland. Ingolf gave the elder Herjolf and his men land between Våg and Reykjanes. Herjolf the younger lived first at Drepstokk; his wife's name was Thorgerd, and their son was named Bjarni and was a young man of much promise. At an early age he was eager to sail to foreign lands, and he won both fame and fortune and spent the winters alternately abroad and with his father. Soon Bjarni owned his own vessel for trading. The last winter that Bjarni spent in Norway, Herjolf set off for Greenland together with Eirik the Red and sold his farm.

On board Herjolf's ship there was a Christian man from the Hebrides. He composed the Hafgerðingadrápa; it contains the following refrain:

> I beseech the immaculate
> Master of monks
> To protect my journey.
> May Heaven's Lord bless me
> And hold His hand
> Over me.

Herjolf made his home at Herjolfsnes; he was an admirable man. Eirik the Red lived at Brattahlid; he was highly respected and everyone recognized his authority. These were Eirik's children: Leif, Thorvald, and Thorstein. His daughter was named Freydis. She was married to a man by the name of Thorvard and they lived at Gardar where the bishop's seat is now situated. She was an arrogant woman, but Thorvard was of little account. She had married him for the sake of his wealth. The people of Greenland were heathens at that time.

The same year that his father had sailed away in the spring Bjarni arrived in his ship at Eyrar [in Iceland] in the summer. He was greatly shocked by the news [of his father's departure] and did not want to bring his cargo on shore. Then his shipmates asked him what he proposed to do. He replied that he wanted to adhere to the old custom and stay with his father during the winter.

'I shall sail my ship to Greenland, if you are willing to accompany me.' They all replied that they would do as he decided.

Then Bjarni said: 'Foolhardy will our voyage seem, since none of us has ever sailed the Greenland Sea.' But they set out to sea as soon as they were able and sailed for three days (*døgr*)* until the land sank below the horizon. But then the fair wind failed them, a north wind and fog set in, and they did not know in which direction they were sailing. They continued thus for many days.

Eventually the sun appeared, and they were able to get their bearings (*deila ættir*). They then hoisted sail and sailed on for a whole day, when they sighted land. They spoke among themselves as to what kind of land that might be, but Bjarni said that he did not believe it to be Greenland. They asked him whether he wanted to sail in to shore or not. He replied: 'It is my advice that we sail in close to the shore.' That they did, and then they saw that the land had no mountains and was covered with woods and there were low hills.

They then left the land on the port side and let their sheet turn towards the land. They sailed for two days and then sighted a new land. The crew asked Bjarni whether he thought that this was Greenland. He replied that he did not think that this was Greenland any more than the previous land, 'for it is said that there are huge glaciers in Greenland.' They soon approached the land and noticed that it was flat and covered with forests.

Then the wind died down. The crew talked about wanting to go ashore, but Bjarni would not allow it. They were of the opinion that they needed both wood and water, but Bjarni replied: 'You are not in need of either.' For this he had to listen to angry words from his men.

He then ordered them to hoist sail, and this was done. They turned the prow away from the land and sailed out to sea before a south-westerly wind for three days and they then sighted a third land. This land was high and mountainous, and there were glaciers there.

The crew asked Bjarni whether he wanted to land there, but he said that he did not want to, 'for this land seems to me to be worthless.' They did not lower their sail but proceeded along the coast and saw that it was an island.

Once again they set their prow away from the land and sailed out to sea before the same fair wind. Soon a gale began to blow, and Bjarni ordered his men to shorten sail and not to sail harder than ship and rigging could stand.

They sailed for four days and then saw a fourth land. They asked Bjarni whether he thought that this was Greenland or not. He replied: 'This land resembles most closely what I have been told about Greenland, and here we will go in to land.' This they did, and towards evening they reached the shore, close to a cape. There was a boat by the cape, and on the cape lived Herjolf,

---

* *Døgr* is, as formerly mentioned (page 36), interpreted as 'day and night (twenty-four hours)' in connection with the Vinland voyages. In this book *døgr* will be translated by 'day' or 'days'.

Plate 6. The ruins of the Sandnes farm in Vesterbygd in Greenland, at the head of the Ameralik Fjord. The farm probably belonged to the Vinland voyager Thorfinn Karlsefni and his wife Gudrid. (Photograph: Helge Ingstad.)

Plate 7. Arrow-head made from quartzite, found in the cemetery a short distance from Thorfinn Karlsefni's farm. It is assumed to be of Indian origin and might have been brought to Greenland by the Vinland voyagers. (Photograph: National Museum of Copenhagen.)

Plate 8. The Oseberg ship. This ship was excavated from a burial mound at Oseberg in south-east Norway. A high-born woman was buried in the ship, and given all kinds of finery and equipment to take with her on the voyage to the realm of the dead. About the ninth century. (Photograph: Collection of Antiquities, University of Oslo.)

Plate 9 (*over*). The Gokstad ship. This ship was excavated from a burial mound at Gokstad in south-east Norway. A chieftain was buried here, with various kinds of equipment. In a similar type of ship the Vinland voyagers set out across the great ocean to Greenland and North America. (Photograph : Collection of Antiquities, University of Oslo.)

Bjarni's father. For this reason the cape has been called Herjolfsnes ever since.

Bjarni now went to his father's home, gave up his trading, and stayed with Herjolf as long as he lived, and later carried on farming as his father's successor.

Leif Eiriksson Discovers Vinland

The next thing that happened [after the death of Olaf Tryggvason in the year 1000] was that Bjarni Herjolfsson sailed from Greenland to Earl Eirik [in Norway] and that the earl received him well. Bjarni told him about his travels and about the lands he had seen, and people thought that he had shown a great lack of curiosity since he did not have more to say about these countries, and he was criticized for this.

Bjarni became a retainer of the earl's, and the next summer he returned to Greenland.

There was now much talk of voyages of exploration. Leif, the son of Eirik the Red of Brattahlid, came to see Bjarni Herjolfsson and purchased his ship and engaged a crew — they were thirty-five men in all.

Leif asked his father Eirik to lead the expedition. Eirik tried to excuse himself, pointing out that he was too old now and did not have the strength to endure all hardships as he had done before. Leif maintained that he was the one in their family who commanded the most luck as a leader. Eirik then gave in to Leif, and as soon as they were ready they rode off to the ships. But when only a short distance away from the houses, Eirik's horse stumbled, and he fell off and hurt his foot. Then Eirik said: 'It is not my fate to discover any more lands than the one in which we now live. We shall not travel together any farther.'

Eirik returned home to Brattahlid, but Leif went on board the ship with thirty-five men. Among them was a Southerner, whose name was Tyrkir.

Now they prepared their ship and put out to sea as soon as they were ready, and they found first the land which Bjarni had seen last. They sailed in to the shore, cast anchor, lowered a boat, and went ashore, but they did not see any grass there. The uplands consisted of huge glaciers, and between the glaciers and the shore the land was just like one single slab of rock. The land seemed to be of no value.

Then Leif said: 'At least it has not happened to us what happened to Bjarni in this land, that we did not go ashore. Now I will give this land a name, it shall be called Helluland (Flat Stone Land).' They then returned to their ship.

They put out to sea and found the second land. This time too they sailed in to the coast and cast anchor, lowered a boat and went ashore. The country was flat and covered with forests, and wherever they went there were white sandy beaches sloping gently down to the sea. Then Leif said: 'We shall give this land a name according to its natural resources, and call it Markland (Forest Land).' After that they hurried back to their ship.

They then sailed out to sea before a north-east wind and were at sea two days before sighting land. They sailed in towards it and came to an island which lay north of the mainland. There they went ashore and looked around, and the weather was fine. They saw that there was dew on the grass, and it came about that they got some of it on their hands and put it to their lips, and they thought that they had never before tasted anything so sweet.

They then returned to their ship and sailed into the sound which lay between the island and the cape projecting northward from the mainland. They sailed westward past the cape. It was very shallow there at low tide. Their ship went aground, and it was a long way from the ship to the sea. But they were so impatient to get to land that they did not want to wait for the tide to rise under their ship but ran ashore at a place where a river flowed out of a lake.

As soon as the tide had refloated the ship they took their boat and rowed out to it, and brought the ship farther up the river and into the lake. There they cast anchor and carried their leather bags ashore and put up their booths. They later decided to winter there, and built large houses.

There was no lack of salmon in the river or in the lake, and they were bigger salmon than they had ever seen before. The land was so bountiful that it seemed to them that the cattle would not need fodder during the winter. There was no frost in winter, and the grass hardly withered. Day and night were of more equal length than in Greenland and Iceland. On the shortest day of the year the sun was visible in the middle of the afternoon as well as at breakfast time.*

When they had finished building their houses, Leif said to his men: 'I now intend to divide our party into two groups and explore the country. One group is to stay here at the houses, the other is to get to know the country, but not to go so far away that they are not able to get back home in the evening, and they are not to be separated from each other.' This they did for a time, and Leif took turns, at one time going off with those who explored the land, at other times staying by the houses.

Leif was a big and strong man, and very impressive in appearance. He was shrewd and clever, temperate, and highly respected in every way.

It happened one evening that one man was missing, and it was Tyrkir, the Southerner. Leif was much distressed by this, for Tyrkir had been with his father for a long time and he had been very fond of Leif when he was a child. Leif spoke harsh words to his companions and prepared to look for him and took twelve men with him. But when they had gone only a short distance away from the camp Tyrkir came walking towards them. They were very happy to see him. Leif could see at once that Tyrkir's spirits were high.

Tyrkir had a bulging forehead and a small freckled face with roving eyes;

---

* Literally: 'the sun had *eyktarstaðr* and *dagmálastaðr* on the shortest day.'

he was a small and insignificant man but was handy at all sorts of crafts.

Leif said to him: 'Why are you so late, foster-father, and why did you not stay in the company of the others?' Tyrkir at first spoke a long time in German, rolling his eyes and grimacing, but the others did not understand what he was saying. A little later he said in the Norse tongue: 'I did not walk much farther than you, but I can report on something new: I have found vines and grapes.' 'Is that true, foster-father?' Leif said. 'It is certainly true,' Tyrkir replied, 'for I was born where there is no lack of vines and grapes.'

They slept there that night, but in the morning Leif said to his crew: 'From now on we shall have two tasks to do and we shall alternate them so as to do each job every other day. We shall gather grapes, and we shall cut vines and fell timber, to make a cargo for my ship.' This was done. It is said that their pinnace was filled with grapes.

A full cargo was cut for the ship, and in the spring they made ready and sailed away. Leif gave the country a name in accordance with its resources, and called it Vinland (Wineland).

They then sailed out to sea and had a good wind until they sighted Greenland, and the mountains below the glaciers. Then a man spoke up and said to Leif: 'Why are you steering the ship so much into the wind?' Leif replied: 'My mind is on my steering, but there is also something else to pay attention to. Don't you see anything strange?' They answered that they could not see anything out of the ordinary. 'I cannot tell,' said Leif, 'whether it is a ship or a reef that I see.' Now the others noticed it also, and said that it was a reef. But Leif had sharper eyes than they; he noticed that there were men on the reef.

'We must beat up into the wind,' Leif said, 'so that we can get close enough to help them if that is necessary. But if they are not peaceful men, then it is we and not they who are masters of the situation.'

They then sailed up close to the reef, lowered the sail, cast anchor, and launched the other pinnace that they had with them. Tyrkir asked them who was the leader [of the shipwrecked party]. His name was Thorir, their leader replied, and he was a Norwegian. 'But what is your name?' Leif told them who he was. 'Are you a son of Eirik the Red of Brattahlid?' the man asked. Leif said that that was so. 'And now I ask you all to come aboard my ship and take along with you as much of your goods as the ship can hold.'

So they did, and they all then sailed up Eiriksfjord with this cargo until they reached Brattahlid. There they unloaded the ship. Afterwards Leif invited Thorir and his wife Gudrid and three of their men to stay with him. He also found lodgings for the winter for the rest of the crew, both Thorir's men and his own.

Leif rescued fifteen men from the reef. He was later called Leif the Lucky. Thus Leif gained both wealth and honour.

That winter a severe sickness afflicted Thorir and his men. Thorir died, as did also a great part of his crew. Eirik the Red also died that winter.

Thorvald Eiriksson's Vinland Voyage

There was now much talk of Leif's expedition to Vinland. His brother Thorvald was of the opinion that the exploration of the land had been confined to too narrow an area. Leif said to Thorvald: 'If you wish, brother, then go to Vinland in my ship. But first I want to fetch the timber which Thorir had on the reef.' This was then done.

Thereupon Thorvald made preparations for the voyage, taking with him thirty men, and his brother Leif gave him good advice. They made their ship ready and sailed out to sea, and there is nothing to tell about their voyage until they came to Vinland, to Leifsbudir. There they laid up the ship and remained quiet over the winter, catching fish for their food.

But in the spring Thorvald ordered them to make their ship ready and some of the men were to sail in the pinnace westward along the land and explore the country during the summer. They thought that it was a beautiful country; it was covered with forests, and the woods came down close to the sea. There were white sandy beaches, many islands, and shallows. They did not see any traces of human beings or of animals, but on an island in the west they found a grain-holder made of wood (*kornhjálm af tre*). They found no other handiwork of men, and they turned back and arrived at Leifsbudir in the autumn.

Next summer Thorvald sailed towards the east with the large ship and then along the more northerly part of the country. They encountered heavy weather off a cape and went aground, breaking the ship's keel. They stayed there a long time while mending the ship. Then Thorvald said to his companions: 'I would like us to raise up the keel here on the cape and name it Kjalarnes (Keelness).' And so they did.

Afterwards they sailed away from there and eastward along the land and into the nearest fjord mouth and to a headland which was jutting out there. It was completely covered with woods. There they moored their ship and put out the gangway to the shore, and Thorvald went ashore with his entire crew.

Then he said: 'This is a beautiful place; here I should like to make my home.'

Thereupon they returned to the ship. But then they saw three mounds on the beach beyond the cape. When they came closer they saw that they were three skin-boats, and under each boat lay three men. Thorvald and his companions divided forces and captured all of them, except one who got away in his skin-boat. They killed the eight men, and then walked back to the cape, and from there they could see inside in the fjord some mounds which they thought to be human habitations.

After this there came over them such a heavy drowsiness that they could not keep awake, and they all fell asleep. Then a cry sounded above them, so that they all woke up. The words cried out were: 'Wake up, Thorvald and all your men, if you want to stay alive. Return to your ship with all your men and leave this land as fast as you can!'

Then came from inside the fjord a great number of skin-boats heading directly towards them. Thorvald said: 'We must put up breastworks on the gunwales and defend ourselves to the utmost, but attack as little as possible.' This they did. The natives (Skraelings) shot at them for a while, but then fled, each one as quickly as he could.

Thorvald inquired whether any of his men had been wounded; they replied that none of them had suffered any wounds. 'I have got a wound under my arm,' he said. 'An arrow flew in between the gunwale and my shield, and under my arm. Here is the arrow, and it will cause my death. My advice to you is that you return home as soon as possible. But first you shall carry me to the headland where I wished to make my home. Perhaps I spoke true when I said that I should dwell there awhile. Bury me there and put crosses at my head and feet, and call the place Crossness for ever more.'

Greenland was at that time Christian, but Eirik the Red had died before the coming of Christianity.

Then Thorvald died. They did everything he had asked of them, and afterwards they sailed away and rejoined the other members of the expedition, and they told each other such tidings as they knew.

They stayed there [at Leifsbudir] that winter and gathered grapes and vines as cargo for their ship. The following spring they made ready for the return voyage to Greenland, and arrived with their ship in Eiriksfjord. Then they could tell Leif great tidings.

Thorstein Eiriksson's Unsuccessful Vinland Voyage

... Thorstein Eiriksson was now intent on voyaging to Vinland in order to fetch the body of his brother Thorvald. He made ready the same ship and selected his crew for their strength and size. He took with him twenty-five men and his wife Gudrid, and as soon as they were ready they put to sea and out of sight of land.

They were tossed about in the open sea all summer, and did not know where they were. But after the first week of winter they reached land at Lysefjord in the Western Settlement in Greenland ...

Thorfinn Karlsefni's Vinland Voyage

That same summer [that Gudrid, Thorstein's widow, was brought to Eiriksfjord] a ship came from Norway to Greenland. Its captain was a man named

Thorfinn Karlsefni; he was the son of Thord Horsehead, the son of Snorri Thordarson of Hofdi. Thorfinn Karlsefni was a man of great wealth, and he spent the winter with Leif Eiriksson at Brattahlid. He soon became fond of Gudrid and asked for her hand; she replied that Leif would have to answer on her behalf. She was then betrothed to Thorfinn, and the wedding was celebrated that same winter.

There was still the same talk about Vinland voyages, and both Gudrid and the others kept urging Karlsefni to set out on an expedition. It was then decided that he should make the voyage, and he gathered a company of sixty men in addition to five women. Karlsefni and his men entered into an agreement that they should all have an equal share in the profits that the venture might yield. They brought along with them all kinds of livestock, for it was their intention to settle in the country if they could possibly do so. Karlsefni asked Leif if he could have the houses he had put up in Vinland, but Leif replied that he would lend him the houses, but he did not want to give them away.

Then they sailed out to sea and reached Leifsbudir safe and sound and carried their skin bags ashore. They soon made a splendid catch, for a whale had been stranded there, and it was both big and fine; they went down and cut up the whale, and thus there was no lack of food.

The livestock was put ashore there, but it was not long before the males became frisky and almost unmanageable. They had taken one bull with them.

Karlsefni ordered trees to be felled and trimmed to make cargo for the ship and laid the timber on a rock to dry. They took advantage of all the natural resources of the country, both in the way of grapes, all kinds of game and fish, and other things.

After the first winter came summer. Then they saw natives (Skraelings) — a great number of them emerged from the woods. The livestock was near by, and the bull began to bellow and carry on in a frightening manner. Then the natives were terrified and ran off with their packs, which consisted of grey furs and sables and skins of all kinds. They ran towards Karlsefni's house and wanted to get inside, but Karlsefni placed guards at the doors. Neither party could understand the other's language. The natives unslung their packs, untied them, and proffered their wares. They asked for weapons in exchange, but Karlsefni forbade his men to sell them weapons.

Then he thought of something else; he told the women to carry out milk to them, and as soon as they saw the milk they wanted to buy nothing else. Thus the outcome of trading was that the natives carried away in their stomachs what they had obtained through barter, while Karlsefni and his men obtained their bales and pelts. After that the natives went away.

The next thing to relate is that Karlsefni had a formidable stockade built round his houses, and that they made preparations [to defend themselves]. At this time Gudrid, the wife of Karlsefni, gave birth to a boy who was named Snorri.

Early next winter, natives came to visit them once more; they were more numerous than before, but proffered the same kind of goods. Then Karlsefni told the women: 'Now you shall carry out to them the same kind of wares which there was most demand for last time, and nothing else.' And once the Skraelings saw that, they threw their bales over the stockade.

Gudrid was sitting in the doorway beside the cradle of her son Snorri when a shadow fell across the door and a woman entered dressed in a black close-fitting dress. She was rather short, wore a band round her head and had light-brown hair; she was pale and had such large eyes that their equal had never been seen in a human head. She walked over to where Gudrid was sitting and said: 'What is your name?' 'My name is Gudrid, but what is your name?' 'My name is Gudrid,' she replied. Then Gudrid the housewife held out her hand and bade her sit down next to her. But all of a sudden Gudrid heard a loud crash and the woman had vanished.

The very same instant one of the natives was killed by one of Karlsefni's men because he had tried to steal weapons. Then the natives ran away as fast as they could, leaving their clothes and goods behind. No one but Gudrid had seen the woman.

'Now we had better put our heads together,' said Karlsefni, 'for I believe that they will come here a third time, and then they will be hostile and come in full force. Let this be our plan: ten men are to go out on the headland over there, letting themselves be seen; all the others are to go into the woods and make a clearing for the livestock; there it can stay when the enemy comes out of the forest. And then we will take our bull and have him march ahead of us.'

The place where they intended to meet the enemy host was situated with a lake on one side and forests on the other. Karlsefni's plan was followed, and the natives came right to the spot where he had planned that the battle would be joined. The fighting began, and many natives were killed. There was one tall and fine-looking man among the natives, and Karlsefni surmised that he must be their chief. One of the natives had picked up an axe; he stared at it for a while, then he swung it at one of his comrades and gave him such a blow that he fell dead at once. The big man seized the axe, looked at it for a while, and then flung it as far as he could out into the water. Then they fled into the forest, each as best as he might, and that was the end of the battle.

Karlsefni and his men spent the entire winter there, but in the spring Karlsefni let it be known that he had no wish to stay there any longer. He wanted to sail to Greenland. They then made ready for the voyage and took along with them many valuable wares, such as vines, grapes, and pelts. They sailed out to sea and arrived safely in their ship at Eiriksfjord, and they spent the winter there.

Freydis's Vinland Voyage

Once more there was much talk about voyaging to Vinland, for it appeared that such an enterprise could lead to both fame and fortune. The same summer that Karlsefni returned from Vinland a ship arrived in Greenland from Norway. The ship was commanded by two brothers, Helgi and Finnbogi, and they stayed in Greenland over the winter. The brothers were Icelanders by descent and came from the Eastfjords.

The next thing to be told is that Freydis Eiriksdøttir made a journey from her home at Gardar to meet with the two brothers, Helgi and Finnbogi. She proposed that they should come on a voyage to Vinland in their own ship, and then they were to share equally with her in all the profits the expedition might yield. They agreed to this. Then she went to her brother Leif and asked him to give her the houses that he had built in Vinland, but he made the same reply as he had done before: he would lend her the houses, but he did not want to give them away.

The agreement between the brothers and Freydis was to the effect that each party should bring along thirty able-bodied men on their ship, in addition to womenfolk. But Freydis broke the agreement immediately; she brought along an additional five men and concealed them, so that the brothers did not know of this until they reached Vinland.

Then they put to sea, and they had agreed that the ships would sail as close together as possible. There was not much distance between them, but the brothers arrived in Vinland just ahead of Freydis and carried their cargo up to Leif's houses. But when Freydis and her crew landed, they unloaded their ship and carried the cargo up to the houses. Then Freydis asked: 'Why have you brought your stuff in here?' 'Because we assumed that all agreements between us would be kept,' they said. She retorted: 'It was to me that Leif lent these houses, not to you.'

'We brothers do not possess enough wickedness to make us a match for you,' said Helgi. Then they carried their possessions out of the house and built themselves a house farther from the sea and by a lake and put everything in order there, while Freydis had timber felled to make a cargo for her ship.

Winter set in, and the brothers suggested that they should arrange games and other entertainment to pass the time. This was done for a while, but then they began to speak ill of each other, it led to ill feeling, and the games came to an end. There was no longer any visiting between the houses. This state of affairs continued for most of the winter.

Then early one morning Freydis got out of bed and dressed, but did not put on shoes or stockings; the weather was such that there had fallen a heavy dew. She put on her husband's cloak and walked over to the house where the brothers were living and went up to the door. A man had just gone out and left the door ajar. She opened the door and stood in the doorway for a while without saying a word.

Finnbogi was lying in the bed farthest from the door, and he was awake. He said: 'What do you want here, Freydis?' She replied: 'I want you to get up and come outside with me; I want to talk to you.' He did so, and they walked over to a tree-trunk that was lying next to the house, and sat down on it.

'How do you like things here?' she asked him. He answered: 'I think highly of what the country has to offer, but I dislike the ill feelings that have come between us, and I think that there is no reason for it.' 'True enough,' she said; 'I feel the same as you do. But I came to see you in order to exchange ships with you brothers, for you have a larger ship and I want to leave here.' 'It is so agreed,' he replied, 'if that will make you content.' With that they parted. Finnbogi went back to bed and Freydis walked home.

She climbed into bed with ice-cold feet, and this made Thorvard wake up; he asked why she was so cold and wet. She answered excitedly: 'I went over to see the brothers in order to exchange ships with them, as I wanted a larger ship, but they got so angry that they beat me and maltreated me. You, you coward, will never avenge my humiliation or your own, and now I realize that I am no longer in Greenland, but I will divorce you unless you avenge this.'

At last he could not bear her taunts any longer. He ordered his men to get up at once and take their weapons. They did so and went straight to the house where the brothers lived, and marched in on the sleeping men and tied them up and led them outside one after the other. Freydis had each one killed as he came out.

Now all the men were killed, but the women were left, but no one was willing to kill them. Then Freydis said: 'Give me an axe.' They did so, and she turned upon the five women that were there, and left them dead.

After this terrible deed they returned to their own houses, but Freydis gave no other impression than that she thought she had done very well, and she said to her companions: 'If we are so fortunate that we ever get back to Greenland, then I shall kill any man who says anything about what has happened here. We must say that the others stayed behind when we sailed away.'

Early in the spring they made ready the ship which the brothers had owned, and loaded it with all the produce they could get and as much as the ship could carry. Then they sailed out to sea, and had a good voyage and brought their ship to Eiriksfjord early in the summer. Karlsefni was still there; he had just made his ship ready and was waiting for a favourable wind, and people say that a ship more richly laden than the one which he commanded had never left Greenland.

Chapter Five

Eirik the Red's Saga*

Leif Eiriksson Discovers Vinland

... Leif and his men sailed away from the Hebrides [to which he had been driven off course on his way from Greenland to Norway] and came in the autumn to Norway where he proceeded to the court of King Olaf Tryggvason. The king bestowed great honours on him and thought him to be an outstanding man.

One day the king came to Leif and said: 'Is it your intention to sail to Greenland this summer?' Leif answered: 'Yes, it is, if you approve of it.' The king said: 'I think it a good thing. You shall go there on a mission for me and preach Christianity in Greenland.'

Leif said that that was for the king to decide, but he added that he did not think that it would be an easy task to carry out in Greenland. The king said that he did not know of anyone who was better suited for such work than Leif. 'You will bring luck to the work,' he said. Leif replied: 'Only if you add your luck to mine.'

Leif put to sea, but he was driven by storms for a long time, and he found a land whose existence he had never suspected. There were fields of wheat growing wild, and there were vines as well. There were also those trees which are called *masur*, and of all these things they took samples. [H: Some of the trees were so big that they were used for house-building.]

Leif [H: found some shipwrecked men and] brought them home with him and gave them all lodging for the winter. In this [H: as in many other ways] he showed magnanimity and courage. He was [H: ever after] called Leif the Lucky.

Thorstein's Unsuccessful Vinland Voyage

... There was now much talk about finding again the land which Leif had discovered. Thorstein Eiriksson was the most eager, and he was a good man, wise and well liked. Eirik was also asked to go with them, for men thought that he had good luck and good judgment; he was reluctant for a long time but

* Translation from *Skálholtsbók*. Extracts from *Hauksbók* are added in brackets and are denoted by H.

did not refuse when his friends urged him. They then made ready the ship which Thorbjørn had brought to Greenland, and the crew consisted of twenty men. They had little cargo with them, mostly weapons and provisions.

The morning that Eirik rode from home he took a small chest containing gold and silver, and hid it. He then rode on his way; but he had not gone far when he was thrown from his horse and broke some ribs and injured his shoulder-joint. He cried out: 'Aiai!' Because of this mishap he asked his wife Thjodhild to fetch the gold and silver that he had hidden away, and he believed that he had been thus punished for hiding it away.

Then they sailed out of Eiriksfjord, in high spirits and with great hopes for a successful voyage. But they were storm-tossed for a long time on the ocean, and they did not reach the destination they had intended. They came within sight of Iceland, and they saw birds from Ireland. Their ship was driven backwards and forwards across the ocean, and in the autumn they set course for home and were in a miserable condition. They reached Eiriksfjord [H: at the beginning of winter] ...

Thorfinn Karlsefni's Expedition to Vinland

... That winter there was much discussion at Brattahlid [H: about searching for Vinland the Good, and it was said that it was a profitable country to visit]. They played draughts, told stories, and occupied themselves with other activities to pass the time. Karlsefni and Snorri wanted to set out and find Vinland, and the plans were discussed. They made their ship ready and wanted to sail to Vinland that summer [H: spring]. Bjarni and Thorhall also wanted to join the expedition with their ship and with the crew which they had brought with them.

There was a man by the name of Thorvald,* the son-in-law of Eirik the Red [H: he came along, and also Thorhall, who was called 'the Hunter']; he had been with Eirik a long time as a huntsman and had been charged with the responsibility for many things. Thorhall was a huge, swarthy man who looked like an ogre; he was getting on in years, was bad-tempered and of few words, taciturn and cunning but nevertheless abusive in speech and always inciting [H: Eirik] to that which was evil.

He had cared little about the Christian religion since it had come to Greenland. Thorhall had few friends, yet Eirik had for a long time listened to his counsel. He was on board the ship with Thorvard [H: with Thorvard and Thorvald], for he had wide knowledge of remote regions. They had that same ship in which Thorbjørn had come to Greenland. Most of the crew were Greenlanders. Altogether there were a hundred and sixty men on board the ships.

* *Hauksbók* has 'Thorvard, who married Freydis, an illegitimate daughter of Eirik the Red, and Thorvald Eiriksson'.

First they sailed to the Western Settlement and from there to Bjarneyar. They sailed from Bjarneyar before a northerly wind and were at sea two days. Then they found land and rowed ashore in the ship's boats to explore it. They found there many flat slabs of stones that were so big that two men could easily stretch out on them sole to sole. [H: many of them were twelve ells (i.e. eighteen feet) across.] There were many white foxes there. They gave the land a name, and called it Helluland.

They then sailed for two days before a northerly wind [H: and changed their course from south to south-east] and then they saw a land ahead with large forests and many animals. South-east of the land there was an island, and there they encountered a bear and called the island Bjarney, Bear Island. The land with the forests they called Markland.

After two days they sighted land again and sailed in towards the coast [H: Then they sailed southward along the coast for a long time and came to a cape]. There they arrived at a cape; they sailed along the land and had it on their starboard side. It was an open harbourless shore with long sandy beaches. They rowed in to the shore and found [H: there on the cape] the keel of a ship and called the place Kjalarnes. They also gave a name to the beaches, calling them Furdustrandir ('Wonder Beaches'), because it took them so long to sail past them.

Then the coastline became indented with bays, and towards [H: one of] them they steered their ships.

When Leif Eiriksson had been with King Olaf Tryggvason and the king had asked him to preach Christianity in Greenland, the king had given him two Scots; the man was called Haki and the woman Hekja. The king had told Leif that he ought to use them if he ever needed something done in a hurry, for they could run faster than deer. Leif and Eirik had let Karlsefni take them on his expedition.

When they thus had sailed past Furdustrandir they put the Scots ashore and bade them run in a southerly direction and explore the country's resources and return within three days.

They were dressed in the type of garment which was called *bjafal* [H: *kjafal*]; it had a hood on top, was open at the sides, and had no sleeves, but was fastened between the legs with a button and a loop. Besides that they were naked.

The ships cast anchor and lay there a while. When three days had passed the Scots came running down from the land, and one of them was holding grapes [H: clusters of grapes] in his hand, the other one wild [H: newly sown] wheat. Karlsefni said that it seemed that they had found a good land.

They were taken on board, and the voyage continued to a place where the land was indented by a fjord. They steered their ships into the fjord. Beyond its mouth lay an island, and around it there were strong currents. They called the island Straumsey [H: Straumey]. There were so many birds [H: eider ducks] that there was hardly any place to step between the eggs.

They steered into the fjord and called it Straumsfjord [H: Straumfjord] and there they carried their goods off the ships and prepared to stay. They had brought all kinds of livestock, and they looked round to see what the land had to offer. There were mountains,* and it was a beautiful country. They did nothing except explore the country. There was an abundance of grass.

They stayed there that winter, but it was a severe winter and they had not put aside any provisions, and now they ran short of food, and both hunting and fishing failed. They then went out to the island in the hope that the hunting and fishing would be better there or that something that could be eaten would drift ashore. But there was little food to be found there, although the cattle throve. Then they prayed to God that He would send them something to eat, but their prayers were not answered as quickly as they wished.

Thorhall disappeared, and men set out to look for him, and they did so for three whole days. On the fourth day Karlsefni and Bjarni found Thorhall on a crag. He was staring up at the sky with eyes and mouth and nostrils wide open, and he was scratching and pinching himself and mumbling something. They asked him why he had come to that place, but he replied that it was none of their business, they should not be surprised, and he had lived so long that they could save themselves the trouble of worrying about him. They asked him to come back with them, and that he did.

A little later a whale was driven into the fjord and they began to cut it up, but no one knew what kind of whale it was. Karlsefni had much knowledge of whales, but he did not recognize the type. The cooks boiled a part of the whale, and they ate it, but they all became ill.

Then Thorhall walked up and said: 'Was it not so that the Red Bearded One [Thor] was stronger than your Christ? This was my reward for the poem which I made in honour of Thor, my patron. Seldom has he failed me.' But when the men heard this, no one would eat the meat, and they threw it over a cliff and committed themselves to the mercy of God.

Then it became possible to go out fishing [H: the weather had improved] and they got enough to sustain life. In the spring they sailed into Straumsfjord and they obtained supplies from two sources, meat from hunting on the mainland, and eggs and fish from the sea.

They now discussed their expedition and made plans. Thorhall the Hunter wanted to proceed north beyond Furdustrandir and Kjalarnes and search for Vinland there. Karlsefni wanted to travel southward along the coast† and east

---

* H. does not mention mountains.
† The rest of the sentence is missing in *Hauksbók*.

of it, for he believed that the country was larger the farther south they got, and
he thought it best to explore the land in both directions.

Thorhall made ready his ship out by the island, and there were not more
than nine men going with him; the others all went with Karlsefni. One day
when Thorhall was carrying water out to his ship, he drank a mouthful, and
composed this poem:

> Bravest men gave promise
> that when here I came
> the best of drinks awaited.
> I could curse this country.
> I who wore a helmet
> carry water buckets
> and must grovel at a spring.
> Not a drop of wine
> ever touched my lips.

Then they put to sea, and Karlsefni accompanied them out past the islands.
Before they hoisted sail Thorhall made this verse:

> Let us all sail homeward,
> Greenland's coasts are calling,
> Ship and men be tested
> by the sea's expanse,
> while the eager warriors,
> they who praise the country,
> stay at Furdustrandir,
> boiling whales.

Then they left the others and sailed northward past Furdustrandir and
Kjalarnes and wanted to steer in a westward direction from there, but they met
with a storm and they were driven right across to Ireland. There they were
badly treated and made slaves. And it was there that Thorhall lost his life
[H: according to what traders tell].

It must now be told that Karlsefni sailed southward along the land, accompanied by Snorri, Bjarni and the rest of the expedition. They sailed for a long
time and at last they reached a river that flowed down from the land and into
a lake and from there out into the sea. There were large sand-bars outside the
mouth of the river, so that they could not sail up the river except at high tide.
Karlsefni and his men sailed into the estuary, and they called the place Hop.*

---

* *Hop* means a bay or a lake, with a narrow channel or river through which the tide rises and
falls. There are many such *hops* along the coasts of North America and Greenland

There they found fields with wild wheat growing on the low-lying land and vines on all the higher ground. In every stream there was plenty of fish. They dug trenches where the land and the sea met at high tide, and when the tide went out there were halibut in the trenches. In the forests there were animals of all kinds.

Karlsefni and the others stayed there for half a month enjoying themselves, and did not notice anything unusual. They had taken their livestock with them.

But early one morning as they were walking about they caught sight of nine [H: a great number of] skin-boats. Those on board were swinging wooden staves which made a noise like flails, and the staves were swung with the sun.

Then Karlsefni said: 'What is the meaning of this?' Snorri Thorbrandsson replied: 'Perhaps it is a token of peace; let us take a white shield and carry it towards them.' This was done. Then the strangers rowed towards them, stared at them with astonishment, and came ashore. They were small [H: dark] ugly men with coarse hair; they had big eyes and broad cheekbones. They stood there for a while, marvelling, and afterwards rowed away in a southerly direction past the headland.

Karlsefni and his men had built their dwellings away from the shore; some of the houses were close to the lake, while others were farther away. They stayed there that winter; no snow fell, and the livestock grazed out of doors.

When spring came, early one morning they saw a multitude of skin-boats being rowed from the south past the headland, and they were so many that it seemed as if the bay was sown with coal. This time, also, staves were being waved in every boat.

Karlsefni and his men raised their shields, and then they began to trade. What the natives most wanted was red cloth [H: and offered in return furs and grey pelts]. They also wanted to purchase swords and spears, but Karlsefni and Snorri forbade that. [H: For a black pelt the natives got one span (nine inches) of red cloth, which they tied round their heads.] The trading continued like this for a while. But when the cloth began to run short, they cut it up in such a way that the strips were no wider than a finger. The natives gave just as much for it, or even more.

Then it happened that a bull which Karlsefni owned came running out of the forest, bellowing loudly. The natives took fright, ran to their boats, and rowed south along the shore. After that they did not see the natives for three weeks.

But at the end of that period they saw a multitude of native boats approaching from the south, pouring in like a torrent. This time all the staves were swung counter to the sun's motion, and all the natives were howling loudly. Then Karlsefni's men raised their red shields which they carried against them. [H: The natives ran from their boats and] Then they clashed and fought fiercely. There was a hail of missiles, and the natives used war-slings also. Then Karlsefni and Snorri noticed that the natives were putting up on poles [H: a pole] a [H: very] large blue-black ball-shaped object [H: more or less resembling a sheep's stomach]. This they sent flying [H: from the pole] through the air towards Karlsefni's men, and it made a hideous sound where it came down. This so frightened Karlsefni and his men that their only thought was to flee up along the river [H: for they believed that the natives were attacking them from all sides. They did not stop until they came] to some steep cliffs, and there they made a resolute stand.

Freydis came out and saw that Karlsefni and his men were fleeing. She shouted: 'Why do you run away from these wretches? Such brave men as you are, I should think, would be able to slaughter them like cattle. If I only had weapons, I would fight better than any of you!'

But they paid no heed to her. Freydis wanted to join them, but she was slow on her feet since she was with child. She followed them into the forest, pursued by the natives.

Then she saw in front of her a dead man — it was Thorbrand Snorreson — with a flat stone buried in his head; his sword was lying by his side, and she picked it up in order to defend herself with it. And the natives came rushing towards her. Then she pulled out her breasts from under her shift and slapped them with the sword. The natives were so terrified that they ran off to their boats and rowed away.

Karlsefni and his men came over to her and praised her courage. Two of their men had been killed and four [H: many] of the natives, even though the natives had great superiority in numbers. They then returned to their houses [H: and dressed their wounds] and pondered what force it had been that had attacked them from the land side. Then they realized that they had fought only against the attackers who had come from the boats, and when they thought there had been others as well, it must have been a delusion.

It happened that the natives found a dead man, with an axe lying next to him. [H: One of them picked up the axe and chopped at a tree with it, then the others did the same and thought that a splendid thing which could cut so well.] One of them hacked at a rock with it, and then the axe broke. He did not think it worth much since it could not cut stone, so he threw it away.

Karlsefni and his men now realized that, even though it was a good land, because of the natives fear and strife would always be a part of life there. They made ready to leave and wanted to sail back to their own country. They sailed in a northerly direction, and while under way they came upon five natives sleeping in their skin clothing [H: by the sea], and they had with them wooden containers in which was animal marrow mixed with blood. They thought that these men must have been sent out from that country (as scouts?) and they killed them. Then they discovered a headland and many animals. The entire headland could be likened to a huge cake of dung, for the animals used to stay there during the winter [H: during the night].

Then Karlsefni and his companions came back to Straumsfjord [H: where there was an abundance of everything they needed]. Some men say that Bjarni and Freydis [H: Gudrid] stayed behind there with a hundred men and did not sail any farther. Karlsefni and Snorri sailed south with forty men, and did not stay more than two months at Hop, and returned that same summer.

Karlsefni set off with one ship in order to search for Thorhall the Hunter, while the rest of the party stayed behind. He sailed north past Kjalarnes, then in a westerly direction with the land on the port side. There was nothing but desolate forests [H: to be seen ahead, with hardly any open spaces]. When they had sailed for a long time, they came to a river which was flowing from east to west down from the high land. They sailed into the river mouth and anchored off its southern bank.

One morning Karlsefni and his men noticed a speck above the clearing; there was something that gleamed at them, and they shouted at it. It moved, it was a uniped, and it jumped down to the river bank where they were. Thorvald, Eirik the Red's son, was sitting at the helm, and the uniped shot an arrow into his entrails. He pulled out the arrow and said: 'I have fat round my entrails; we have found a good land, but I shall hardly be able to enjoy it.' Thorvald died from the wound soon afterwards.

The uniped ran off to the north; Karlsefni and his men pursued the uniped and caught a glimpse of him now and then. The last they saw of him was his leaping into some river or other. Karlsefni and his men then turned back.* Then one of the men composed this stanza:

> The men were chasing,
> and it is true,
> a uniped
> down to the beach.
> This weird creature
> streaked away,
> sank in water.
> Hear, Karlsefni!

Then they sailed away and back to the north. They thought they had sighted the land of the unipeds. They were unwilling to risk the lives of the men further.

---

* Some of the details in the account given in *Hauksbók* are slightly different, but it agrees on the whole with the one here given.

They intended to explore all the mountains, those at Hop and those that they had now discovered. [H: They thought that the mountains at Hop and those they had now discovered belonged to the same mountain range, and that these places therefore were directly opposite each other, and that the distance from Straumfjord was the same in both directions.]

They sailed back and remained at Straumsfjord that third winter. There were bitter quarrels among the men [H: because of the women] for the unmarried men ran after the married women. [H: This led to serious disturbances.] Karlsefni's son Snorri was born there that first autumn. [H: He was three years old when they left.]

[H: When they sailed from Vinland] they got a south wind and came to Markland. There they found five natives — one man with a beard, two women, and two children. Karlsefni captured the two boys, but the others got away and disappeared into the ground. They took the two boys with them, taught them their language, and baptized them. They said that their mother's name was Vætildi, that their father was called Uvægi, and that there were kings ruling the land of the Skraelings, one of whom was called Avaldamon and the other Valldidida. There were no houses there; the people lived in caves and in dens. They said that there lay a land on the other side, directly opposite from theirs, where the people went about in [H: lived who wore] white clothes and shouted loudly, and went about with [H: carried] poles with patches of cloth attached. It was said that this was Hvitmannaland* [H: or Ireland the Great].

Then they came to Greenland and spent the winter with Eirik the Red.

---

* This name recurs in the legendary accounts about Ari Marsson in the Icelandic *Landnámabók* and about Bjørn in the *Eyrbyggja Saga* (see page 29).

Chapter Six

Sailing Information and Topographical Descriptions in the Sagas

Bjarni's Voyage

The saga account of Bjarni's voyage is as plain as a ship's log and has the stamp of credibility. The authenticity of the story is further buttressed by the fact that his contemporaries did not look upon the voyage as a great achievement but as something to be criticized, for the reason that he did not explore the new land which he had glimpsed from the sea. In short, Bjarni was an ordinary sailor who had lost his way and had only one thing on his mind: to reach his original destination.

Bjarni had sailed from Norway to Iceland and there he had been told that his father had sailed to Greenland and settled there. Although he had never sailed across the Greenland Sea, Bjarni set out for his father's new home. He encountered a north wind and fog, and lost his bearings for many days.

After a time he glimpsed a foreign land, one that 'had no mountains and was covered with woods and there were low hills'. This description fits the north coast of Newfoundland extremely well. He would have been drifting at about nine degrees of latitude in a southward direction from Greenland and would have covered about 1,350 nautical miles from Eyrar in Iceland.

Bjarni did not want to go ashore but kept the land on his port side and let the sheet turn towards the land. They sailed on for *two days* and saw a new land which was *flat country* and *covered with woods*, but Bjarni still would not go ashore. The description of the regions which had been reached fits the area round Cape Porcupine in Labrador very well. Here the country is extremely flat and the forests come all the way down to the shore. It is also noteworthy that the distance from the north coast of Newfoundland to Cape Porcupine is about two hundred nautical miles, and that it would have taken close on two days and nights (*døgr*) to cover that distance.

They then sailed seaward before a south-west wind for *three days* and discovered a new land which was high and mountainous, with glaciers. It proved to be an island. This may have been Loks Land, adjacent to tremendous glaciers on the south coast of Baffin Island, or perhaps Resolution Island. The

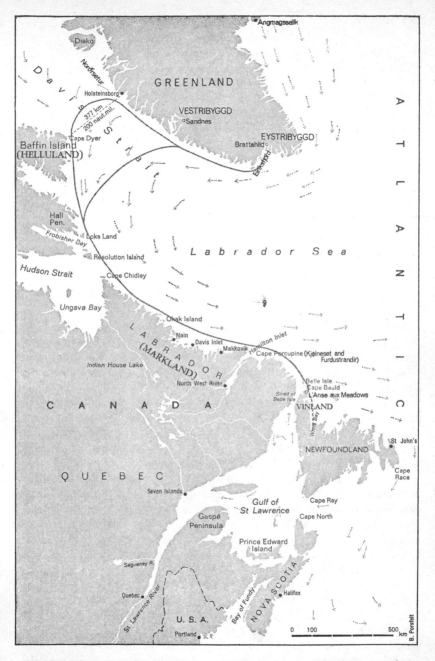

The solid lines indicate the routes that Leif Eiriksson and other Vinland voyagers are supposed to have followed from the Norse settlements in Greenland to Vinland.

distance from Cape Porcupine to Loks Land is about five hundred nautical miles and it could have been covered in three days without too much difficulty.

Bjarni did not go ashore here either, but continued sailing for *four days* before a strong wind and reached his father's farm at Herjolfsnes at the southern tip of Greenland. The distance from Loks Land to this place is about 570 nautical miles, and it seems just about right that he took four days to cover that distance.

In all, then, he sailed for nine days from the land that he sighted first, and if we calculate from an average speed of 150 nautical miles in twenty-four hours this makes about 1,350 nautical miles. If we look at the whole voyage on the assumption that he sailed from the north coast of Newfoundland to Cape Porcupine, and then from Loks Land to the southernmost point in the Eastern Settlement in Greenland, then the total distance can be seen on a map to be about 1,300 nautical miles. The difference between these two figures is so small that we are justified in saying that there is a remarkable correspondence between them over such a great distance.

Leif Eiriksson's Voyage

The voyage of Leif Eiriksson is described quite differently in the two sagas. We shall first consider the few lines in Eirik the Red's Saga concerning Leif's great discovery. It says very curtly that during his voyage to Greenland from Olaf Tryggvason's court in Trondheim he was storm-driven for a long time and discovered a new land where there were fields with wild wheat, vines, and trees called *masur*. He reached Greenland that same year, and on the way back he rescued a shipwrecked crew.

This is the essence of an account which is entirely different from the detailed description in the Greenlanders' Saga, which also contains an observation of the sun, the authenticity of which has not been contested.

The version given in Eirik the Red's Saga seems improbable. It may have been included in order to increase the prestige of the Church, in view of the fact that Leif's voyage was made out to be a missionary venture. He had been given the assignment by the king of introducing Christianity in Greenland. It is also possible, as we have mentioned before, that the details regarding Leif's voyage became, in time, of less interest to the saga-tellers in Iceland than the account of Karlsefni's achievements.

In the Greenlanders' Saga Leif Eiriksson's voyage appears as a well-planned expedition launched for the purpose of exploration. The essential prerequisite — as is the case with most great expeditions of exploration — was that he had some knowledge of the lands which he was seeking. His knowledge was based on the experiences of Bjarni on his voyage. He bought Bjarni's ship, and with a crew of thirty-five men he set out towards the new lands. But he took the *opposite route*, that is, he sailed first towards the northern parts which Bjarni had seen last.

In this northern land he did not see any grass, but only huge glaciers, and between the glaciers and the sea the land was like a single slab of rock. He gave the land the name Helluland; it must have been somewhere on the southeastern coast of Baffin Island. It is of importance to note that there are no glaciers farther south, either in Labrador or in Newfoundland.

Then they set out to sea and found *the second land*. It was flat and covered with forests, and there were extensive white sandy shores and the water was shallow far out into the sea. He called it Markland (Forest Land). This runs parallel to Bjarni's account, with a descriptive addition about the long and extensive beaches. This piece of information also agrees with the long and extensive beaches (Furdustrandir) at Keelness included in the account of Karlsefni's voyage. As originally shown by W. A. Munn[1] and V. Tanner,[2] the beaches at Cape Porcupine, stretching for miles, are the only ones of their kind along the shores of Labrador, a fact which I myself have corroborated. It is consequently probable that Leif made a landfall on these beaches, which are visible from far out at sea.

This fact provides us with a better basis for calculating the distance to *the third land* than can be derived from the account of Bjarni's voyage. The saga says that they then sailed out to sea before a north-easterly wind and remained at sea *for two days* before they sighted land. From the extensive beaches at Cape Porcupine to the north coast of Newfoundland it is, as previously mentioned, about two hundred nautical miles, and that distance would require about two days' sailing time.

Having covered that distance Leif came to an island which lay north of the land. It may perhaps have been Great Sacred Island, or possibly Belle Isle, both of which are conspicuous landmarks for the seaman. We are also told that there was a cape pointing towards the north, how shallow the sea was where they landed, and that there was an abundance of grass and forests. Later on in this book I shall show how these descriptive details seem to fit L'Anse aux Meadows, where the ancient house-sites were found.

There is, however, one aspect of this description which seems surprising, and that is the reference to a *hop* — a lake with a river up which they dragged their ships at flood-tide. The fact is that we have an identical description in Eirik the Red's Saga dealing with the more southerly explorations of Thorfinn Karlsefni, and it would be strange indeed if two different expeditions in two widely separated regions of North America had encountered the same conditions and made the very same kind of arrangements where they settled down. There is much that seems to indicate that the reference to a *hop* may derive from Eirik the Red's Saga or another, common source.

The distance covered from a likely point of departure in Labrador and the general information given indicate that the north coast of Newfoundland was probably Vinland, the 'third land'. The saga tells us that Leif and his men carried their leather bags ashore and put up temporary shelters there; then they decided to stay over the winter, and they built 'large houses'. Leif gave the country a name in accordance with its resources and called it Vinland.

Thorvald Eiriksson's Expedition

I have previously mentioned the fact that Eirik the Red's Saga says that Thorvald took part in the Thorfinn Karlsefni expedition. But this part of that particular saga is marked by so many improbabilities that the sober account in the Greenlanders' Saga about Thorvald's independent expedition must be considered to be the true version.

Here we are told that Thorvald's brother, Leif Eiriksson, lent him his ship and advised him to take along thirty men. It says further that there is nothing to be said about the voyage until they arrived in Vinland, at Leifsbudir. This sounds authentic, since the route to northern Newfoundland is far from complicated and may be described in a few words. It is also probable that some of Leif's men had come too, to give Thorvald the benefit of their knowledge.

This expedition is the first one whose purpose was settlement in America, for it is clear that Thorvald explored the country thoroughly with a view to building permanent living quarters.

The coastline towards the west was explored during the first year. They found a beautiful forest-covered land with many islands and extensive shallow coastal waters, a description which fits the north coast of Newfoundland very well.

The next summer Thorvald sailed with his biggest ship eastward along the northern part of the land. They met with rough weather outside a cape, the ship's keel was broken, and they had to repair the ship. They called the cape Kjalarnes, or Keelness. In the account of Karlsefni's expedition (Eirik the Red's Saga) there is also mention of a Keelness, but it has an entirely different location, namely, on the extensive beaches of Markland, about two days' sailing to the north of Vinland. It is possible that this is the result of a mix-up, but it is also possible that two different land formations were given the name Keelness because they made one think of the keel of a ship. At any rate, the course taken by Thorvald according to the saga excludes the possibility that he was as far north as Labrador.

It could be that the northerly land explored by Thorvald was the low mountain range near Cape Bauld, in the north of Newfoundland. We are told that he sailed along the coast to the east of the land, which may mean that he sailed along the east coast, and that he sailed into a fjord mouth and up to a headland

Plate 10. The author and his wife Anne Stine on board the *Halten*. (Photograph: National Geographic Society.)

Plate 11. The *Halten* in the Labrador Sea. A Norwegian rescue vessel built of oak, the *Halten* was designed by Colin Archer, who also built Fridtjof Nansen's famous ship *Fram*. (Photograph: Erling Brunborg.)

Plate 12. The women members of the *Halten* expedition: Anne Stine Ingstad (*left*) and Benedicte. (Photograph: Erling Brunborg.)

which he found there. Everywhere they saw forests. They went ashore, and here the pioneer settler found what he had been looking for, and exclaimed: 'This is a beautiful place; here I should like to make my home.'

Soon after, he encountered the natives and an armed clash ensued. Thorvald was hit by an arrow, and was buried on a promontory which was named Crossness. The members of the expedition stayed at Leifsbudir one more winter. Thorvald was the first European who is definitely known to have encountered the natives of North America.

Thorfinn Karlsefni's Expedition

All the voyagers to Vinland so far had been Greenlanders; Thorfinn Karlsefni, on the other hand, was an Icelander who just before his great expedition had been visiting Greenland. The saga says that he belonged to a distinguished family, was wealthy, and a good seaman.

The following summary will in the main be based on Eirik the Red's Saga, but note will be taken of the somewhat different version in the Greenlanders' Saga.

Thorfinn Karlsefni probably set out from Brattahlid around the year 1020, as Gathorne-Hardy[3] maintains. There were three ships in all, with about one hundred and sixty men and women, among them his wife Gudrid. (The Greenlanders' Saga says that there were in all sixty men and five women.) In addition they took livestock with them. Many of the participants were Greenlanders. The main purpose of their boldly conceived plans was to establish a Norse colony in the newly discovered land.

The ships first sailed northward to the Western Settlement, then to Bjarney whose location we do not know. Benefiting from a northerly wind, they must then have crossed Davis Strait to Baffin Island. The voyage lasted *two days* (*døgr*), and that seems very plausible. It is doubtful if the expedition reached exactly the same place that Bjarni and Leif had seen, but that is of lesser importance. In the land he did find there were Arctic foxes and large flat stones; he called the land Helluland. A very significant piece of information in the Greenlanders' Saga makes it quite clear that Helluland must have been the south-eastern part of Baffin Island. In the account of Bjarni's Vinland voyage as well as in that of Leif Eiriksson we are told that in the northernmost land they had arrived at there were large glaciers and that Leif called it Helluland. As mentioned before, there are no glaciers in Labrador, nor are there any farther south.

They then sailed for *two days* before a northerly wind and arrived in a land with huge forests and many wild animals. This cannot have been any place but Labrador, very probably its northern part — the northern limit of the forest belt is at about 57° N. The animals seen were probably caribou. He called the land Markland.

They then sailed on for *two days* and passed a cape which they gave the name Keelness (Kjølneset), and long sandy beaches, which they called Wonderstrands (Furdustrandir) because it took them such a long time to sail past. As mentioned before, similar beaches and shores are mentioned in the story of Leif Eiriksson's voyage, and there seems little doubt that they must have been the twenty-mile-long beaches not very far south of Hamilton Inlet. The cape is shaped like a capsized boat, and the name Keelness is very suggestive.

The voyage continued, very probably in a southward direction. The account now becomes somewhat less clear, not least because the fairy-tale motif of Haki and his wife Hekja who find wild grapes and wild wheat is a disturbing element. We are succinctly told that he sailed on to a fjord, which he called Straumsfjord, and stayed there. Where can that possibly have been?

We should first take note of the fact that northern Newfoundland must have been clearly visible at long range, and lay right in the middle of the ships' course when the expedition came sailing south along the coast of Labrador. One might think that the expedition would have made its quarters on the north coast of Newfoundland, where the Strait of Belle Isle, whose powerful current can be felt far and wide, opens into the ocean. The island nearest to the mainland may have been Great Sacred Island or Belle Isle. The allusion to the mountains does not fit with the facts very well, but it is quite possible that it refers to mountains that could be seen farther to the south. *Hauksbók*, however does *not* mention mountains. When the saga says that there was plenty of grass, this agrees very well with the north coast of Newfoundland but not with Labrador.

The description of the hard winter and the difficulties faced by the expedition in the course of it—partly due to the fact that an adequate food supply had not been assured through hunting and fishing—also point to a more northerly latitude. It is also implied that there were no grapes in that locality. This is confirmed by the fact that the next year Karlsefni undertook a long voyage of exploration southward, and this would not have made much sense if he had already arrived in a southerly and fertile region. We are also given the interesting piece of information that he sailed east of the land and then in a southerly direction. If he had settled in Labrador, this would not have seemed a reasonable thing to do. Of special interest in this connection is his opinion that the land would be 'larger' farther south. This implies that the region in which he had gone ashore was one of limited extent, and such a description does fit the north coast of Newfoundland, the northernmost part of which is an elongated narrow peninsula. It would have taken him only several hours to sail along that part of the coastline facing north.

In the Greenlanders' Saga we are told that Karlsefni asked Leif if he could have his houses in Vinland, the answer being that he could borrow them. It is expressly stated that Karlsefni's expedition stayed at Leifsbudir. It seems rather strange that Eirik the Red's Saga does not mention that they built houses, a fact which would seem to be of signal importance inasmuch as it entailed dwellings for no less than one hundred and sixty persons. The Greenlanders' Saga says that all the Vinland expeditions stayed at Leifsbudir. It is also noteworthy that in the account of Karlsefni's southward voyage of exploration, on which he took a limited number of persons and on which dwellings cannot have been of the greatest importance, we are told that houses were built, and we are given quite a detailed description of their location.

Is it possible that an element of rivalry has played a role here, that Karlsefni's Icelandic posterity has found it not strictly necessary to emphasize in the saga account that he stayed in the buildings originally put up by Leif Eiriksson, the discoverer of Vinland?

On the whole, many circumstances point to the fact that Karlsefni made his quarters at Leifsbudir on the north coast of Newfoundland. Later on I shall revert to the fact that at L'Anse aux Meadows, where the old sites were excavated, we found a spindle-whorl, made of soapstone, and unquestionably of Norse origin. This shows that women must have been there, and we know that women did participate in Karlsefni's and Freydis's expeditions, but not in those of Leif and Thorvald.

As regards the voyage made by Karlsefni from his headquarters in a southerly direction, the saga does not contain any sailing directions that might help us to identify the places visited. As mentioned before, he sailed east of the land and southward, which may mean along the east coast of Newfoundland. We are also told that he brought his ship up into a river and into a lake (*hop*) at flood-tide and built his houses there, but the difficulty is that there are so many places that fit this description along the coasts of the North American continent.

There is no doubt that the Norwegian archaeologist and historian A. W. Brøgger is right in maintaining that the story of Karlsefni gives a clear impression of various sources having been mixed up and that it contains many self-contradictory and bewildering bits of information. We are told, for example, that Thorhall the Hunter wanted to sail back, in a northerly direction, past Wonder Beaches and Keelness in order to search for Vinland. That means that he wanted to sail for two days northward along the forbidding coasts with which he had become acquainted in the voyage to the south and where he must surely have known that there was no chance of finding any sizable grasslands. It is equally improbable that Karlsefni set out a year later in the same direction in order to search for Thorhall. Instead of getting lost in philological speculations we should remember that these men were experienced and practical seamen with an eye for everything that a country could offer. This part of the Karlsefni account contains other curious elements that do not seem very authentic. We are told about the uniped who kills Thorvald with an arrow, and that the latter makes a remark which must have been borrowed from the story of Thormod Kolbrunarskald in the Saga of Saint Olav. *Hauksbók* goes on to say that the mountains to the north seem to be the same as those seen at *Hop*, in a region in which Karlsefni had been after he had sailed in a *southward* direction from his headquarters. It is equally meaningless to infer that Karlsefni, following his encounter with the uniped, sailed towards the north in order to get back to Straumfjord.

The important thing to remember, however, is that in many essentials the sagas seem to contain reliable information. What they have to say about Vinland points, as already mentioned, to the north coast of Newfoundland.

Freydis's Voyage

In its account of the Thorfinn Karlsefni expedition, Eirik the Red's Saga also relates an episode dealing with Freydis. As mentioned already, this is probably because Icelandic tradition has in the course of time incorporated into the story of their great hero much material that belongs elsewhere. The story about Freydis as it appears in the Greenlanders' Saga seems more plausible, however. According to that version, she launched her own expedition to Vinland together with the brothers Helgi and Finnbogi who had come from Norway in their own ship. Thus two ships with sixty-five men, in addition to a number of women, set sail for Vinland.

The story of Freydis's voyage is not a pleasant one. She must have been a ruthless woman, but that type of woman was to be found in the Viking Age. She wanted to exchange ships with Helgi and Finnbogi, a suggestion which caused bitterness, and in the end the brothers and their entire crew, including their women, were killed. Stories about murder on expeditions to far-away places might easily lead to exaggeration when retold through the centuries; thus the story about Freydis may have a kernel of fact which has provided tempting possibilities for embroidering the truth.

Disputes and fighting make up the central theme in this account. We are not told anything about the voyage or about the lands visited; the saga merely says that the expedition arrived at Leifsbudir and decided to stay there. Once more we get the impression that the route to be followed to reach Vinland was uncomplicated and comparatively well known.

If we take an overall view of the sailing directions and the descriptions of the new-found lands as they appear in the various sagas, it is astounding how much the really important pieces of information are in agreement, and how much there is that agrees with the actual geographical features.

All the accounts emphasize that the voyagers came to three different lands, which we must assume were separate. They were Helluland, Markland, and Vinland. The sailing distances and the time spent at sea are all reported as so short that there is hardly any question but that the three lands were Baffin Island, Labrador, and northern Newfoundland. The most striking thing about it all, perhaps, is that those distances which we can determine on the basis of the sailing time coincide in large measure with those which we can measure on a map. This is especially true of Bjarni's voyage and of Leif Eiriksson's voyage from 'the white sandy beaches' (probably the beaches at Cape Porcupine) to Vinland. The entire story must also be read with reference to those scattered sources outside the sagas; we are told, for instance, in ancient Icelandic geographical descriptions that it is not very far from Markland to Vinland (see page 31).

It is also worth noting in this connection that Adam of Bremen calls Vinland an island, that the island of Newfoundland juts out like a man's arm into the ocean, and that a ship sailing from the north along the coast of Labrador would have a straight course towards the northern coast of that large island. All in all, the sailing directions and the descriptions of the land point to the fact that the Norsemen settled on the north coast of Newfoundland and that it was this area that was known as Vinland.

Chapter Seven

Grapes and Skraelings

It is important to ascertain whether any further information given in the sagas might be of value in determining the location of Vinland. Would this also, like the sailing directions and the description of the land, indicate that Vinland is northern Newfoundland, or would it point in another direction?

Grapes and the Name 'Vinland'

The northern limit along the east coast of North America for the growth of wild grapes is at approximately 42° N., in Massachusetts. In the interior of the country the limits are a bit farther to the north. If the Norsemen found grapes at their headquarters in Vinland, it would mean that they must have made a voyage covering about two thousand nautical miles from Baffin Island, and this would have taken them about fourteen days and nights, probably more. If that were so, we should have to disregard completely all the sailing directions involving only a few days, even though such information is usually considered the very nucleus of the accounts told by experienced sailors.

The sagas proffer various items of information about grapes which are very peculiar:

In the Greenlanders' Saga's account of Leif Eiriksson's voyage we hear about a participant in the expedition who has been away for some time and returns to the houses in a confused condition, evidently from eating grapes. This man, who is also rather strange-looking, tells the others that he has found vines and grapes, and he adds that 'it is certainly true, for I was born where there is no lack of vines and grapes.' We are also told that he has the curious name Tyrkir and that he is not a Norseman but hails from more southerly climes. The whole story gives a strong impression that the saga-teller has felt it necessary to make use of this southerner to prove his point, since a Norseman would not have recognized grapes even if he had seen them.

Later on Leif says, 'We shall gather grapes and we shall cut vines and fell timber, to make a cargo for my ship.' And we are told that the ship's boat was filled with grapes.

In the account of Thorvald's Vinland voyage (the Greenlanders' Saga) we are also told that the members of the expedition collected grapes and vines as cargo for the ship. This is supposed to have happened in the winter or the spring!

From the account of Karlsefni's expedition (Eirik the Red's Saga) comes the curious story of the two Scottish runners Haki and Hekja, who set out on a reconnoitring journey into the interior of the country and came back after three days with grapes in one hand and wild wheat in the other. Here also it has been found necessary to have foreigners to identify the grapes. And the finding of the grapes occurs during the southward journey to Vinland, evidently in chilly Labrador and before their arrival at the headquarters at Straumfjord, where, on the contrary, no grapes were found. This episode has all the characteristics of a fairy tale.

In Straumfjord Thorhall complains that he is not getting any wine, but does not mention grapes, and sails back. When Karlsefni, having completed his exploration, sails from the same spot towards Greenland, it says in *Hauksbók* that 'they sailed from Vinland' in spite of the saga having made it clear that grapes were not found there.

About Karlsefni's voyage of exploration towards the south and to the *hop* the saga says: 'There they found fields with wild wheat growing on the lowlying land and vines on all the higher ground.'

The sagas' peculiar information about grapes is significant. It is not least revealing that the crew cut down vines to be used as cargo for the ship. A critical evaluation cannot lead to any other result than that those who incorporated the information about the grapes into the saga had no knowledge of grapes or vines. But how then are we to explain the fact that the episode of the grapes has been given such an important place in the sagas?

There is first of all one aspect of the matter which cannot be disregarded, namely, the fact that down through the ages various popular views and ideas of distant lands have been connected with grapes, wine, and wild wheat. Such conceptions were the symbols of the riches of the new lands and appealed strongly to the popular imagination. From the time of the Pentateuch onwards there are numerous examples of this. Fridtjof Nansen[1] has strongly emphasized this aspect and pointed to fables such as that of Isidor's Fortunate Isles — *Insulae Fortunatae* — where there grew wild vines and fields of grain. From a later time we have a number of Irish legends dealing with sea voyages and in these the mention of grapes has a conspicuous place, and the sailors, like Tyrkir, become inebriated from eating the grapes. The most famous of these Irish legends is *Navigatio Sancti Brandani*[2] — an account of St Brendan's voyage across the sea, lasting seven years, with the objective of finding the 'Promised Land'. Here we are told, among other things, of a 'fortunate island' with dense forests of 'wine trees'. When the travellers left the island, they did the same thing as Leif Eiriksson, they filled the ship's boat with grapes.

In the accounts of early voyages to North America it is not difficult to find the fertility of the region in question greatly exaggerated; we notice, for instance, that grapes are not only mentioned wherever they are found but also where they cannot possibly have grown. It is also of interest to note that William Alexander's[3] 1624 account of Nova Scotia mentions a kind of 'red wine-berries', which were very probably wild currants or squash-berries but cannot have been grapes. Quite significant is Nicolas Denys's[4] comment of 1672 on the French colony in Canada: he deplores the fact that people are very apt to condemn a newly discovered country if there are no grapes which can be used to make wine.

These circumstances may have contributed to the fact that grapes and wine were mentioned in the sagas. On the other hand, it is hard to accept this as the entire explanation. There is reason to believe that the stories about grapes did have a factual basis.

One starting-point might have been the Lay of Thorhall the Hunter in Eirik the Red's Saga which is probably one of its original sequences. Thorhall complains that he had been promised the sweetest of beverages, but no wine has so far passed his lips. This is indeed a blunt remark; there is no embroidering, and it has all the hallmark of authenticity. *But there is no mention at all of grapes*; he may simply have been referring to wine made from wild berries.

I shall discuss in another context the multitude of varieties of wild berries to be found in northern Newfoundland, not least in the neighbourhood of the house-sites at L'Anse aux Meadows (see pp. 140, 174–5). The Vinland voyagers may have made wine from wild gooseberries, from the squash-berries* that grow in clusters on bushes, from currants, or from other kinds of wild berries. It is also characteristic of this region, and this agrees very well with the incident concerning Thorhall, that the climate in summer is very changeable. This is the reason why there may be a surfeit of berries one year, and the next year very few to be found.

It is reasonable to assume that the people in Norway knew at that time how to make wine from wild berries.† It is quite evident that alcohol played a considerable role in the life of the people during the Viking Age. We know that they drank mead (made from honey) and beer; they were in other words familiar with the process of fermentation. It would be curious indeed if they did not utilize for wine-making the very great quantities of berries that grew near the farms, and especially in places where there was difficult access to the ingredients for the brewing of mead and beer.

---

* Probably *Viburnum pauciflorum*. They are red and very tasty berries, somewhat larger than European currants. They are abundant in Newfoundland, and they are also used for making wine.

† According to V. Tanner, the Nascapi Indians of northern Labrador are also supposed to have been able to make intoxicating liquors from wild berries. See *Acta Geographica* (Helsinki, 1914), p. 675.

We are told that King Sverri[5] in the twelfth century tried to have wine made from wild berries accepted as altar wine, but that Pope Gregory IX did not agree to this. It is safe to assume that wine-making was not invented in King Sverri's time, but that it was a process whose origins in the north reached far back in time.

Emigrants to Iceland and Greenland probably took with them across the seas the knowledge of the simple fermentation process — together with so many other traditions. Apart from that, Eirik the Red was born in Norway, and Leif Eiriksson had stayed there a whole year.

If the Vinland voyagers did make wine from wild berries, this fact alone would have captured the popular imagination and it would have been fairly certain to have been included in their account of the voyage, not least because they had found such an abundance of different kinds of berries completely unknown in Greenland and Iceland, where the only species to be found are blueberries, cranberries, and whortleberries. A thing such as this must have made an impression on the explorers of the new land.

The sagas dealing with the Vinland voyages have been handed down orally through the centuries, from one generation to another, and included in this tradition is Thorhall's poem, which expressly mentions wine but not what it was made from. Subsequent saga-men, who were further removed from the more detailed knowledge of the Vinland expeditions, must have thought that the wine which is mentioned in the poem had been made from grapes. They did not mean to falsify the saga, but it could easily happen in the course of a few hundred years that saga-men who did not know what grapes were would add an explanatory sentence on this tempting popular subject, if they thought that in other respects they were standing on firm ground. And the marvellous fables concerning grapes which were current at that time all over Europe played their part. In the course of time, the misunderstanding crystallized into a definite oral tradition, and this was subsequently written down in the manuscripts.

We can also believe it possible that Vinland may have been situated in a more northerly region if we can suppose that the saga text may be interpreted to the effect that the Vinland voyagers made wine from berries which they *thought* were grapes, as for example squash-berries. The same would be true if they used berries which they might have called *vinbær*, as currants are called even today in the district of Trøndelag and in Sweden — in northern England and Scotland they are called 'wine-berries'.

To substantiate the contention that it was grapes that they found, it has been mentioned that the manuscripts use the word *vínber*, meaning 'grapes'. But this implies nothing more than that the saga-writers put down what they *believed* was correct. They cannot have known that in the course of centuries this matter could have been distorted – that originally the old narratives spoke of berries growing wild and of a wine being made from them. As regards the name Vinland, there is *no* indication in the Icelandic manuscripts, apart from *Flateyjarbók*, which was written down as late as *c.* 1380, that its meaning is 'the land of grapes'. The name would in that case have been written with a long 'i': Vínland, whereas it was actually written with a short 'i': Vinland. In this case, the meaning of the name would be 'grassland', in the same way that Snorri Sturluson in his *Heimskringla* uses the name Viney for Denmark, because of the abundance of grassland (see page 75).

There is another important source that has a bearing on this matter, namely, the work written down about A.D. 1070 (see pp. 28–9) by the German ecclesiastic Adam of Bremen. In it we read:

In addition he has mentioned still another island which many have found in this great ocean, and which is called Vinland, since there grow wild grapes and they give the best wine. There is also an abundance of self-sown wheat there; we know this not from legends but from reliable accounts made by the Danes ... Beyond this island, he says, there is to be found no inhabitable land in this great ocean, but everything beyond is filled with intolerable ice and terrible fog. About all this Martianus says: 'One day's sailing beyond Thule the ocean runs together.' This the experienced Harald Hårdråde, the king of the Norwegians, was to learn. When he wanted to investigate the breadth of the Northern Ocean by ship, there finally formed such a fog in front of the gates of the end of the world that he, after being in great distress, just managed to save himself from the awful abyss by going back on his course.

How much importance should we assign to the information given here about grapes? First of all, we must remember that Adam of Bremen's account is in many ways very unreliable. On the other hand, it is possible that many tales were told and retold about Leif Eiriksson and others having made wine in the newly discovered country, and a German, especially, might without further ado draw the conclusion that the wine was made from grapes and not from wild berries.

Apart from this, another part of his account seems to contradict his information regarding grapes. He says that beyond the newly discovered island there is no inhabitable land in the great ocean, but everything beyond is filled with intolerable ice and terrible fog. This description fits Newfoundland very well, since it is not only an island but is within the borders of the drift-ice, where a heavy and extensive fog over the ocean and far to the north is a very characteristic phenomenon. If Adam of Bremen is correct in his mention of grapes, then we shall have to search for his island far to the south, in the region of wild grapes whose northern limit would be at approximately 42° N. If we think of places like Massachusetts, Rhode Island, New York or Virginia in this connection, his description will not come anywhere near the facts. It would have been strange indeed if he had described this region, and the green and fertile coast far to the north, as being characterized by fog and an icy polar climate.

Facts like these also warrant a great deal of scepticism when we are told by Adam of Bremen that the name Vinland was given to the country because wild grapes were growing there. And our scepticism is buttressed by the fact that he employs similarly peculiar explanations with regard to other lands and in other connections. Thus, he tells us that the name Greenland derives from the fact that the people living there have blue-green faces. Kvenland (the Norse name for Finland) is in his view the Land of Women (*Kvinneland*), and he connects the Huns with dogs (*Hunde*) ... and so on.

As regards the meaning of the name Vinland, it is of some importance for us to keep in mind the Norsemen's background and point of view. Thus, we must ask ourselves: What did they have in mind when they gave a name to a new land? We are here concerned with practical men, hailing from a barren land far to the north, where they had to work hard to secure for themselves the amenities of life. Their most important industries were cattle raising, hunting, and fishing. That which their livestock provided them with—milk meat, and wool—was a most significant element in their existence. And when they came to a new land, the natural thing to do was to give it a name which would reveal something of its practical possibilities.

Such a principle for the naming of a new land was followed on the more important occasions, such as Greenland (the green land), Helluland (the land with stone slabs), and Markland (the wooded land). From the sagas we also learn the interest of Vinland voyagers in the growth of grass in the new lands—they were thinking of their livestock and how good the land might be for grazing.

This agrees very well with the interpretation of the name Vinland offered by the Swedish philologist Sven Söderberg.[6] In his view, the prefix *vin* in Vinland does not refer to grapes but is the old Norse word for 'grazing land' or 'meadow', as it exists in Norway today in names such as Vinås and Vinje.

It has been claimed that the word *vin* (meadow) went out of use in Scandinavia before the Viking Age, but an authority like Magnus Olsen[7] is of the opinion that there is no reason for setting a date beyond which the word was not used. He mentions as an example the name Viney which was used for Denmark by the skald Bragi the Old in the ninth century and quoted by Snorri Sturluson in his *Heimskringla* (c. 1230).

Vin is often found in place-names in Norway, as for example Vinjar, Vinås, Hovin, Bjørgvin, and so on. The same is true in the Shetland Islands, where *vin* in most cases is a prefix; in Sweden, too, there are areas in which *vin*-names occur. In the Faroes and Iceland, on the other hand, there are no place-names with *vin* as prefix or suffix. Söderberg thinks that this is because in these two countries there are no areas which fit the geographical concept represented by the word *vin*. Social conditions may also have played a certain role in this respect. But that does not mean that the word did not exist in the language spoken in those countries at that time.

We should also recall that the father of Leif Eiriksson, Eirik the Red, came from Jæren in south-west Norway, and according to Magnus Olsen there are relatively many place-names there ending in -*vin*. We know what an important role tradition played, especially in the great families, and it is very probable that the place-names of the old home districts were kept in mind—and perhaps used again in the new lands.

Söderberg also believes that Adam of Bremen heard the name Vinland mentioned in Denmark, but did not know what it meant and offered the kind of explanation which would come first to mind among Germans.

As mentioned previously, the account of Karlsefni's expedition relates that the region in which his headquarters Straumfjord was located was called Vinland, in spite of the fact that it is quite evident that it was a comparatively northerly land and that there were no grapes growing there.

In addition, it is noteworthy that *nowhere in the Vinland sagas or in other Icelandic sources is it said that the name Vinland has any connection with grapes.* The Greenlanders' Saga says about Leif Eiriksson: 'Leif gave the country a name in accordance with its resources, and called it Vinland.'

The legend on the Icelandic Skálholt map (from *c.* 1590) (see page 81), which is supposedly based on older sources, says: 'Here lies Vinland which on account of the fertility of the soil and other useful things is called Vinland the Good.' The fertility of the soil—splendid grazing lands where Norse people could settle down with their livestock—that was the important thing.

To give the main conclusions: The Vinland voyagers probably made wine from wild berries, of which there abound many kinds along the North American coast. Such berries may have been mentioned in Thorhall's poem and the ancient fables, and this may in the course of centuries have been the reason why grapes were introduced into the sagas. Also, Sven Söderberg must be presumed to be right when he says that originally Vinland means 'grazing land'. This implies that Vinland may have been located in northern Newfoundland, a fact which is also indicated by old sailing directions and the descriptions of the new lands.

Wild Wheat

In addition to grapes, the sagas mention wild or self-sown wheat. It has been contended that this must have been corn or wild rice, but the American botanist M. L. Fernald[8] offers convincing reasons why it cannot possibly have been either of these two cereals. Can it have been sandwort (*Elymus arenarius*)? This is found in many places, such as Labrador and Newfoundland, and can spread over large areas and look like wheat fields. This plant was, however, well known to the Norsemen, who used it to make flour. We may perhaps look for the solution of this problem in the fact that wine and wheat are often mentioned together in ancient fables and theological writings. It is noteworthy that later explorers in North America mention wine and wheat when describing areas where there were actually neither grapes nor wheat.

The Observation of the Sun

The account in the Greenlanders' Saga of Leif Eiriksson's voyage makes an astronomical observation in connection with Vinland. It says: 'Day and night were of more equal length than in Greenland and Iceland; the sun had *eyktarstaðr* and *dagmálastaðr* on the shortest day of the year.' That means that the sun was visible (above the old marks) in the middle of the afternoon as well as at breakfast time on the shortest day of winter.

This is a curious bit of information whose authenticity is generally accepted. The Norsemen did not have clocks or watches; they took the bearing of the sun's position over the horizon in relation to mountains, passes, cairns, etc., which corresponded to a certain division of the day, often connected with the various meal-times.

Many attempts have been made to work out the location of Vinland on the basis of the observation just mentioned. Gustav Storm and H. Geelmuyden[9] added something new when they maintained that *eyktarstaðr* was not a time of day but a point on the horizon which could be sighted. But where was that point? If it could be ascertained, a plain astronomical calculation would give us the latitude at which Vinland was located.

A help in this investigation was the usage of Norwegian farmers, and particularly information in two old Icelandic manuscripts. In the Prose Edda of Snorri Sturluson we read: 'Autumn lasts from the autumnal equinox until the sun sets at *eyktarstaðr*.' And the Icelandic book of laws known as *Grágás* says that 'it is *eykt* (nones) when *utsudrs ætt* [the south-west quarter of the heavens] is divided into three parts and the sun has passed through two of them and has one to go.'

What, then, is to be understood by *utsudrs ætt*? Storm and Geelmuyden came to the conclusion that *utsudrs ætt* is that octant of the horizon which has *utsudr*, that is south-west, in its centre, and that it is *eykt* when the sun has passed two-thirds of that distance. On the basis of this calculation Leif Eiriksson's Vinland was placed by them at 49° 55′ N. — that is, in the northern part of Newfoundland. The Norwegian mathematician Almar Næss[10] in a notable treatise maintained that the bearing of *eykt* is sixty degrees west of south, and his calculations led him to believe that Vinland was situated at 36° 54′ N., that is, on Chesapeake Bay in Virginia.

Other investigators have arrived at various results: M. Wormskiold arrived at 49° N.; C. C. Rafn and Finn Magnusson 41° 24′; Th. Bugge 41° 22′; L. M. Turner 48° 75′; E. Tengström 31°; H. R. Holand 42° North; and L. Löberg the region to the south of 55° (Labrador or Newfoundland).

There is here, in other words, a wide divergence; the northern boundary of Vinland has been thought to have been situated at widely separated places along the far-flung coast stretching from Georgia to northern Newfoundland. Even though some of these scholars may have understood the problem well enough the possibilities of arriving at an unsatisfactory solution are great indeed, for the calculations are not based on measurements made with instruments but merely on an estimate made by man. The horizon does not have to be very irregular for a difference involving several degrees of latitude to result.

It is also quite possible that the above observation was not made at Leifsbudir, but from the southernmost point Leif reached during one of his exploratory voyages. Something similar happened in Greenland, where an observation of the sun was made not in the inhabited settlement but at the northernmost point reached by that particular expedition.[11]

Actually, it seems hazardous to rely too much on the calculations that can be made from the primitive sun observation mentioned in the saga. Nevertheless, it is very significant as an indubitably authentic part of the saga.

The Natives

Thorvald was the first white man to encounter the natives; it happened during an exploratory voyage to the east from Leifsbudir. He saw three skin-boats and three men underneath each boat. They killed eight of them, but one of them got away in one of the boats.

Were these people Eskimoes or Indians? The canoes of the Indians were generally made of birch bark, and skin-boats* may thus indicate that the people were Eskimoes. On the other hand, since the saga was written down several hundred years after the event, the description of the vessels may have been influenced by what was already known about the skin-boats of the Greenland Eskimoes. Three men cannot possibly lie underneath a kayak. It would

---

* The kayak is not known to have been used by the Dorset Eskimoes, who must be supposed to have been living in Newfoundland and Labrador at that time.

be different if it were an *umiak* or Eskimo 'women's boat'; but we are told that the survivor fled in one of the boats, and it would not be possible for one man in a great hurry to launch a big *umiak* all by himself. We are informed by early explorers that the Indians liked to sleep underneath their birch-bark canoes. But three men under one canoe would be too many, unless the canoe was considerably larger than usual.

Thorvald also glimpsed a number of mounds at the head of the fjord, and concluded that they were native settlements. This information makes us think of Eskimo dwellings made from stone and turf. Later on, he was involved in a fight with the natives, was hit by an arrow, and killed.

In the account of an earlier exploratory trip, made in a westward direction from Leifsbudir, we are told that Thorvald's men found a wooden grainholder. It seems clear that this discovery had nothing to do with grain; probably it was something or other left behind by the natives, and what comes immediately to mind is a set of discarded tent poles still standing as a pyramid – as for a tepee – or a cache built for storing meat.

Thorfinn Karlsefni also encountered natives. According to the Greenlanders' Saga this happened first at Leifsbudir, but Eirik the Red's Saga says that the first meeting occurred at Hop during his voyage to the south. Both accounts say that the Norsemen traded with the natives, and the description of this trading and barter sounds very authentic. We are told that the natives offered the strangers grey furs, and marten and other skins. This would indicate that these natives were Indians. It is improbable that a coastal people like the Eskimoes would go hunting far into the large forests for marten and squirrel.

This account, too, mentions skin-boats, and I will merely refer to what I have said above. We are further told that the natives, when they approached in their boats, were swinging their sticks, and that they swung them on one occasion in the direction of the sun's motion, and on another occasion in the opposite direction. Many scholars are of the opinion that these sticks were kayak paddles, but, as Gathorne-Hardy emphasizes, this interpretation can hardly be deduced from the text. This goes on to say that a threshing sound seemed to come from the sticks, and Karlsefni asked what that could possibly mean. Snorri Thorbrandson replied: 'Perhaps it is a token of peace.' It would indeed be a strange thing if these practical seamen could not differentiate between paddles and sticks which emitted a curious sound and seem to have been used for a purpose quite unconnected with the propulsion of the boats.

Finally, a battle ensued between the Norsemen and the natives. The saga says that the natives placed a large blue-black ball on top of a pole; it was then flung at Karlsefni's men and it gave out a terrible sound as it fell to the ground. H. R. Schoolcraft[12] offers a similar description of a weapon used by the Algonquin Indians.

The appearance of the Skraelings is described thus: 'They were small (dark) ugly men with coarse hair; they had big eyes and broad cheekbones.' This information is too sparse for us to be able to determine what kind of people these natives may have been. But the trading with furs of typical forest animals and the above-mentioned weapons seem to indicate that these Skraelings were Indians.

During the voyage northward from Hop to the headquarters at Straumfjord Karlsefni encountered five sleeping Skraelings clothed in furs. After he had killed them, he found wooden containers in which there was the marrow of animals mixed with blood. This has an authentic ring to it, but it does not tell us much as to what kind of people they may have been. I may mention that during a stay among the Indians of northern Canada I found that a mixture of blood and marrow was one of their favourite dishes, but I have also seen a similar dish among the Eskimoes of Alaska.

During the return voyage from Straumfjord to Greenland Karlsefni's expedition met five Skraelings clad in skins, and this would probably have been somewhere along the coast of Labrador. The five consisted of a man with a beard, two women, and two boys. The adults fled, and the two boys were captured and taken along. They said that their parents' names were Vætildi and Uvægi, and that Avaldamon and Valldidida were two kings of the land of the Skraelings. A satisfactory linguistic explanation of these names has not been found. The saga says that the boys also mentioned another land where the people were dressed in white clothes and carried flags. This may safely be put down as fantasy. It was probably the intention of the saga-writers to try to confirm the existence of the legendary Hvitmannaland (see page 29).

The saga descriptions of the Skraelings leave no doubt that the Vinland voyagers met the natives of North America. It is also safe to say that along such far-flung coasts they must have encountered both Eskimoes and Indians. On the other hand, they would hardly have been able to see the difference between them. To the Norsemen they were all Skraelings — strange-looking, dangerous people.

Later in this book I shall deal with the question of how widely the natives were scattered in the old days, but I can mention here that recent archaeological investigations have shown that the Dorset Eskimoes used to live far to the south along the coasts of Newfoundland. It is also more than probable that during the summer the Indians would move from the interior to these same coasts, as they did at the time when North America was rediscovered. Thus,

Plate 13. An Eskimo in his kayak, in western Greenland. (Photograph: Mats Wibe Lund Jr).

Plate 14. Cape Porcupine. South of Hamilton Inlet in Labrador, this peninsula juts like a spear into the ocean. To the north and south of it there are extensive white, sandy beaches. This promontory must have been the Kjalarnes (Keelness) of the Vinland voyagers. (Photograph: Hans Hvide Bang.)

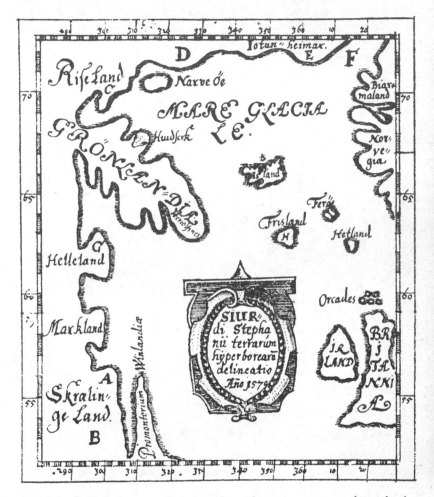

The Icelandic Skálholt map, which dates from about A.D. 1590, was drawn by the learned Sigurður Stéfansson. The original has been lost; this is a copy, drawn in 1670 by Bishop Thord Thorlaksson. The long and narrow peninsula on which has been written *Promontorium Winlandiae* seems to correspond to northern Newfoundland. (Photograph: Royal Library, Copenhagen.)

the Vinland explorers may have encountered both Eskimoes and Indians in Newfoundland.

The information regarding the Skraelings confirms the reliability of the saga texts, but it does not help us when we try to determine the exact situation of the different areas mentioned.

Chapter Eight

Old Maps and Other Pre-Columbian Voyages

So far we have dealt with the most important written sources that have a bearing on the Vinland voyages. They indicate, as we have pointed out, that Vinland must be sought along the north coast of Newfoundland. But there is also extant other source-material, and we shall deal with this in the present chapter.

The Old Maps

The so-called Skálholt map,[1] drawn by the Icelander Sigurður Stéfansson, dates from about A.D. 1590. The original map has been lost, but there is extant a copy of it made by Bishop Thord Thorlaksson in 1670 (see page 81).

Most scholars, among them Professor Gustav Storm,[2] are of the opinion that this, as well as the map by Resen to be dealt with shortly, was drawn on the basis of the descriptions in the sagas and is no more than a rough sketch without any geographical value. There are certain things about the two maps, however, that support a different view, and we must agree with Gathorne-Hardy, who contends that the maps reveal a greater knowledge of certain areas in North America than other cartographers of the period possessed. Without going into details, I must emphasize that both maps show distinctly two fjords in southwest Greenland, indicating the fjords leading to the Eastern and Western Settlements. Moreover, in Resen's map the northernmost fjord in Greenland has been given the name Vesterbygdsfjord, and the one to the south Ericsfjord, which was located in the central part of the Eastern Settlement. This is of considerable significance, since the situation of the Eastern Settlement was in time forgotten, and for a long time it was believed that it had been situated on the east coast of Greenland. These circumstances indicate that both maps were rooted in an ancient geographical tradition.

In Stéfansson's map the elongated headland in the west bears the name *Promontorium Winlandiae*. It is hard to avoid making a comparison with the northern part of Newfoundland, which is a similarly long and narrow peninsula. True, on the map there is a long and narrow fjord instead of a strait on the western side of this peninsula, but we must remember that it was some time after the rediscovery of these regions before it was established that

Newfoundland and Labrador were separated by a strait, the Strait of Belle Isle.

It should also be mentioned here that Carl Sølver[3] has redrawn the Stéfansson map using the correct relation between degrees of latitude and longitude in accordance with Mercator's projection, and he found that the old Greenland route from Hernar in Norway to a point just north of the southern point of Greenland is, according to modern charts, 1,573 nautical miles, while the Skálholt map indicates a distance of 1,360 nautical miles. This is a remarkably close agreement. It is no less astounding that the distance from the southern point of Greenland to Cape Bauld on the northern tip of Newfoundland according to a modern chart is 622 nautical miles and according to the Skálholt map 640 nautical miles. It is indeed remarkable that the distances we arrive at on the basis of this old map are so very close to the real ones.

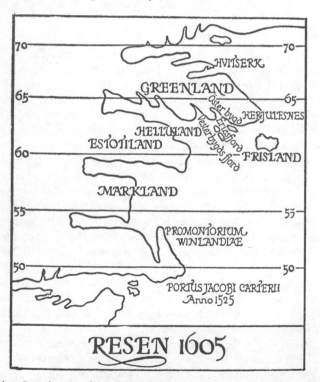

Hans Poulsen Resen's map of the northern lands, drawn in 1605. As on the Skálholt map and the Hungarian map, the name *Promontorium Winlandiae* has been written beside a long, narrow peninsula. The above reproduction of the map is based on a redrawing by Gathorne-Hardy, with many details omitted. (Photograph: Royal Library, Copenhagen.)

The above-mentioned map by Hans Poulsen Resen[4] was drawn in 1605. His map too shows a long peninsula in the west on which has been written the name *Promontorium Winlandiae*. Resen's map is related to the Skálholt map but cannot have been copied from the latter, since it carries a Latin text which expressly states that it is based on a map that at that time was some hundred years old. It is probable that both maps derive from a common source.

I have discovered another map (see Plate 5), which is the only other extant map known of the same type as the Skálholt and Resen maps. Strangely enough, it was found in Hungary, in the old archbishop's residence in the city of Esterom on the Danube. During the Second World War the Germans had their headquarters in the archbishop's residence, and there were pitched battles in the area towards the end of the war. When the city was liberated, the victors found old documents, maps, and books from the archives and the library of the archbishop, together with copperplate engravings and other valuable antique objects strewn over the yard of the residence and also scattered in other places. The map was found in among this litter, and was in the safe keeping of the archivist Géza Szepessy. There are indications that the map was copied by the Jesuits in the former university town of Nagyszombat in northern Hungary.

The Hungarian map displays, by and large, contours and names similar to those of the Skálholt map. But it also exhibits some novel features of considerable interest. I shall confine myself to mentioning some of its most important aspects:

The map has been drawn on old paper made of rags, not of wood pulp; the ink used seems to be what is known as 'bistre', that is, a mixture of beech charcoal and vinegar which was commonly used for writing in the sixteenth and seventeenth centuries: a chemical test of the ink would, however, be necessary. The main title—which has been placed directly underneath the compass card and is surrounded by a sailing vessel, cannon, death's-heads and other symbols—gives the impression, on the whole, of being a later addition, one made, perhaps, to make the map seem more imposing. The date, however, may very well be authentic. For the map must have been based on earlier ones, and it is probable that whoever made the Hungarian map wished to retain the date he found on the older map. It is also quite remarkable that the date on the Hungarian map, 1599, is so close to the year in which the Skálholt map was made, that is, about 1590.

Strangely enough, several place-names in the Hungarian map have been written out in Hungarian runes. Runes are used for the name that spans the entire Atlantic, and also in a text given in the left-hand margin of the map. Professor Knut Bergsland has interpreted the runes and made the following observation:

In the centre of the map and spanning the Atlantic Ocean is the word TENGAR, which may be meant to be the Hungarian word for ocean, *tenger*. The text in the left-hand margin of the map reads as follows: 'North Sea [route], then by [along] northern world/Europe [?] and northern new world, then on to York and Winlandia.

Knut Bergsland is of the opinion that it is a type of Germanic language, and that certain words may be related to English. Professor A. van Loey, who is an authority on Dutch and other Germanic literatures at the University of Brussels, has also gone over the text and says: 'It seems to me that we are here concerned with elements [of a sailors' idiom] which point to continental north-west Europe, that is, Holland or North Germany.'

As for its purely geographical aspects, the number of meridians and parallels of latitude is the same as on the Skálholt map, but we find that on the Hungarian map the distances between the parallels of latitude vary. The northern areas display features which are similar to those on the Skálholt map. That there are other features which do not exist on the Icelandic map is not difficult to understand, in view of the fact that it was a common practice to add new discoveries to older maps.

Greenland has been placed in about the same position as on the Skálholt map, but the Hungarian map shows it as an island. This is also the case in three other old maps: John Dee's map of 1552, Humphrey Gilbert's map of 1567, and Mercator's world map of 1569. The contours of the east and west coast are essentially the same as in the Skálholt map, showing bays at the locations of the Eastern and Western Settlements. At the southern tip of Greenland appears the name York, instead of the Herjolfsnes of the Skálholt map. The Hungarian map also has two points plotted north of the two settlements; they may refer either to later expeditions or to Nordrsetur, the far northern hunting grounds of the Greenlanders.

In the north-western part of the map there is marked off a York which possibly has some connection with Martin Frobisher's expeditions of 1576-8. The indentation towards the west must be Hudson Strait. If we follow the coastline in a southerly direction, we see the name York appear twice more, and there are additional places plotted: these may have some connection with later expeditions.

Both maps show the long peninsula on which appears the name *Promontorium Winlandiae*. But here we note an interesting difference. On the Hungarian map the northern tip of the peninsula has been sharply delimited by a heavily marked off black area. The name *Winlandiae* has been placed directly above it, as if to indicate that it does not apply to the whole of the peninsula, but only to the northernmost point as shown on the map. (The Norse house-sites discovered and excavated by my expeditions were located at the northern-most tip of Newfoundland.)

The route drawn in on the map is called '*hoyerweg*', the meaning of which is probably 'main route'. It goes from England to Norway and then in a west-ward direction to Iceland, Greenland, Helluland, Markland, and Vinland. The question then is whether this route represents conjecture or something more concrete.

The Hungarian map, it will be seen, presents us with a number of problems. It displays some marked weaknesses—it was evidently copied by an amateur geographer who had a poor knowledge of Latin, and for some reason or other wished to give his map an imposing appearance by adding the ornate title decoration. But it also displays some remarkable features which cannot pos-sibly have been thought of afterwards. No matter how one might interpret certain doubtful aspects, it is nevertheless clear that we have here an old European-made map of the Skálholt and Resen type—the only one known apart from these two. It may have been derived from a copy of the Skálholt map, or more probably from an older and perhaps common Icelandic source.

We ought to be cautious in assigning too great a significance to this map, but it is tempting to believe that it may provide us with a valuable perspective. Like certain written sources, this map indicates that Europeans had greater knowledge of the old Norse sea routes than we have realized hitherto.

If we look at the three maps together—the Skálholt map, Resen's map and the Hungarian map—there seems good reason to believe that they all are based on older maps which have been lost and which had their roots in old Icelandic geographical tradition. Various circumstances make it probable that *Promon-torium Winlandiae* is identical with northern Newfoundland.

Since the original Norwegian edition of this book was first published in 1965, Yale University Press have issued a remarkable volume entitled *The Vinland Map and the Tartar Relation*, in which the well-known scholars R. A. Skelton, Thomas E. Marston and George D. Painter discuss the more recently discovered 'Vinland map' and the volume into which it had been bound. Thus the Vinland map was not taken into consideration at the time this book was originally written, but the map does seem to agree very well with the views and conclusions that I have recorded here. I shall take the opportunity some other time to deal more fully with the Vinland map, but I will discuss here a few of its more significant features.

The map is related to the atlas of the Venetian B. Andrea Bianco, issued in the year 1436, but it also contains features not found in his maps. The Vinland map is considered to be pre-Columbian, dating from about A.D. 1440. The map-maker is unknown, as is also the source on which he based his work.

Iceland, Greenland, and Vinland appear in the northern and north-western part of the map. Vinland is shown as a large island in a northerly area west and south-west of Greenland. From the east coast two elongated fjords extend almost as far as the west coast, and to the south there is a large and very noticeable promontory jutting out into the ocean.

Next to the northernmost part of the island the following sentence appears in Latin: 'The island Vinland discovered by Bjarni and Leif in company (?).' Above 'Vinland' and partly above 'Greenland' we read the following text in Latin:

> By God's will, after a long voyage from the island of Greenland to the south towards the most distant remaining parts of the western ocean, sailing southward amidst the ice, the companions (?) Bjarni and Leif Eiriksson discovered a new land, extremely fertile and even having vines, the which island they named Vinland. Eirik [Henricus], legate of the Apostolic See and bishop of Greenland and the neighbouring regions, arrived in this truly vast and very rich land, in the name of Almighty God, in the last year of our most blessed father [Pope] Pascal [II], remained a long time in both summer and winter, and later returned north-eastward towards Greenland and then proceeded [home to Europe?] in most humble obedience to the will of his superiors.

There are circumstances, in my opinion, which indicate that this map may be authentic and of considerable age; however, I do not at present wish to deal with the question of its exact date. One detail that carries much conviction is the reference to the Vinland voyage made by the Greenlandic bishop Eirik Gnupsson. It supplements in a curious way the brief statement which appears in the Icelandic Annals for the year 1121, which reads as follows: 'Eirik, bishop of Greenland, set out in search of Vinland' (see pages 30, 94). Also of some significance is the fact that the account has been couched in such plain and modest terms and carries the imprint of the usual ecclesiastical style, even though his sensational voyage to Vinland would have given ample cause to use more colourful language.

In the heated debate about the Vinland map some of the participants have voiced their doubts about its genuineness. In my opinion, it would indeed be strange if any forger possessed the wide historical knowledge needed to make such a map. It might also have been expected that he would have put a date on the map, or at least some indication of its being so sensationally ancient. In fact, the great age of the map has been ascertained only through painstaking scientific analysis.

Objections have been raised to the effect that Greenland is shown to be an island, that this is a unique feature in old maps, and that consequently it must be a forgery. To this may be said that there are extant at least four maps from

Plate 15. Forests, lakes, bogs and rivers characterize the land west of Cape Porcupine (Keelness). The land is flat, and the forests come right down to the sea, as the sagas pointed out. (Photograph: Hans Hvide Bang.)

Plate 16. The extensive beach north of Cape Porcupine in Labrador. This beach is about forty miles long, and up to two hundred feet wide. It may be seen from a long way out to sea, and the Vinland voyagers could not help noticing it when they came sailing from the north. This must have been the *Furdustrandir* (Wonder Beaches) of the sagas. (Photograph: Hans Hvide Bang.)

Plate 17. An Eskimo from Makkovik in Labrador. (Photograph: Hans Hvide Bang.)

the sixteenth century, all of which show Greenland to be an island (see page 86). Moreover, the contention has been made that the outline of Greenland in the Vinland map corresponds so closely to the actual coastline that it must have been drawn in modern times. To this contention a few comments may be made: Those areas that exhibit a certain similarity to modern maps comprise roughly the areas in which the Greenlanders, according to the sources, must be supposed to have sailed quite frequently — that is, along the major part of the west coast and a deal of the east coast, probably as far north as Scoresby Sound. In the course of several centuries it was inevitable that the Greenlanders should gain a thorough knowledge of these coasts.

If we set in its proper context what we know of Greenland's history through five centuries, it is reasonable to believe that some of the people's geographical knowledge was passed on to Europe. The prime conveyor of such knowledge would be the Catholic Church; in Greenland the Church owned seventeen churches, two monasteries, and one bishop's manor, and in time was to become the owner of the most favourable land areas, including a large island off the east coast on which polar bear hunts took place. The main interest of the Church was the maintenance and survival of the Christian faith, but economic factors were not neglected: the Greenlanders paid not only tithes, but also a tax to help pay for the Crusades. Under such circumstances it is reasonable to believe that the Archbishop in Norway, or the Vatican itself, would not be satisfied with a dim and hazy picture of a distant Arctic country, but on the contrary would wish to learn what the country looked like in order to know where the various properties of the Church were situated. It should also be recalled that we know some documents from the Vatican archives which deal with Greenland. And we know of a number of Greenlandic bishops, and that several of them returned to Europe after completing their term of office. It is especially interesting to note that the text on the Vinland map seems to indicate that Bishop Eirik Gnupsson also returned to Europe. He must have brought with him knowledge of the new lands in the west and must in addition have possessed a detailed knowledge of Greenland after having lived there several years.

It is also of great interest in this connection to note the fact that an English Minorite in the year 1360 completed a long voyage of exploration northward along the west coast of Greenland (see page 95). He seems to have had with him an astrolabe with the help of which he could determine the various latitudes, and this instrument he later gave to a Greenlandic priest, probably Ivar Bárdarson, who was in charge of the bishopric of Gardar.

Another very interesting feature of the Vinland map is the fact that the name Vinland is associated with an island and that this island has a northerly location. The two deep indentations divide the country into three parts. The narrow and most northerly indentation which terminates in a lake makes one think of Hamilton Inlet in Labrador. The somewhat broader fjord to the south may be the Strait of Belle Isle, and the adjacent elongated peninsula may represent the northernmost point of Newfoundland.

Even though it is difficult to say anything definite with regard to the geographical questions, it is nevertheless quite remarkable that three other ancient maps – the Skálholt map, the Resen map, and the Hungarian map – all depict a similar fjord and characteristic elongated peninsula. On the first two maps the peninsula carries the name *Promontorium Winlandiae* and on the Hungarian map the northernmost point of the peninsula (also called *Promontorium Winlandiae*) has been made black, directly underneath the name *Winlandia*. When I put forth my hypothesis of a northerly location for Vinland I maintained *inter alia* that these maps were based on ancient geographical tradition and that the elongated peninsula referred to northern Newfoundland. And it was at the northernmost point of Newfoundland that the Norse sites were discovered.

Possible Traces of the Vinland Voyagers in America

It has been maintained that the so-called Kensington Stone is proof of the presence of the Norsemen in America. This is a stone with a runic inscription found in Minnesota at the end of the last century. The inscription tells how eight Swedes and twenty-two Norwegians set out on a journey of exploration westward from Vinland, how ten of the participants were killed on the way, and how ten men were keeping watch over the ships that were fourteen days' journey away.

Hjalmar R. Holand[5] spent the best part of a lifetime trying to prove the Kensington Stone genuine, but in a case like this one cannot disregard the verdict of the greatest authorities in the science of runology. The foremost specialists on runic writing in our day are of the opinion that the description is not genuine.

The Newport Tower in Rhode Island has attracted a great deal of attention, as a building that Norsemen may have erected some time before Columbus. It is probable, however, that it was built in colonial times, even though it must be admitted that it displays certain features which point to the Middle Ages. We shall discuss the tower in greater detail at a later point in this book (see page 100).

Not far from Beardmore, Ontario, there have reportedly been found in the earth several implements made of iron, and it is certain that they date from the Viking Age.[6] But there is serious doubt attaching to the original report of the find, and a Norwegian who brought various Viking artifacts with him from Norway is involved. The whole matter is so open to doubt that the authenticity of the Beardmore find cannot be regarded as having been proved.

Other finds, too, especially inscriptions on various stones, have been put forward with claims that they are Norse, but none of them has so far successfully withstood scholarly criticism.

In 1501, eleven days after Gaspar Cortereal's return from his expedition to Newfoundland, Pietro Pasqualigo,[7] who was the Venetian ambassador to the Portuguese court, wrote to his brother in Italy. He wrote about the expedition, about the land and the fifty-seven natives whom Cortereal had brought back with him from the new country, and went on:

> The language which they [the natives] speak cannot be understood by any one, even though all kinds of languages have been attempted. In that land there is no iron, but they make swords from a type of stone and arrow-heads of the same material. There has also been brought here a piece of a broken sword, inlaid with gold, which we are convinced was made in Italy, and one of the children had in his ears two pieces of silver which most certainly seem to have been made in Venice—a circumstance which leads me to believe that their country is part of the continent, for it is obvious that if it had been an island which ships had reached earlier, we would have heard about it.

This statement, made right after the return of the expedition, has the hallmark of authenticity. Pasqualigo had seen the natives and had talked with the returning sailors. But it is rather surprising that the Venetian ambassador states in such a decisive manner that a part of a sword comes from Italy, and even that a few pieces of silver had been made in Venice. There is reason to believe that his evaluation is not unbiased. This was only nine years after Columbus's discovery, the name of the great Italian was on everyone's lips, and the matter in hand concerned another discovery made by a rival explorer.

The question then is: From which expedition can the broken sword and the pieces of silver have originated? Hardly from Cortereal's expedition of the previous year (1500), for if the articles could be ascribed to that expedition there would not have been anything worth noting about it. Then we have John Cabot's expeditions of 1497 and 1498 which may have reached the shores of Newfoundland, although we cannot be sure of it. The information that comes down to us regarding these expeditions is very sparse. It appears that he returned and probably participated in a British-Portuguese expedition to Greenland in 1501. It is also very curious that Pasqualigo does not connect his countryman Cabot's discovery, which must have been known in Portugal and Italy, with the land that Cortereal had discovered.

There is, in other words, no great probability that the piece of the sword and the lumps of silver may have originated with Cabot's expeditions, which were the earliest then known. The question then is whether they originated with Norsemen of the time before the rediscovery of North America. I refer here particularly to Newfoundland, where my expeditions have unearthed sites of Norse settlements from about the year 1000. We know that the Norsemen fought the natives, who killed some of them; we can also take it for granted that the natives very carefully picked up from the ground everything in the settlements of the strangers that they thought was valuable. As mentioned before, there were later Norse voyages to North America, and it is of interest to note in this connection that the Norsemen in Greenland disappeared around the year 1500, in other words, just about the time that North America was rediscovered. This opens up fascinating perspectives, but nothing certain can be said about this matter.

Traces of the Vinland Voyages in Greenland

In the Western Settlement in Greenland there was once a farm at the head of Ameralik fjord (Lysefjord), which around the year 1000 probably belonged to the Vinland voyager Thorfinn Karlsefni and his wife Gudrid. The farm was excavated in 1930 by the Danish archaeologists Poul Nørlund and Aage Roussell,[8] and many interesting finds were made.

One of the most curious finds was a lump of coal which was dug up from the depths of the main building. In the fireplaces they only found wood-ash, and this is the only piece of coal ever found among the Norse ruins in Greenland. The most mysterious aspect of the find was the fact that the lump was anthracite coal — since this type of coal does not exist in Greenland.

No attempt was made to explain the find. How it had got there was obviously a fascinating question; where could a lump of coal have come from that was found deep in the ground in the farmhouse of the Vinland voyager Thorfinn Karlsefni?

The sources inform us that ships in the Greenland trade sailed to and from the mother countries, that is, Iceland and Norway. But in Iceland there is no coal, and in Norway there are only insignificant deposits far to the north, and it is not anthracite coal. The very circumstance that the lump was found in a deep layer indicates that it is somehow related to the very earliest years of the Greenland settlement, and it is very difficult indeed to imagine that English and German ships, for instance, can have called at this remote part of the Arctic island at such an early date.

It is most probable that the piece of coal originated in North America. But was anthracite coal actually to be found in coastal areas which the Vinland voyagers could possibly have visited? Subsequent investigations show that there are only two deposits of anthracite coal along the east coast of North America, and they are both to be found in Rhode Island. Is it possible that Thorfinn Karlsefni got as far as that? In the saga we read, as mentioned above, that from his first and more northerly situated headquarters he undertook a long voyage to the south and then stayed for some time in a very fertile region (Hop). And later on there may have been other Norse expeditions sailing quite far to the south.

In addition, it is curious that this has a parallel, namely an object found in the vicinity of Karlsefni's dwelling. In the north-west corner of the cemetery there has been found an arrow-head of quartzite, of a type which is unknown in the huge Eskimo material collected in Greenland. The Danish archaeologist Jørgen Meldgaard[9] states categorically: 'It is a pure Indian type.' Here, in other words, is concrete proof of the Vinland voyages. Is it connected with the fighting in Vinland, during which the natives killed some of the Norsemen? Was the arrow-head, perhaps, imbedded in one of the dead Norsemen who were brought back to Greenland to be buried in consecrated ground?

Later Norse Expeditions to North America

From the foregoing, it will be seen that we have evidence from various sources that Norsemen sailed from Greenland to North America about a thousand years ago. Their swift ships traversed the coastal waters stretching from Baffin Island in the north to Newfoundland and probably even farther to the south, the men on board gazing in wonder towards the unknown coasts. They settled down, built houses, remained there one or two winters, and explored the new country.

For the young sailors from an Arctic region it must have been a strange experience. A new land—so rich, so wonderful. What they related when they returned to their homes in Greenland must have spurred others into making similar voyages. They may have had second thoughts when 'Skraelings' were mentioned, but as far as adventures in unknown lands are concerned, mankind has always shown the greatest optimism.

The Norse Greenlanders dreamed of the meadowlands for grazing, and of the incredibly huge forests, which obviated the need for collecting driftwood along the beaches for material for boats and houses. They also dreamed of the multitude of game and fur-bearing animals. The voyage was a short one, the route was uncomplicated and well known.

And considering that the Greenland settlements existed for almost five hundred years following the first Vinland expeditions, it would indeed have been strange if the people had not made a number of voyages to North America in the course of time. It is also possible that there were people in Greenland who had enough of the hard life there and seized the opportunity to emigrate to the favourable land lying to the west.

Some scattered sources tell us what we might have expected, but they are no more than a few isolated glimpses seen through mist. All primary sources from Greenland have disappeared, and the Icelandic sources pay most attention to noteworthy events concerning their own country, the Church, or men of high birth. What the common man in Greenland was doing was of less interest, and what was known about him was also limited.

The Icelandic Annals for 1121 contain the curious item of information about Bishop Eirik of Greenland who set out in search of Vinland. As mentioned previously (see pages 30 and 88), it is probable that he had a fixed destination in mind, and that he was going to visit Norsemen who had settled in North America.

The Annals of the learned Bishop Gisle Oddson for the year 1637, which are based on old sources, say about 1342: 'The inhabitants of Greenland voluntarily left the Christian faith and turned to the American people.'[10] This sentence may refer to a Norse emigration to North America, and this is the opinion of the great Norwegian historian P. A. Munch.[11]

The Icelandic Annals for the year 1347 record the fate of the ship from Greenland that had been to Markland (Labrador) and was driven by storms to Iceland (see page 30).

Around the year 1350 the deputy bishop of Greenland, Ivar Bárdarson,[12] journeyed to the Western Settlement in order to drive out the 'Skraelings'. When he arrived he found the entire settlement deserted of people, and only ownerless horses and cattle. There is no mention of any traces of a struggle with the Eskimoes, and it is also obvious that the latter in such a case would have slaughtered the horses and the livestock for the sake of the meat. There seems little doubt that the people who lived in the Western Settlement had emigrated and had only left behind them the animals for which there was no room in the ships.

But where did the people of the Western Settlement go? If their destination was Norway or Iceland, it is probable that their first stop would have been the Eastern Settlement. If so, the leader of the Church, Ivar Bárdarson, and the rest of the people would have known about this exodus, and his own voyage northward to the Western Settlement would never have been undertaken. The most likely explanation is that the people of the Western Settlement emigrated to North America.

For the year 1355 there is recorded an expedition which was quite extraordinary in many ways and which was initiated by Magnus Eiriksson, king of Norway and Sweden.[13] He authorized Paul Knutsson of Onarheim to fit out an expedition to Greenland. This was only a few years after the ship mentioned above had come to Bergen from Markland (1347) and it is possible that it had a valuable cargo on board. But that is all the information we have about the Paul Knutsson expedition. We can only conjecture that its objectives may also have included a visit to the shores of North America.

In 1516 the Norwegian archbishop Erik Valkendorf[14] planned an expedition to Greenland, and for that purpose he took steps to collect information about conditions in that far-away land. In his notes we are told that there were black bear and marten in that country. A similar and quite independent piece of information appears in a work by Absalon Pedersen Beyer[15] in 1567. He relates that in Greenland there were sable, marten, deer, and huge forests; but none of these are, in fact, found in Greenland, and the black bear is not even to be found in Norway.

Both Valkendorf and Absalon Beyer lived in Bergen, the centre for the Greenland trade. In that city there must have been available lists of products that originated in Greenland, not least because both King and Church collected taxes on them. For that reason it seems likely that some of the information cited by Valkendorf and Beyer was based on such lists of imports — but these lists, on the other hand, would not specify whether certain commodities, such as sables and the furs of black bears, had come from Greenland or from North America via Greenland. This implies the possibility that Norsemen at that time hunted fur-bearing animals in North America and sold the skins to Greenlandic merchants who then sent them to Norway.

The Norse community in Greenland probably disappeared at the end of the fifteenth century and we don't know why. Did some of the Greenlanders at that time emigrate to North America?

The Norse Routes and the Rediscovery of North America

As a conclusion to this chapter I shall consider the rediscovery of those regions in North America where the Norsemen had made their landfalls. There is much to indicate that sailors of the fifteenth and sixteenth centuries had a much greater knowledge of the ancient routes across the North Atlantic than we are led to believe by the scanty source-material.

There is extant information from about the year 1360 about an English monk, a Minorite of Oxford,[16] probably Nicholas of Lynne, who sailed to the Norse settlements in Greenland. From there he set out on a voyage towards the North Pole and later on he wrote a book about his experiences, *Inventio Fortunata*, which has unfortunately been lost. This seems to presuppose that the English at that time knew where Greenland was and how to get there. And the monk's writings must have given quite a large circle of Englishmen further details about Greenland and the adjacent seas.

We know that an English fleet of fishing vessels used to arrive in the waters

The Arctic regions, as shown in Mercator's map of 1569. From Jomard: *Monuments de la géographie*. Mercator partly based his work on information relating to a polar expedition on which an English monk and astronomer set out in about 1360 from Austerbygd in Greenland. This monk was probably Nicholas of Lynne.

round Iceland every year after 1412, and before that the English used to carry on a lively trade with Bergen. Those were the places where the traditions regarding the route to Greenland and on to North America must have been very much alive. When seamen met and discussed ships and the sea, information of that kind would be passed on from one to another.

We also know of a Norwegian-Danish-Portuguese expedition which set out in 1476, with the Norwegian Jon Skolp[17] as navigator, and probably reached Labrador. It was at about the same time that the Norwegian nobleman Didrik Pining and Hans Pothorst sailed to Greenland.

Then, in 1497, John Cabot's expedition led to the actual rediscovery of North America. It set out from Bristol, and we know that his son had applied for permission to fish in Icelandic waters. In that country he may have received information about the routes leading to the west.

Plate 18. The Nascapi Indians' camp in the interior of northern Labrador, west of Davis Inlet. (Photograph: Hans Hvide Bang.)

Plate 19. A Nascapi Indian girl in the wilderness west of Davis Inlet, Labrador. The young girls provided the firewood for the camp, and they certainly knew how to swing an axe. (Photograph: Hans Hvide Bang.)

Greenland comes into the picture at that time mainly as a port of call. It is of considerable interest in this connection that the people disappeared at about the time of the voyages that led to the rediscovery of North America.

It was probably in the year 1500 that João Fernandes sailed to Greenland. The following year an English-Portuguese expedition also arrived there. Gaspar Cortereal probably sailed along the east coast of Greenland in 1501, and from there he continued to Newfoundland. But the Cantino map of 1502 is so surprisingly good that it seems to indicate that Cortereal must have been preceded by other expeditions.

An especially interesting piece of information comes down to us from the Sebastian Cabot expedition which may have taken place between 1507 and 1509. We are told that, with three hundred men, he sailed the *Icelandic route*[18] towards Cape Labrador, which at that time was the name of the southern tip of Greenland. He probably reached present-day Labrador or Newfoundland. It appears from this that the 'Icelandic route' was a well-known term among seamen and navigators.

Thus, a number of factors seem to indicate that there was a continuous tradition from Leif Eiriksson's Vinland voyage to the later westward voyages of the Norse Greenlanders, down to the rediscovery of North America.

Chapter Nine

Along the Coast of North America

In the preceding chapters I have dwelt on some of the views and opinions which I originally put forward in my book *Land under the Pole Star*, which was written after my expedition to Greenland in 1953. On the basis of this material I came to the conclusion that Vinland had a comparatively northerly situation and would probably have to be sought in Newfoundland.

The main reasons for this point of view, as given above, may be summarized as follows: The name Vinland must be interpreted as 'the land with grazing lands or meadows'. The brief sailing times mentioned in the sagas have probably been recorded fairly accurately, in the tradition of a seafaring people, and seem to fit the three lands – Baffin Land, Labrador and northern Newfoundland – which probably correspond to the sagas' Helluland, Markland and Vinland. Fragmentary Icelandic sources mention that it is not far from Markland to Vinland and this corresponds with the Greenlanders' Saga, which gives a sailing time of two days (*døgr*). The 'Wonder Beaches' in Eirik's saga can most likely be identified with the long beaches near Cape Porcupine in Labrador, thus indicating a northerly Vinland. The Skálholt and Resen maps, on which Vinland is marked, must be supposed to be based on old Icelandic geographical tradition. The route from Greenland to northern Newfoundland is simple. The Vinland voyagers would, on account of the ice, probably make a fairly late start from Greenland, and it must have been important for them to settle as soon as possible in the New World in order to make preparations for the winter. And these people from a polar country would want to settle in a land where they felt at home, where they might live according to the old pattern of Nordic culture.

I contended furthermore that it should be possible to find traces of the buildings put up by the Vinland voyagers if one went about it in a thorough manner and searched the coast by boat and plane.

This is the background for the eight archaeological expeditions which I organized and led to the east coast of North America during the years 1960–8 and which led to the discovery and excavation of a group of Norse pre-Columbian sites on the northern tip of Newfoundland (at L'Anse aux Meadows).

*

98

My theory regarding the location of Vinland and my plans outlining a search for the Norse sites met with considerable scepticism. This might perhaps have been expected, for a sizable number of books by well-known scholars had maintained for the past two centuries that Vinland lay far to the south, in the region of wild grapes. This had become something of an axiom. It was also to be expected that my plans for a search to be made along the coasts of North America for thousand-year-old house-sites were generally characterized as 'looking for a needle in a haystack'. Naturally, there were many difficulties to be surmounted, but I thought that my theory was soundly based and that it ought to be possible to find what I was looking for through systematic investigations and with a certain amount of luck.

In any case, there were a few authors and scholars who in the course of time had held to the view that Vinland might have been in northern Newfoundland. Of especial interest is a small and little-known pamphlet by W. A. Munn,[1] who himself lived in Newfoundland. It is not a scientific treatise, but it is characterized by practical and sound judgment as well as an intimate knowledge of the area. He was of the opinion that Vinland might have been situated at the head of Pistolet Bay on the north coast of Newfoundland. The very same conclusion was arrived at by the eminent Finnish scholar V. Tanner. Arlington H. Mallery[2] and Jørgen Meldgaard[3] have more recently carried out investigations in Pistolet Bay, but no traces of Norsemen were to be found.

In 1960 I organized my first voyage of investigation along the east coast of the North American continent. At first I travelled alone but during the latter and more important part of that voyage my daughter Benedicte joined me in the work.

I had planned to set out in the spring and to begin my exploration fairly far to the south. I wanted first to have a closer look at some of the areas where in the opinion of so many eminent scholars Vinland was to be located. One of these was Rhode Island, a state which also was of special interest because of the occurrence of anthracite coal in that area and its possible relation to the piece of anthracite coal excavated from the deep layers in the floor of Thorfinn Karlsefni's house in Greenland (see page 92).

I planned to make my way gradually northward and at the same time have a good look at the coasts which might have been visited by the Norsemen during their voyages of exploration from their headquarters in the north, or by their descendants during the five hundred years when the Greenland settlements were in existence. Such a voyage would provide me with a comprehensive picture of both land and water as far as northern Newfoundland, the region which in my opinion was the Vinland of old. I would arrive there just about the time when the drift-ice had disappeared and the grass was green, and that is where I wanted to carry out my most systematic investigations.

On a warm day in spring I was sitting in a bus rolling across Rhode Island, the smallest state in the American Union. The sun was shining brightly over the green hills and colourful flowers, and the blue sea seemed to intrude itself everywhere into the landscape. The countryside was beautiful, and it reminded me of more southerly lands.

I arrived in Newport, a small seaside town with old and honourable sea-faring traditions. Here is also found the old tower which in the opinion of some was built by the Norsemen before Columbus's discovery of the New World. My hotel was appropriately enough called the Viking. In the dining-room there were huge paintings along the walls showing dragon ships under sail and sinister bearded Vikings brandishing their bloody swords above the heads of the flesh-and-blood diners.

I went for a walk in the town's beautiful park, known as Touro Park, and there in its centre, surrounded by chestnut trees, stood the famous tower. It is indeed a curious ruin, so entirely different from anything else that has survived from the ancient past of North America. It is twenty-six feet tall, constructed from mortared stones, in the form of a cylinder, and it has eight arches supported by round columns. There used to be an upper storey, but the floor dividing the two storeys has disappeared, although there are traces of former stairs. Above the arches there are four apertures or windows, three of which face out to sea. There are also some narrow openings in the walls and on the inside a number of small square niches. On the ground floor there are traces of an open fireplace.

There has been a great deal of debate about this tower. Some have been of the opinion that it was built in colonial times, having been put up in the seventeenth century by Englishmen, Dutchmen, or Portuguese. Others have contended that it was built by Norsemen before the time of Columbus. The town of Newport was founded in the year 1639, and the tower was mentioned for the first time in 1677. What can its function possibly have been? The experts give us a number of different answers: watch-tower, windmill, church ...

The archaeologist William S. Godfrey[4] in 1948 and again in 1949 excavated the ground around and inside the tower. His finds all dated from colonial times; his results, however, are questioned by some people in view of the fact that other excavations had been made in the same area a hundred years earlier. But, all archaeological and historical facts considered, it seems likely that the tower was indeed put up by English colonists in the early part of the seventeenth century.

The next thing was to visit one of the localities where coal is to be found. The coal deposits in Rhode Island are of the kind called meta-anthracite, and appear in various forms, even as graphite. In earlier times and in certain localities the coal was mined, but its quality was poor and the work came to a halt.

I visited Willow Lane, about seven miles from Newport. There should have been an old coal-mine in the area. A hill covered with wild flowers sloped down to the sea, and below, on the level ground, I noted the curious remains of an old building which must have been connected with the mine. Everything was overgrown with mosses and grass, and along the brick walls slender stems were twining upwards, looking exactly like grape vines. I had indeed, it seemed, come to the land of wild grapes!

I was looking round among grass tufts and hillocks when suddenly I saw something gleaming in the sun—coal. There was something fascinating about the black lump; it felt heavy in my palm and had a peculiar metallic sheen. My thoughts reverted to another lump of anthracite coal, the one that had been found on the Greenland farm of the Vinland voyager Thorfinn Karlsefni.

Could this have been the spot to which he came on his southward voyage of exploration—the 'Hop', which the saga describes in such vivid language? I looked out over Narragansett Bay, where here and there a white sail was set off against the blue; I saw small islands and pleasant shores, whose vivid green colours told of a fertile land.

However, I could not find any river or lake which might fit the description of Karlsefni's 'Hop'. I took along with me a few pieces of coal in order to carry out a comparative analysis of these lumps and the piece of coal that had been found in Greenland.

After crossing part of Rhode Island, I travelled slowly northward to the area around Cape Cod, then along the coast to Boston, New Hampshire and Maine. This is the area in which the majority of scholars think that Vinland was located. It is indeed possible that the Norsemen in the course of time reached as far south as this but I do not believe that they covered the immense distance from Greenland to New England in one stage. They must have had a more northerly headquarters.

In any event, it seems to be a next to hopeless task to find traces of ancient settlements in these southerly areas. Such remains would be well hidden by vegetation, or they would have vanished in cultivated fields or underneath houses, roads or factories. More northerly areas, where the vegetation grows more slowly and built-up areas are more scattered, seemed to offer much greater possibilities.

As I travelled along the coast of North America, I was struck again by the immense beauty of the land, its forests, fields, lakes, rivers, and mountains. I thought again of the first immigrants, who arrived here when it was a virgin land. These men from a densely populated Europe must indeed have experienced a sense of wonder, and they must have thought it a great and splendid thing to be able to pick and choose as much land as they wanted on this fertile and untouched continent!

And I thought of the Indians, the free men who originally owned the country: their half-naked hunters, vigilantly roving through the forests with bow and arrow, their birch-bark canoes gliding along the rivers, men and women at peace in front of the tents, from which the smoke rose slowly into the air. A world that perished, and not very long ago!

I left the land of the wild grapes and crossed over to Nova Scotia. Here I immediately came to a more northerly clime; it was noticeable in the ocean breezes and in the vegetation. A deeply indented coastline extends far to the north-east.

Near the southernmost point of Nova Scotia lies Yarmouth. Here there has been found a hotly debated stone with an alleged runic inscription. It is probable that the marks in the stone surface were made by men, but they are definitely not runic writing.

After some days spent in exploring the coast I arrived in Halifax, a thriving port and city. Here I met the Norwegian-born shipowner Karl Karlsen, whose firm is active in fishing, sealing and whaling, and who knows more about the coast and this area in general than most men. He was at this time, and also during subsequent expeditions, to provide me with valuable assistance. I also greatly appreciated finally meeting someone who believed in my plans, who thought that it might indeed be possible to find traces of Norse house-sites. His positive attitude may perhaps be explained be the fact that he hailed from the district of Sunnmøre in western Norway, from where so many Vikings sailed in olden times.

In his classic work on the Vinland voyages, Professor Gustav Storm[5] emphasizes that Vinland must be sought in Nova Scotia, more particularly along the east coast of Cape Breton Island. He supposes that Cape Breton was the Kjølneset (Keelness) of the Norsemen and that the extensive 'Wonder Beaches' and Vinland must have been situated somewhat farther to the south. This theory has been accepted by many scholars.

I sailed along these coasts and investigated the topography of the land but could not find any features that would specially single them out as the land mentioned in the sagas. I did not, for instance, see any beaches long enough to fit the description of the unusual natural landmark which the Norsemen called 'Wonder Beaches'.

But the scenery was beautiful, not least in the neighbourhood of old Fort

Louisburg, which played such an important role in the history of eighteenth-century Canada. Here, as in many other places, raged the battle between France and England for supremacy in this new and far-off land, a struggle from which England was to emerge victorious.

The old ramparts, overgrown with green grass, tell of what once was. The fields inside the walls are now almost deserted, but once upon a time there were rows of houses here, and a multitude of people were busily engaged in activities quite different from those of today. The huge country lay all around them; hunters and trappers and other pioneers already called it their own, but immense areas were still only wilderness, and its sea-lanes were ruled by the ships with the largest number of guns. Frigates with rows of gun-ports would sail into the little bay by the fort, and eager sailors would go ashore and search for rum and women.

Excavations have been carried out at Louisburg, and in the little museum there are to be seen a number of beautiful objects from the time of the French.

If it was true, as Gustav Storm maintained, that Nova Scotia was the land in which the Norsemen settled, there was in my opinion a particular spot that was a much more probable landfall than the one he had selected, namely the elongated north-west promontory of Cape Breton Island. But if the Norsemen had come there, they would most probably have sailed through the Strait of Belle Isle and then southward, and it would then have been a more natural thing for them to have headed for Cape North, the northernmost point of Nova Scotia.

I made for this part of the country and came to a small fishing village called Dingwall, lying on the east coast a short distance south of Cape North. There was nothing but a few scattered houses in this remote settlement, where people seemed to live an existence quite separate from the rest of the world. When I met some of the men on the pier or along the path leading up to the houses, they would doff their caps to the stranger and say in a friendly manner, 'How do you do, sir?' Old Scottish traditions and culture still prevailed among them.

It was a curious experience to encounter the name Dingwall in this remote and out-of-the-way place. The name is of Norwegian origin and means 'the field where the parliament meets'. As is the case in so many place-names along the coast of Scotland, it harks back to the time of the Norwegian Vikings. Scottish emigrants had subsequently brought the name of their home town with them when they settled in the New World.

I found a room in the house of an elderly lady called Margaret Seely. Friendly and hospitable, she was a splendid pioneer type of woman, a little bent and worn, but with a very active mind and full of courage. One night some young people had sneaked into her barn to see what they could steal, but she had heard the noise, had grabbed her two old pistols, and had run after them, firing several shots.

In a corner of the parlour there hung an old sabre, and Margaret informed me that it had been used by her great-grandfather in the battle of Waterloo. She also had many interesting things to tell of the early struggles of the pioneers, and I gained a vivid impression of the sufferings of the people during the war between the English and the French. She told stories of French families who had to flee their farms and hide for a long time in the mountains.

I explored the east coast of Nova Scotia from Dingwall far to the south. Once I got a real surprise, for on White Point I found traces of old building-sites, and at first glance they greatly resembled those that I had seen in Greenland. But they turned out to be remains of buildings put up by early French settlers. Nevertheless, it would be useful to have them excavated, since they seemed to be fairly old and might throw light on the early history of North America.

The land and the vegetation reminded me in many ways of certain coastal districts in Norway. There was grass for the cattle and some farming, but the farms could only be small. Rowan trees and wild cherry trees were in flower and in some places they looked like white gardens against the background of the blue ocean.

I continued my search northward, as far as Cape North, and passed on the way a sandy beach with a number of strange-looking lagoons, but it did not seem to be conspicuous enough to fit the saga description. The Nova Scotians believe that John Cabot, the rediscoverer of North America, went ashore here in 1497, but great men are often claimed by many different communities. At last I came to Cape North, a fairly high mountainous area which must be visible far out to sea. But I did not find any traces of old sites and no one could tell me about remains of any kind.

The day came for me to take my leave of Margaret, the friendly pioneer woman. She stood in her yard, supporting herself on a stick, and looking after me as I left.

I crossed the eighteen-hundred-foot high ridge in the middle of the cape, which is covered with pine forests; then I travelled along the western shore of the long peninsula. Here too I investigated a number of places but soon realized that the coastline was too exposed to the sea, would not provide suitable harbours, and consequently would not have been considered very inviting by the Vikings.

At last I came to the town of Sydney. I had by then explored hundreds of miles of coastline in these southern regions, where other scholars had thought that Vinland was located, and where, in any case, Norsemen might have landed on their voyages from a headquarters farther north. To the north lay the large island of Newfoundland, where according to my theory the Vinland voyagers had settled and built their houses. Would a lucky star light my path?

Chapter Ten

The Discovery

Newfoundland is a remarkable island which lies farther east than any other territory or island belonging to the North American continent. Its contours are odd, as if Nature in a wilful moment wanted to make an abstract work of art: to the south there is a large sprawling lower body with the strangest indentations, and from it a long promontory, looking more like a horn than anything else, reaches out northward.

The area of the island is about 43,000 square miles, so that it is a little larger than Iceland, and it is situated between latitudes 46° 36' and 51° 40' N., the same as the northern half of France. It is a hilly country with extensive forests of pine, spruce and larch, and deciduous trees of many kinds, and scattered ridges and mountains that do not reach any great height. The longest and highest mountain formation is Long Range Mountains, which run along the northern peninsula. A multitude of lakes and numerous rivers give life to the scenery. The Strait of Belle Isle separates Newfoundland from Labrador. Down through the ages this narrow passage has had a very special significance as a main highway of the sea and as a place for fishing and hunting seals and whales — by Indians, Eskimoes, and white men.

Newfoundland has a maritime climate and the winters are considerably milder than in continental Canada to the west. Along the east coast the frigid Labrador Current drives southward, and at times brings huge masses of ice along with it, which has its effect on the climate. But the Gulf Stream, too, makes its influence felt.

Newfoundland is not primarily an agricultural country, but here and there one will encounter fairly substantial farms. Along the coast and on the off-shore banks there is an abundance of cod, which since the time of the re-discovery of the country has been of the greatest economic significance. Other kinds of fish also abound. Beside these, there are whales and harp (or Greenland) seals, which breed on the ice along the Labrador coast and in the Gulf of St Lawrence.

The great forests have made forestry one of Newfoundland's most important industries. Among the indigenous wild animals in the inland areas are caribou, black bear, lynx, otter, marten, beaver, musk-rat, fox and hare, but they are not so numerous as they used to be. In certain areas there is an abundant bird life, and in the rivers there are trout and salmon.

The original inhabitants of the country were the Beotuk Indians, but of them none are left. In the past there also used to live a number of Eskimoes along the coast.

Following Columbus's discovery the very knowledge that the New World was out there in the west served to incite kings, traders, seamen and adventurers to seek fame and fortune in these lands. People believed that this was the road to India, and thought about Cibola's seven fabulous cities and similar myths.

As a forerunner for the rediscovery of the northern areas of North America must be reckoned the Norwegian-Danish-Portuguese expedition which had the Norwegian Jon Skolp as navigator. Several sources indicate that this expedition reached Labrador in about A.D. 1476.

In 1497 and 1498 John Cabot sailed out from Bristol and reached a land which was probably Newfoundland. Thereupon Portugal entered the scene, represented by Gaspar Cortereal, who came to Newfoundland in 1500 and again in 1501. His last expedition probably landed in Notre Dame Bay. The huge trees, which could be used to make the tallest ship's masts, the abundance of cod, salmon, and herring, and a wealth of wild game, made a deep impression. The land was named Terra Verde — the Green Land. But what pleased the Portuguese most was the large number of natives who could be sold as slaves; they took back with them to Lisbon fifty-seven men, women, and children. Cortereal's ship disappeared on his last voyage; two years later his son Miguel set out with three ships to search for him, but he also disappeared without a trace.

These discoveries were the reason for a number of ships crossing the ocean to the new lands in the west; lured, first and foremost, by the opportunities for fishing and whaling, and also for trading in furs. In a surprisingly short time a considerable fleet of fishing and whaling vessels was active off the coast of Newfoundland, and it was not long before the waters off Labrador and the Gulf of St Lawrence were also exploited. Many nations were represented, the majority, however, being Frenchmen, Englishmen, Basques, and Portuguese.

Newfoundland became the key area for the exploration of lands farther to the west and north. We shall not go into detail, but only mention here the voyages of the pioneer explorer Jacques Cartier in 1534, 1535, and 1541. He sailed through the Strait of Belle Isle and into the Gulf of St Lawrence, and his longest voyage took him up the St Lawrence River as far as the Iroquois settlement called Hochelaga, which was situated where we find the city of Montreal today.

Apart from expeditions like these, whose explicit purpose was to explore these new lands, there were others who came in contact with them while looking for the north-west passage—the route that was thought to lead to India. We must here mention the expeditions of Martin Frobisher (1576–8: three expeditions), John Davis (1585–7: three expeditions), George Weymouth (1602) and James Hall and John Knight (1606).

What we know of the history of Newfoundland and Labrador during the years after their rediscovery is very sparse and often hazy. These were new lands, to which ships from many nations set out in order to fish, catch seals and whales, purchase furs from the natives, explore the land and also go in for piracy. It was a colourful, but also a harsh and lawless era, in which the main purpose was to grab as much as possible for oneself. Fishermen, hunters, and fur traders were usually interested in keeping their voyage a secret in order to keep the best areas for their own use, and that is one of the reasons why a veil has been drawn over a great many things from this pioneer era.

During the eighteenth century more information became available, not least because the sovereignty over the area became hotly contested by France and England. The bitter struggle ended with the Treaty of Utrecht of 1713, which confirmed British sovereignty over Newfoundland.

My journey subsequently took me to the capital of Newfoundland, the city of St John's, which is a fishing and seafaring town with old traditions. First I had to decide on which parts of the island to investigate. Even though I believed that Vinland must be sought in the northern part, it also seemed important to conduct a search along the east coast. According to the accounts in the sagas, both Thorvald Eiriksson and Thorfinn Karlsefni were supposed to have headed expeditions from their northern headquarters in that direction, and other Norse expeditions not known to us might also very well have been active in that area.

I carried out a number of investigations northward along the east coast. It soon became clear to me that there was such a multitude of fjords, bays, and islands that it would be no easy task to find what I was looking for. A scattered population, mostly fisherfolk, made their homes on this weatherbeaten strip of coast facing the Atlantic, the small villages usually lying in coves and inlets. The people here lead a simple life, and they were friendly and hospitable.

Again and again I spoke with the people I met and tried to question them about traces of old house-sites. No one knew anything, and I often got the impression that they felt it was too much to expect them to take their minds off fishing and concentrate instead on the curious questions that the stranger raised. The reaction elicited by my questions might range from surprise to the ill-concealed suspicion that I must have a screw loose, spending my time looking for traces of people who lived a thousand years ago instead of doing useful work.

Once I came to a fishing village where a big fellow was standing on the pier attending to his nets. I walked over to him and asked him the usual questions. He gave me a quick glance and said: 'What do you want with old things like that?'

'To dig them up,' I said.

'That's what you say, but you don't fool me.'

I did not get the drift of what he meant, but he continued in a sharp tone of voice: 'Any treasure that is supposed to have been buried around here we'll be able to find by ourselves.'

As time went by I was to encounter many stories of hidden treasure along the coast. People firmly believed in them, and there were quite a few who from time to time would set out with pick-axe and spade to search for old chests or kettles supposedly filled with golden and silver ducats. Most often it was said that they had been left behind by pirates who ravaged these coasts in the old days. The stories had an air of mystery—the pirate ship was supposed to have come inshore in the dead of night, the sailors had gone ashore carrying something very heavy, which was buried in the earth. Then the ship disappeared. Often the story-tellers were *almost* sure of where the treasure had been buried. If I were to venture a remark indicating doubt, it was immediately countered with fascinating details originally supplied by relatives or others who had long been dead. That the treasure did exist was an incontrovertible fact.

I returned to St John's in order to join my daughter Benedicte, who was arriving from Norway in order to participate in the last and most important part of the trip. We first made a trip by air over a large part of the east coast, a trip which came about through the courtesy and co-operation of the government of Newfoundland. This trip afforded me a useful bird's eye view of that part of the country, mainly consisting of fjords, a multitude of islands, small villages, and limitless forests.

Then we sailed north in the coastal vessel *Baccalieu*. This voyage could be compared with a trip to North Norway, although there were differences. Among our fellow-passengers was a typical group on their way to northern Newfoundland and Labrador. A lean Catholic priest in a black gown with a finely chiselled face, a lively Eskimo girl from Battle Harbour in Labrador, an Eskimo from a district still farther north, a weatherbeaten fur trapper, a trader, a silent Indian, and others. Most of them were very typical people of the northland.

We called at a number of remote fishing villages, at each of which the arrival of the steamer was looked upon as an event. The people standing on the jetty seemed to know most of the travellers on board. Many of them walked up the gangway to greet acquaintances, have a cup of coffee with them, and discuss the latest happenings; others helped with the loading, and no one seemed to be in a hurry. There are indeed still to be found places both inland and by the sea which the hustle and bustle of civilization have not reached as yet.

We went ashore at St Anthony, a village situated about thirty-five miles to the south of Newfoundland's most northerly point. The place to a great extent bore the stamp of the Grenfell Mission, an unusual organization which does marvellous work in assisting the people in northern Newfoundland and Labrador.

At the turn of the century the conditions in which Labrador Indians, Eskimoes and 'settlers'* lived can hardly be described. The few people who lived in scattered settlements along the coast were to all practical purposes left entirely to their own devices and became an easy prey for swindlers who sold them rum and cheated them out of their furs and their fish. Medical aid in case of sickness was practically non-existent. The people were starving, and disease took a heavy toll.

When the Scotsman Sir Wilfred Grenfell, during an inspection trip, became aware of all this misery, he was deeply moved, and he devoted the rest of his life to helping these people. He began in 1892, without any financial means, but by dint of his enthusiasm and his administrative ability he succeeded in creating an international organization supported by private contributions. Modern hospitals were built at St Anthony and at North-west River at the head of Hamilton Inlet, in addition to several bigger or smaller clinics along the coast. Then the aeroplane was enlisted in the work, and today they have come so far that whenever anyone becomes seriously ill, a message is sent over the radio-telephone, and within a short time the patient will be picked up and flown to a hospital. I don't know of any other northern area in which aid like this is organized as effectively as here. It is an example worthy of emulation all over the world.

A spirit of idealism still characterizes the work, which at the present time also includes an expanded programme of care for Indian and Eskimo children, many of whom are sent to school or receive various kinds of training. The superintendent of the Mission is Dr Gordon Thomas, who has devoted many years of his life to service in that part of the north.

I arrived as a stranger and told Dr Thomas about my plans, and at once he took a lively interest in them and offered assistance in any way he could. During the eight years in which I had expeditions in the area, his co-operation was to be of very great significance to us.

I told him that it would be of the greatest interest to explore the north coast

* The term used for the inhabitants of Labrador who are of neither Indian nor Eskimo stock. As a rule they are of mixed origin.

of the island, and that I should have to hire a fishing boat. He replied that the hospital boat, the *Albert T. Gould*, was due to sail up the north coast in a few days; wouldn't it suit me to go along as a passenger? The nurse was to call at all the fishing villages in order to vaccinate the inhabitants, and there would be plenty of time to look round and get to know the country. I agreed that nothing would suit my purpose better.

The *Gould* set out on its voyage; it was a nice little ship, forty-four feet long, and its skipper was the old-timer Norman Small. In addition there were a cook and an engineer. The nurse's name was Pamela Sweet; she was English, young and charming, and became very interested in our plans. Soon we felt as if we all belonged to the same family.

First, we sailed a short distance to the south, to Hare Bay, a long fjord that slices deeply into the peninsula and where dense forests come down to the shore almost everywhere. To the north we could see White Mountain, which is nearly a thousand feet high, and to the south-west we could glimpse the Long Range Mountains. My thoughts once more reverted to the Vinland voyagers. If they had their headquarters in the northern part of Newfoundland, they could hardly have avoided coming upon this large fjord on their voyages of exploration eastward along the Newfoundland coast. The area round it must have looked attractive, especially because of the thick forest and the rivers abounding in salmon.

We called at a few fishing villages, and for the first time I got a good idea of the way people lived along this northern coast: small houses that seemed to have been nailed together without any plans, a few potato and vegetable patches, sleeping dogs, sturdy sleds of the type used by the Eskimoes put aside for use in winter, rows of low racks constructed from wooden sticks and beams used for drying fish, boats at the jetties, and children everywhere. They were a quiet, unassuming, and hospitable people, with a ready smile for a stranger. Fishing for cod from small boats and with home-made gear is not a very profitable occupation, but the people seemed to be satisfied with their lot.

At last we were on our way to the north coast, to those areas which I thought must be the Vinland of old, and where so much indicates that Leif Eiriksson built his 'large houses'. Would my lucky star stay with me?

This part of the east coast was treeless and appeared rather barren, but at the head of the fjords the country took on a fairer aspect. We visited one fishing village after another. Wherever we stopped Sister Pamela had her hands full vaccinating all comers, and there was plenty of time to talk to people and to look round the neighbourhood. It was of particular interest to me to ascertain whether there was much grassland in the area, in other words, good grazing for the cattle, a feature of the land to which the Vinland voyagers evidently attached great importance. But in that respect the east coast was a disappointment. I did not see any place that might have looked tempting to the Norsemen, and the people I met did not know of any traces of ancient sites.

We made our way through the narrow sound near Quirpon Island, whose northernmost tip is the well-known landmark Cape Bauld. Then we sailed westward along the north coast, passing a few fishing villages which we were scheduled to visit on our return. One of them was L'Anse aux Meadows.

From the ship I got a good view of the north coast. The landscape was fairly flat, with low hills but no mountains. There was not much forest to be seen, but, as I shall point out later, the woods did come close to the shore a few generations ago. I could not help thinking about Bjarni's description of the first land to which he came and which is probably identical with Leif Eiriksson's Vinland: 'The land had no mountains and was covered with woods and there were low hills.' We sailed past many islands and skerries, the scenery fitting very well the description of what Thorvald saw on his exploratory voyage westward from Leifsbudir. The largest and most conspicuous of these islands was Great Sacred Island, the outermost island facing the ocean.

We were sailing too far from the shore for me to form a firm opinion about the vegetation, but it struck me that the green level country at L'Anse aux Meadows looked very promising.

But for the present we sailed right past and came to the big fjord called Pistolet Bay, which looked like a huge gulf opening up towards the north. A little east of this fjord, we put in at the head of Ha-Ha Bay, at Raleigh, an attractive fishing village. Here there was some stunted spruce growth and grasslands, and the people kept cattle, but no one knew of any traces of ancient sites either here or in the Pistolet Bay area.

As has been mentioned, W. A. Munn and V. Tanner endorsed the theory that Pistolet Bay was the place where the Vinland voyagers settled, and later on a few investigations were carried out in the area, but no traces of the Norsemen were found. In the company of two fine young fellows, Harvey and Abel, I set out on a trip along the eastern shores of the fjord in order to have a look round. It was an interesting trip, indeed, especially as these two wide-awake young fellows were so eager to show me what their country had to offer. They came running towards me with curious-looking sea shells and large crabs, and they found birds' nests in the grass and gooseberry, currant and squashberry bushes. In several places we encountered sandwort waving in the breeze, making one think of wheat.

At last we came to an idyllic little lake, encircled by pine forests, reeds, and grass. A short river emptied into the lake, but it was, at least at the present time, too shallow for any Viking ship to be dragged up into the lake. The river-system includes a few bigger lakes, where there is a run of salmon.

Plate 20. A Montaignais Indian girl, living on the north shore of the Gulf of St Lawrence. (Photograph: Erling Brunborg.)

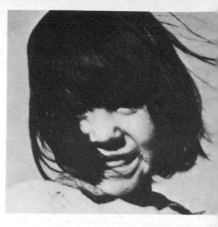

Plate 21. An old Nascapi woman from Davis Inlet, Labrador. (Photograph: Hans Hvide Bang.)

But here too the facilities for grazing seemed to be too limited for the Vinland voyagers to have chosen to settle here. The same is true of the heavily wooded areas at the head of Pistolet Bay, which I investigated a few years later.

By now, I had been carrying out my investigations since early spring and had travelled several thousand miles along the coast of North America, from Rhode Island northward, by boat and aeroplane, and on foot – and I had met with nothing but disappointments. And it looked as if I would have no luck on the north coast of Newfoundland either, the very area which I had pinned my hopes on. Once more I took a hard look at all the reasons which indicated that there just had to be Norse remains in this area, and I said to myself: 'The old Icelandic map cannot possibly lie.' But it was a poor consolation.

It was then that I happened to meet someone and put, almost automatically, the same questions to him that I had asked people along almost the entire length of the North American coast. 'House-sites,' he said, and scratched his head. 'Yes, I seem to have heard about something like that over at L'Anse aux Meadows. But George Decker is the only one who knows anything about it; he's the boss over there.'

I felt as if I had hooked a large salmon. It was true that I had experienced bitter disappointments earlier, after I had been given some very promising bits of information, but this time everything seemed more promising. It was not only that L'Anse aux Meadows was situated on the north coast, but I also remembered that when we sailed past it I had noticed the open, inviting, verdant countryside. And I thought of 'Meadows', which is the same as 'grasslands' or the old Norse *vin*, just what the Norsemen were looking for. The *Gould* was to call at L'Anse aux Meadows on the return trip, and I would in any case have been informed about the house-sites by George Decker, but this advance information was to me like a ray of sunlight in the winter darkness.

On the return trip we called first at Ship Cove, which is situated on the western shore of Sacred Bay where it opens out into the ocean. The little fishing village looked very attractive with its green hills and well-kept houses. Here I met a wonderful old lady, Berthe Decker, who was ninety-four years old and had lost her sight. She had beautiful silvery hair, and there was a certain kind of dignity in her finely chiselled features, still tinged, it seemed, with youth. There was something about the old lady which made me think that she would have been able to hold her own among women of any milieu or social class whatsoever.

Her memory was fabulous. She told us in great detail about her youth, about fights between English and French fishermen, about the hunting of seals, and also of polar bears, and the Arctic fox that followed the drifting ice southward in the spring, about terrible shipwrecks, and about the Eskimo Maggishoe, who at one time lived on Sacred Bay. This particular Eskimo and his family were, as far as is known, the last of their race to live in northern Newfoundland. She, too, knew about the sites at L'Anse aux Meadows and she said that they had been there when the first white people settled in the area. 'But no one knows who built them, and it must have been a very long time ago,' she added.

We headed for L'Anse aux Meadows, our last port of call on the north coast.

While sailing past islets, skerries, and shallows, I was at first struck by the fact that this landscape was so very different from everything we had seen up to then. Ahead of us a wide green plain opened up and reached as far as a promontory to the north. And farther away there stretched an undulating land with small hills.

The fishing village is situated on the eastern side of the plain, and we headed in that direction. We detected eight or nine houses, and I got a strong impression that this must be a very lonely spot. There is no road leading to the outside world,* and the coastal steamer does not stop here. A small isolated community facing the sea.

A man came walking towards me. It was George Decker. He was a stocky man of about sixty; his bearded face was weatherbeaten, with a keen expression, but in his eyes there was warmth and a humorous gleam. There was something both bold and authoritative about him, revealing that he is the kind of man who knows what he wants.

I asked about old sites, and he replied immediately: 'Yes, there is something like that over by Black Duck Brook.'

'Has anyone ever dug there?' I asked.

'No strangers have ever seen them, and no one comes to L'Anse aux Meadows without my knowing about it,' he answered, with the emphasis of one who has a position of authority.

Then we walked along a path in a westerly direction across the wide plain. A number of cows were grazing in the meadows, and on a small hillock there was a flock of sheep.

After a ten-minute walk we came to a bay—Épaves Bay—and it was easy enough to see that it was very shallow; the tide was out, and from the shore and far out into the bay the sea bottom lay high and dry. A river, with the beautiful name of Black Duck Brook, emptied into the bay. It wound its way through the level country, in among the heather, willows, and grass.

A short distance from the bay an ancient marine terrace arched towards the river, about twelve feet or so above sea level. This must be the place! Along the terrace I noted a number of indistinct overgrown elevations in the ground, practically level with the grass and the heather. There was no doubt about it,

---

* A road was constructed in 1966.

these must be sites of houses, and very old ones. There seemed to be at least five of them, but it was quite possible that there were more; the faint irregularities in the terrain seemed to indicate this.

'Who were the people who lived here?' I asked Decker.

He shook his head and said: 'No one knows. They were here before the fishermen came to L'Anse aux Meadows and other places along the north coast. And my family were the first people to settle here.'

'But how about the whalers and fishermen of olden times?'

He pointed to the bay, where the low tide had exposed the sea bottom for a great distance, and said: 'They must have had a screw loose if they settled here where their boats could not dock. They would have had to wade ashore with the whales on their back.'

I looked out across the plain and to the north, to the islands and the sea. In the distance I could make out Belle Isle and the coast of Labrador, which the Vinland voyagers must have followed on their way south. And I recalled that Viking ships needed no docks but could be pulled ashore no matter how shallow the bays were.

I had a distinct feeling of recognition. There was so much here at L'Anse aux Meadows that reminded me of what I had seen of the surroundings of the Norse farms in Greenland: the green fields, the rippling stream, the open country, the view of the sea, and perhaps something else that was not so easy to fathom. Here the people from the Arctic island would have felt at home.

But so far everything was uncertain; only digging could reveal to us the secrets in the ground.

Chapter Eleven

First Flight over Labrador

Autumn was not yet over, and it would still be possible to accomplish a number of useful things in preparation for the archaeological expedition to be organized the following year. I planned to use a boat of our own, not only so that we should not have to depend on anyone else in getting to the area of excavation, but also in order to enable us to explore other coasts, and not least the coast of Labrador. I intended to take enough people along for these exploratory voyages to be undertaken without any interruption in the work of excavating the site which we had already found. The coast of Labrador and its fjords and bays were of particular interest; the route of the Vinland voyagers had lain in this area, and their landmark, the 'Wonder Beaches'; here they had probably sailed to fetch timber, and it was also possible that some Norsemen had settled in Labrador in the course of the centuries.

It would be very useful for us to get to know this huge country before the exploration to be carried out the following year in our own ship. I shall dwell here on a few aspects of this first highly interesting trip, when we saw the coasts and the interior from another angle than we did later—for we went by air. The Grenfell Mission gave us permission to travel in their plane; besides this, the Department for Fire, Fish and Wildlife placed a plane at our disposal for several days. In short, I met with a wonderful spirit of co-operation.

Labrador is about half a million square miles in area. It is situated roughly between 51° and 61° N., that is, on the same latitude as the area lying between London and the Shetlands. The cold Labrador Current, which flows southward along the coast, has a decisive influence on the climate.

On a sunny day we set out for the huge land, largely a wilderness, which rose out of the sea to the north. A bird's-eye-view of Labrador is a fascinating sight: a seemingly endless coastline, with innumerable fjords indenting the land, a multitude of islands, flocks of birds soaring below us, large icebergs drifting south, and only faint traces of human habitation. The coast seemed barren and cold, but in the interior there spread out a virtually endless wilderness, the forests looking like a green carpet as far as the eye could see, with here and there bogs and mountainous areas, and everywhere gleaming lakes and numerous rivers making such curious loops that it seemed as if they were about to join up with themselves.

It was in Sandwich Bay that a plane was put at our disposal, and we flew along the coast in various directions. We flew at a low altitude so that it was possible to get a good look at the land and its many inlets.

One day we landed at Muskrat Lake, not far from the source of the Eagle River, which is well known for its abundance of salmon. Here we met three men in a tent; they were foresters on the look out for forest fires, the greatest scourge in this land. We were warmly received. A large and newly skinned hide of a black bear was stretched out for drying near the tent, and one of the men told us with a somewhat offended air that the animals of the forest had made nightly visits to the rubbish heap and that this was all right as long as they did not disturb one's sleep. But then they began to paw on the tent walls and woke people up – and that was going a little bit too far!

We tried our luck at fishing in Muskrat Lake – and agreed that we had never before come upon such an abundance of fish. The bait was no sooner in the water than char jumped at it; and they were good-sized creatures, from two to six pounds, who fought to the finish, churning up the water and jumping in the air.

We continued our trip in a northerly direction and flew over the beaches at Porcupine Point, a place we were to investigate more closely the following year. The coastline had the appearance of a long, wide and white fringe along the edge of the forest. The land itself seemed to be quite flat.

Then we flew over the mighty fjord called Hamilton Inlet and as far as North-West River at the head of the fjord. There were a number of houses around the Grenfell Mission Hospital. Its superintendent is Dr Padden, who is a veteran in this kind of work and has taken the northerly regions as his own province. He offered to take us along on one of his planes going farther north.

But first I wanted to talk to people in the area, in order perhaps to obtain some information or see something or other that might prove helpful on the following year's expedition.

We stayed in the home of a trapper, who in later years had turned to salmon fishing as well. His name was Sidney Blake, and he was a man who knew more about the wilderness than most men, as for years he had made a good living from trapping. In the Labrador forests there are marten, beaver, musk-rat, mink, lynx, bear, fox, caribou, and other animals. Not very long ago about a thousand beaver skins and several thousand skins of marten and mink used to be put on the market every year by the trappers in this area.[1]

On the other side of North-West River we could glimpse a number of tents in among the bushes. We crossed the river to pay them a visit. Salmon had been placed for drying on a wooden frame, an old woman was kneeling in front of a fire, and skinny dogs were lying all around. Having lived among Indians and Eskimoes in Alaska and Canada, I felt at home in a place like this, and soon became acquainted with the Indians living here. The girls crowded round Benedicte, the contrast between them being quite striking: a blonde Norwegian girl surrounded by a group of brown-skinned, black-haired teenagers of the wilderness.

These were Montaignais Indians; they have lived in this area from time immemorial. In the past they wandered far and wide, setting out every autumn in their canoes, going upriver and staying in the interior during the winter. The caribou was at that time the focus of their existence. But times have changed, civilization has arrived even here, and the people's life-force seems to have become paralysed. They are amply provided for, but one cannot help thinking: it is bad not to help these natives, but it is worse to help them too much.

We flew in a north-easterly direction towards the coast and right across a comparatively level tract of wilderness, with forests, countless lakes, and great rivers. In certain places the ground gleamed like a yellowish white carpet – it was reindeer moss. Deer and other animal trails could easily be spotted from the plane.

We landed at Makkovik, where smiling Eskimoes greeted us at the pier. These were coastal people, of an entirely different type from the more reserved Indians, the sons of the great forest. The two peoples are not only quite different in their behaviour but also in their temper and disposition, and the old enmity between them is not difficult to explain.

The Moravian Mission is active here. This institution has made a splendid contribution to northern Labrador ever since 1752, when life in this region was extremely hazardous for the white man. In the course of time the mission has built a series of stations along the coast, and the Eskimoes have looked to them for help. In later years the most northerly stations, in areas where the hunting was best, such as Killinek, Ramah, Hebron, and Okak, have been closed down. There may have been several reasons for this, but it seems that differing opinions as to how the natives are to be treated have been the decisive factor.

We met Käthi Hettasch, the daughter of the late missionary Paul Hettasch, whose name is remembered for his magnificent work spanning many years. Through her we made the acquaintance of the Eskimoes. The most interesting group were the Hebron Eskimoes, who had been moved south a short time ago when the mission in their area was closed down. There seemed to be a primitive forcefulness about these people, which was lacking in the others. They now live in small houses specially built for them, standing in a drab, city-like row; here young and old were ambling about seemingly without much purpose. These people do not freeze, they are not hungry, but it seems as if the joy of living has been extinguished in them. I talked with one of the older Eskimoes, and his eyes shone when time after time he reverted to *his* country away up north, with its endless coast and the splendid seal-hunting. They had accepted their destiny, as Eskimoes are wont to do, but their longing for their homeland will not soon be eradicated.

My thoughts went back to an event that happened to my wife and me when we visited the Norse settlements in Greenland. We met an Eskimo sitting on a rock outside his house and looking out over the ocean. He was just sitting there. We got into conversation with him and were told that his home was away up north, but the government had moved everyone in the village farther south. We then talked about the war, which he had barely heard about. We told him a few things about that world-shaking event, and my wife mentioned that her father had been taken by the enemy and had been a prisoner for a long time. The word 'prison' sounded strange to him, but he recognized it as one of the worst things that could happen to a human being. Quietly he said, 'They moved him.'

The old Hebron Eskimo also provided me with many interesting bits of information about the land and about ruins along the coasts. He was especially interested in some ruins which he did not think originated with his own people, because they were different. In response to my question he said that they were probably remains of the Tunnit people. The old traditions about this people were encountered not only here but also at other places along the coast. The Tunnit people are thought to be identical with the strange Dorset Eskimoes, whom the Vinland voyagers very probably met, but they are now extinct. I shall revert to them in another connection.

The Eskimoes living along the northern coast of Labrador were much more numerous in the past. They were known by the beautiful name of Serkinermiut, which means 'people living on the sunny side', or on the coast facing east. They were divided into several groups. The plagues that civilization brings in its wake had also hit these Eskimoes hard. During the Spanish influenza epidemic of 1918, for instance, no less than two hundred and sixteen out of a population of three hundred and ten died in the village of Okak. Their existence, however, has been altered during the last few decades, in that they now also take part in the cod-fishing industry. They still hunt seal, but the stock has been reduced. In the autumn they fish the Arctic char, which swim up the rivers in great numbers at that time. The hunting of the caribou is done on a modest scale. The time of the kayak is over, the Eskimoes use motorboats, but they still have dogs and sleds, and the Labrador dog is a strongly built and beautiful animal. Thus the new age has brought with it many changes, but in the mind of the Eskimo ancient traditions and views are still deeply rooted.

We flew farther north, towards Nain. The coastline was protected against the might of the ocean by numerous skerries, small islands, and shoals. These features are characteristic of a large part of the coast all the way from Belle Isle to the south. The Vinland voyagers would very probably have kept far out to sea, away from the dangerous shoals and skerries, and would hardly have taken the risk of landing in a strange country unless the coastal waters looked fairly safe and inviting.

Looking from the plane out over the ragged coastline and the ocean, I thought of the Vinland voyagers and their small open boats pushing south, centuries ago. The hardy sailors would look searchingly at the strange land passing on their starboard side: Was it rich enough, or should they sail farther on to the south?

Where the land faced the ocean, trees had taken root only in scattered and sheltered spots, but throughout our northward flight we saw forests covering the land to the west. Deep fjords indented the land, and at their heads there were also forests, and large rivers, such as Kaipokok and Kanariktok, emptied into the fjords. But the grasslands were sparse. In many places along this coast it would have been possible for the Norse Greenlanders to have fetched all the timber they needed. If they stayed through the winter, in order, perhaps, to trap and hunt such animals as marten and beaver for their furs, or to hunt walrus and seal, their life in this country would not have been more strenuous than the one they were used to. There was cod in the ocean, trout, char and salmon in the rivers, and plenty of caribou in the interior of the country.

We flew across Davis Inlet, a beautiful spot surrounded by woods and lying in the shelter of the big island of Ukasiksalik. This is where the most northerly Indian tribe lives; they are the Nascapi Indians, with whom I was to live for a while later on. At the edge of the woods we could glimpse some of their tents.

Nain is a small settlement, with a church situated below a ridge of hills, and with spruce trees covering the slopes above it. The drift-ice had arrived from up north, and our pilot had a hard time of it landing between the ice floes. Nain is at present the northernmost Eskimo settlement along the coast of Labrador.

Once more we experienced the hospitality of the country. We made a valuable acquaintance in Pastor Fred Grub, who is the leader of the Moravian Mission in this area. He provided us with a great deal of useful and highly interesting information about the Labrador coast. So did that remarkable man, a very son of the wilderness, E. P. Wheeler, who together with his wife was about to leave in his canoe for some small hut far to the north, and to stay there through the winter.

Wheeler is a geologist, 'and that I became', he said, 'because geology was the subject which offered me the only chance of living in the wilderness and

Plate 23. The Nascapi Indians pole their canoes upriver, on the way to the interior in late autumn. Their dogs follow on the shore. (Photograph: Hans Hvide Bang.)

Plate 24 (*over*). Aerial photograph of the Norse sites at L'Anse aux Meadows at the northern tip of Newfoundland. They were discovered by the author in 1960 and excavated during the following six years. Sheds have been put up to protect some of the more important sites, as, for instance, the largest, at the lower right, and the smithy, on the other side of the river. (Photograph: Hans Hvide Bang.)

Plate 25. Our camp, situated a little below the Norse sites. In the distance, Great Sacred Island. (Photograph: Hans Hvide Bang.)

at the same time being able to do some useful work.' He has been wandering about, visiting the northernmost areas of Labrador, for about thirty years, in a region where one hardly ever meets anyone but a few nomadic Eskimoes. At times he would join them on their sledge journeys and he learned to speak the Eskimo language. As a rule, he went alone, but in later years his wife would join him on these journeys. His work over the years of mapping hitherto unknown areas has been of fundamental importance.

It is obvious that he likes this kind of life; he always seems to be in high spirits and often bursts out laughing. He is about sixty years old, and his wife is not much younger, but her footstep is as light as a feather and she knows how to use a paddle! They arrange their life in such a way that they stay for two years in the wilderness and then one year in civilization. Their home is in New York State. She told us with a smile: 'When my husband returns to civilization from the wilderness, he wants to drink wine from crystal goblets — the very finest of wines.'

I also met Isaac, an old and friendly Eskimo, who replied to all my questions with alacrity. I was told about the coast and about some ruins that he thought were rather curious. I hoped to be able to investigate them some time in the future. It was, of course, most probable that they had an Eskimo origin, like so many other sites in this region, but when conducting a search in the wilderness it is worth while to pay attention to any information that is out of the ordinary and make an investigation, even if you are likely to be disappointed. It should also be kept in mind that only a few very scattered archaeological investigations had so far been carried out along the far-flung coasts of Labrador.

The trip by air from Newfoundland had given us a very good picture of the route followed by the Vinland voyagers. And I had seen and learned a great deal which would prove useful when my expedition planned for the following year was to sail northward and investigate Labrador in greater detail.

It was late autumn, and much colder. The cod had returned to the great ocean. A large flock of wild geese flew southward, in plough-formation. Very soon Winter would reign, the sea ice would block the coast and snow would cover the wilderness; the people of Nain would be isolated for a long time. Teams of dogs would pull sleds across the ice.

Benedicte and I did the same as the flock of wild geese: we flew southward. And then we were once more over the northern coast of Newfoundland. Down below we could see the wide plain at L'Anse aux Meadows, Black Duck Brook winding towards the sea, and the terrace where we had discovered the old house-sites. What secrets did the earth conceal?

Chapter Twelve

With the *Halten* along the North Coast of the Gulf of St Lawrence

Halten was the name of the boat. She was a rather old Norwegian rescue vessel, forty-seven feet long, built of oak, with strong ribs and equally solid planking. Colin Archer, the builder of Fridtjof Nansen's famous *Fram*, had also constructed the *Halten*, which was also a masterpiece in a way. The austere lines gave the ship character. She had been built to make her way through the roughest of seas. When storms were raging along the Norwegian coast and fishing vessels were smashed to pieces, that was the time when rescue vessels like the *Halten* showed their mettle. She was something out of the ordinary – a personality. When she lay at anchor in a strange harbour, she presented a striking contrast to other boats, and experienced sailors would stop and look at her for a long time. A stalwart and sturdy ship she was – but she could roll!

Her former owner had built a cabin on deck, and consequently the amount of sail had to be reduced; on the other hand there was room for a larger crew. Besides my wife Anne Stine and myself the crew was made up of the following: Paul Sørnes, the skipper, who hailed from western Norway and had long experience in the ice-filled waters off Spitsbergen and Greenland; Odd Martens, our doctor, who was an old boyhood friend of mine and with whom I had gone camping summer after summer in the mountains of Norway; Erling Brunborg, who had sailed round the world in a boat very like the *Halten* and who was also a photographer, a splendid sailor and a jack-of-all-trades; and finally my daughter Benedicte.

Our plan was to ship the *Halten* on a cargo boat across the Atlantic to Montreal. From there we were to sail down the St Lawrence River, then proceed eastward along the north shore of the Gulf of St Lawrence, then pass through the Strait of Belle Isle and finally sail, still in an easterly direction, to L'Anse aux Meadows at the northern tip of Newfoundland. At L'Anse aux Meadows we were to begin the excavation of the ancient sites I had discovered the year before. It was also our intention while under way to investigate the north shore of the Gulf of St Lawrence, since some scholars believe that the

Vinland voyagers made a landfall there. The drift-ice normally blocks the passage through the Strait of Belle Isle until late in the season, and we could not expect to reach the excavation site before the beginning of June.

One day in May the Norwegian cargo boat *Byklefjord* entered the ice-filled Gulf of St Lawrence, and made its way very carefully through the dark open channels. The bright sunshine made the drift-ice gleam far in the distance. The *Halten* was standing upright on the after-deck, tall and sombre, looking naked in a way, as if longing for the sea.

We sailed up the river to Montreal, the metropolis which has grown up where the Iroquois at one time had their village of Hochelaga. A mighty crane lifted the *Halten* up high, and we watched her trip through the air with suspense. Then a splash, and the old ship at last felt water lapping round her sides. We gave a sigh of relief.

Our final preparations were taken care of in Montreal. There are many Norwegian-Canadians and Norwegians living there, and we benefited from their exceptional hospitality and helpfulness. But their unqualified faith in our finding Leif Eiriksson's houses would at times leave me with mixed feelings. Even if I had reasons for being optimistic, everything was uncertain, and I had been disappointed so many times.

We started on May 10th—a huge crowd had come down to the river to see us off, we sailed out into midstream, and the great city disappeared into the distance.

To the south we passed a mostly flat countryside, with small villages scattered about; to the north the landscape was more hilly, and one of these heights provides a marvellous site for the city of Quebec. Large steamers passed us, for this was the time of year when the Great Lakes were being opened up for traffic. It struck me as fantastic that there should be a waterway carrying such heavy traffic going right into the heart of the continent.

Here and there we noticed fences erected off shore in the river, and we were told later that they had to do with the catching of eels. There were many kinds of fish in the river, but in earlier times and according to old accounts there must have been a much greater abundance of fish. Cartier wrote in connection with his voyages of 1534–5 and 1543: 'The river has the greatest abundance of fish that anyone remembers having seen or heard about.' Of special interest is his statement that whale, porpoise, seal, walrus, and beluga were to be found as far upriver as 'Canada', that is to say, Quebec.

The Indians along the river belonged to the Iroquois tribe. They grew maize, but it appears that they were also fishermen to a great extent and that they also knew how to harpoon a whale. I thought of Cartier, who was the first white man to encounter the natives of this region; their villages were situated along the shores of the river, half-naked Indians came in their canoes

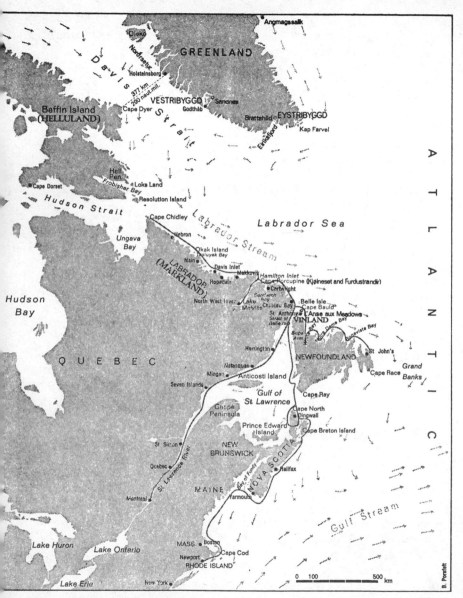

The solid lines show the routes covered by the author's various expeditions along the coasts of North America.

with articles for barter, while, always ready to take flight, they stared fearfully at the big ship and its strange-looking crew.

In this region, the northern limit for the growth of grapes probably extends (or extended) farther to the north than it does on the coast. Cartier has this to say about his journey on the river: 'We found on both sides the most beautiful and the best land that we could hope to see—filled with the most wonderful trees in the world, and so many grape-vines weighed down with grapes that they appeared to have been planted by man and not growing wild, but because they have not been cultivated or grafted the grapes are not as large or as sweet as ours.' There must be some truth in this, but Cartier was capable of great exaggeration when he described the regions he had discovered. Later I spoke with a Frenchman who knew the country inside out, and he had never seen any wild grapes.

We passed the large Orleans Isle, and the river widened out to such an extent that it resembled a fjord. Large flocks of ducks and other kinds of seabird were flying about by the islands and above the extensive shoals. As we approached Île aux Coudres we noticed something white in the water, at first a short distance away, and soon all around us. It was beluga, a small whale which is prevalent in Arctic seas. The animals turned over lazily as they plunged out of the deep, then snorted and puffed and slid down into the water again; at times they would come very close to the ship.

It was a large school; our experienced skipper thought that there must have been at least four or five hundred of them. According to old legends, the Indians 'fished' this whale; they harpooned it and afterwards killed it with bows and arrows. When the animal had been dragged ashore, 'all the chiefs were called together, and they began to sing for joy.'

I thought of the Eskimoes, to whom the beluga was a favourite dish, especially its vitamin-rich skin—*mataq*. They would have enjoyed living here. It is indeed possible that schools of beluga did lure them as far west as this in the past. We know that they came as far as Mingan, and to the far-ranging Eskimoes the trip from there would be no problem at all.

We continued on our course along the north shore of the river and arrived at the small village of St Simon, which is sheltered by the long and narrow Hare Isle. The Danish scholar Professor Steensby thought that this was the place where Thorfinn Karlsefni had his headquarters of Straumfjord. In this case, Hare Isle would have been Straumøy. I investigated the surrounding area, but found it difficult to believe that any Norsemen would have been tempted to settle in a place like this. There were hardly any grasslands, the river was too shallow for boats to ascend it, and I saw no bays in which ships could find shelter.

The Saguenay River surges forth between steep banks of gneiss and granite, and is navigable for large ships for quite a distance upstream. This river was the main highway of the Indian 'kingdom and land of Saguenay', Cartier tells us. We kept on our course for Seven Islands; the night was black and the waves began to get a bit rough. There was phosphorescence in the water, to the rear the propeller whirled a trail of light, and as the *Halten* made her way through the waves cascades of fire were thrown into the night.

Seven Islands is a latter-day Klondyke. Iron is the great thing here. In the wilderness of Labrador have been discovered enormous, easily accessible iron deposits, and American big business is already involved. In hardly any time at all, a railway has been built to the northern deposits, and in Seven Islands, where once the Indians put up their tents, there is now a town of more than fifteen thousand inhabitants, with big stores, jazz music, and chewing-gum. Production totals about twelve million tons of ore a year, and in the course of a season no less than five or six hundred cargo boats call at this port.

It is the Montaignais Indians who have been living here since time immemorial. They constitute a branch of the Algonquin tribe and are related to other groups of Indians to be found along the north shore of the Gulf of St Lawrence and in Labrador. In the past the Indians used to pitch their tents at Seven Islands and stay there during the summer months, but in the autumn the families would ascend the rivers in their canoes as far as the caribou country. There they would stay during the winter and spring, and when the ice broke up in the rivers they would paddle back to their old camping-places by the sea.

What is the situation today? It seems that the tremendous growth of the town and the white man's industries have just about crushed the Indians. At Seven Islands the Indians have a small area to themselves in the centre of the town, with a number of dilapidated houses. They all looked sad and dishevelled. The long voyages into the interior have practically come to an end—at any rate they have been severely curtailed. Their district includes some of the most valuable sites in the town, and the authorities want them to move, and have even offered to build new houses for them. But they do not want to move; this is the place where their tents were pitched in the old days, and here they want to stay; when an Indian doesn't want to do a thing, he won't do it.

From Seven Islands we made a number of trips along the coast and out to the islands in order to explore this region. On the islands there was a multitude of birds, the strangest being the cormorants. Unlike the usual type of cormorant, which nests among rocks, these had their nests in the tops of the spruce trees. The long-necked cormorant mothers made an unusual sight, sitting in one tree-top after another, the same way as the capercailzie.

One day a storm broke, and things looked bad for Anne Stine, Benedicte and Brunborg who were chugging about somewhere in the small plastic dinghy with the outboard motor. The rest of us made our way in the *Halten* through the heavy seas, fearing the worst – but then a bonfire flared up on an island in the distance, and when we approached the shore the tiny plastic boat darted towards us. Its crew were soaking wet and chilled to the bone, but their spirits were as high as ever.

The capelin arrived. Millions of this little fish headed for the coasts, and piles of them were washed ashore. The fishermen were overjoyed, for now the cod could not be far away, and cod-fishing is the main livelihood in this area. The arrival of the capelin was celebrated according to old traditions. As evening fell one bonfire after another was lit along the beaches. The young people arrived in droves, and there was always someone who ran down to the water, scooped up the gleaming fish and carried them over to the fire. The joyous celebration lasted far into the night.

We travelled farther east along the coast. A host of birds – auks, eider ducks, guillemots, gulls, ducks, and others – were everywhere to be seen; some circled the boat, others raced by or clustered together to form large bobbing groups on the surface of the sea. Now and then the black back of a whale would break the surface and gush water high into the air. After a while we could glimpse a faint blue outline far to the south; it was the large island known as Anticosti.

The coastal landscape exhibited very little variation. It was mainly stone and rock, and wooded hills, with more level areas round the mouths of the rivers. The scattered human beings – whites and Indians – who live here are as remote from civilization as if they lived on the moon. They make a living primarily from cod-fishing, but also from trapping and other pursuits. They cannot earn very much. A visit to their villages was a curious experience – it was as if we had entered a world of the past. On this shore time had stood still.

The small communities were headed by Catholic priests. The language was a kind of French that was spoken long ago in the home country, and is difficult to understand even by French Canadians living farther to the west. The history of these people goes back to the time when numerous ships from Europe came to fish and hunt whale and seal in the Gulf of St Lawrence. From time to time the sailors would settle down with Indian wives, and gradually other immigrants were also attracted to the area. Many of the people here do not know much about their forefathers, but I got the impression that not a few descend from people who once lived in northern France.

They were friendly people; they asked us to visit them in their homes, and their houses were neat and clean, the family heirlooms being displayed in the place of honour. In one house I came across an antique clock from Normandy, in another I saw some old French mahogany chairs. A merchant told me that one of the fishermen is supposed to be the owner of a Stradivarius violin, but he does not want to sell it, for he says that it has belonged to his family for generations. Alcoholic beverages were nowhere to be seen. At a young people's festival they served Coca-Cola, and everyone seemed to have a marvellous time. 'Don't they ever dance?' I asked an elderly lady. She replied: 'Yes, at weddings.'

One of the first villages we visited was Mingan, beautifully situated near a river. The Indians had pitched their tents at the edge of the forest. We soon became good friends, and got to know their chief, Damién Mechotakáche, quite well. He even did me the great favour of singing a number of Indian songs, allowing me to record them on tape. The little black-haired, barefoot Indian children who ran about the camp were a sight, especially the girls. They possessed that kind of indescribable grace that is to be found among wild animals, and were irresistible.

These Indians gave the appearance of being more robust and vigorous than the others we had met along the coast. They still set out in their canoes for the interior in the autumn, but perhaps do not go as far inland as before. In the winter they make their dogs pull their toboggans, these being of the usual Canadian type and not the heavy Eskimo sled (*kometik*) which the fishermen use out on the sea ice. Their dogs are small and lean, as is often the case with Indians.

We know that the Eskimoes got at least as far as Mingan in the old days, but the trader George Maloney and the Indian chief told me that once they were to be met with at Seven Islands and farther up along the St Lawrence River.

Tales are still told about the battles of the Eskimoes in the neighbourhood of Mingan. It seems that for a long time they managed to hold their ground in a region which the Indians also looked upon as theirs. Then, we are told, a French frigate gave the Indians flintlocks in exchange for their furs. As a consequence, the Indians became the stronger, and the Eskimoes suffered a disastrous defeat at Point Mort and on Eskimo Island. They were forced to withdraw from the entire area; this occurred some time in the seventeenth century.

Daily life on board our ship had a steady rhythm, but once in a while something unexpected happened. As far as Captain Sørnes was concerned, any surprise that he experienced had to do with the engine, an evil-tempered old semi-Diesel. The engine and Sørnes developed in time a deep enmity for each other, which lasted until the end of the expedition. As the *Halten* was making her way over the bounding waves and the skipper was humming a shanty, the engine would conclude that now was the time to annoy him. It would back-fire, give off a few disdainful puffs, and stop – and the *Halten* would be left a prey to the wind and the waves. The skipper would jump down into the engine room, which the motor had filled with smoke to make things doubly difficult for him. With furious concentration he would throw himself at the

Plate 26. Épaves Bay, at the head of which the Norse sites are located. It is very shallow, and this agrees with the account in the saga, which says that Leif Eiriksson's ship ran aground far from land when the tide was out. (Photograph: Hans Hvide Bang.)

Plate 27 (*over*). View of Épaves Bay and the large grassy plain at L'Anse aux Meadows. Black Duck Brook flows into the sea at the head of the bay. Noddy Head is in the background to the right. (Photograph: Hans Hvide Bang.)

Plate 28 (*over*). View of L'Anse aux Meadows from the low hill lying west of the sites. Our tents may be seen by Black Duck Brook, below the sites. The fishing village lies on the other side of the promontory. (Photograph: Hans Hvide Bang.)

monster and after several hours of struggling he managed to make his arch-enemy behave. Blackened and tired, but never displaying any lack of good spirits, he would then throw himself on the sofa in the lounge, grab his guitar, and begin to sing the 'Song of the Arctic Ocean' with an abandon that an opera singer might envy.

The cook, Dr Martens, took the preparation of our meals so seriously that one began to think this should have been his real vocation. He wore his white chef's cap at all hours of the day, and on his feet he wore the kind of clattering wooden shoes that are tied with only one strap across the toes—which he maintained was healthy. It must be judged as nothing short of a miracle that, favouring that kind of footwear on a slippery and heaving deck, he did not end up in the sea together with his potato peelings. His great speciality and pride was his puddings, which he used to put in the forepeak to cool. It so happened that Brunborg would often duck down the front hatch to get something, and on such occasions footprints would be found in the pudding. It is understand-able that the cook reacted to this.

Brunborg, the photographer and circumnavigator of the world, was some-thing out of the ordinary. To him ships and the sea were the most important things in life. He was indeed a splendid sailor, he always knew what to do, was agile as a monkey in the rigging, never stopped working, and had the Spartan outlook of the Indians. We used to come across him sleeping on a coil of rope or on the floor of the cabin, curled up like a dog.

The women did not have an easy time of it, having signed on in such a small ship and encountering all kinds of weather. But Anne Stine and Benedicte set about their tasks in the best of spirits and not even the stormiest weather would elicit a grumble from them.

And as for the *Halten*—I don't wish to say a bad word about our good old ship, but how she could roll! She rolled in the balmiest of weather, rolled wildly in a fresh breeze, and when there was a storm—enough said!

'Have you seen any sign of the cod?' was the first question directed to us when we met people along the coast. It usually heads towards the shore at the end of May or the beginning of June, but no one had seen it, and it did repre-sent almost everyone's livelihood. Captain Sørnes had a lot of experience of ocean fishing, and from time to time he would be able to spot shoals of cod with the help of the echo-sounding device. Then we would stop and catch quite a few fish over the ship's side. With cleaned cod dangling like strange fruits from the stays and the mast, we would head for the next village. The inhabitants were surprised to see the fish, and when we handed it out all round the ice was soon broken, and contact came naturally.

Havre St Pierre was the name of one of these villages. Upon arriving there I looked up Hector Vigneau, who was supposed to know more about the old history of the region than anyone else. He was a quiet man, in his eighties, with a noble appearance. As for ruins, he knew very little, but with regard to life among the fishermen, the seal hunters, and the Indians of times past, he had a wealth of information to offer.

He let me read his father's diary, a fascinating historical document throwing light on conditions in the region of the Gulf of St Lawrence about a hundred years ago. The diary had a lot to say about fishing and seal hunting (which in those days was much more extensive), driving dogsleds, shipwrecks, and other things. I received a vivid impression of the harsh life and the never-ceasing struggle for existence at that time. It also included a detailed account of a horrible tragedy that took place on Anticosti Island. A ship with nineteen men and women on board was wrecked, and they suffered starvation, and some of them died. A giant mulatto killed the weak survivors and ate the human flesh. When he was found, he was lying next to a full kettle; he had probably died from over-eating, it said in the diary.

In Natasquan – 'the river of the bears' – we met Father Fortin, a young clergyman full of life and energy. I had been told that a number of Indians were living some distance from the town and I wanted to find out what they knew about the country, about ruins, and other things. 'Oh yes, just follow me,' the priest said, and jumped on an old motor-cycle and set off along a narrow path. He was quite a sight, splashing through pools, wobbling over stones, and jumping high when he hit a bump. His black cassock flapped in the breeze, and his rosary swung from side to side.

But I did not get very far with these particular Indians. They just stood there, silent, with a rather hostile expression.

We continued our eastward voyage. As I scanned the coast I was for ever thinking: If the Vinland voyagers had been sailing along these shores, which spot would have looked inviting enough for them to stay and build their houses? I tried to put myself in the place of my seafaring forefathers, to try to think the way they must have done, to imagine myself on board one of their ships, so to speak.

If we sighted a place that looked inviting, we would cast anchor and go ashore. But the result of our investigations was always the same: we found an infertile land, in which even small green pastures were a rarity.

But at the same time, we did encounter much that was of great interest, when we went ashore in the motor-boat. We would sometimes meet fishermen, a solitary trapper or a group of Indians, or we would journey into the silent wilderness where the animals had the world to themselves. At times we would go up some river and through the forest, and might see a bear or two strolling along the river bank or an eagle swoop down for a meal of fresh-water fish. We found stone caches, put up by Eskimoes or Indians, as well as overgrown sites of houses which had once been used by fishermen or fur trappers, and remains of whaling stations.

Kegaska was the first fishing village we came to on our eastward voyage where the inhabitants spoke English. From there we sailed through an ever greater multitude of islands and shoals—difficult and hazardous waters for a boat whose draught was no less than nine feet. Once we actually foundered, but it ended well. It was now the end of May, but still quite cool. The leaves on the trees had not yet turned green, even though we were in a latitude as far south as the English Channel—so great is the influence of the Labrador Current on the temperature in the huge Gulf of St Lawrence and on the climate in the whole region.

We were approaching the Strait of Belle Isle—the narrow channel between Labrador and Newfoundland. Should we be able to get through, or was it blocked by ice? Presently we had a clear view to the north: only a few huge icebergs glittered in the blue sea. We breathed a sigh of relief.

But first we made a detour to visit Bradore Bay. At its head there is a level stretch on which stand a few fishermen's houses. About two hundred and fifty years ago, however, it must have presented an entirely different picture, for it was here that the Frenchman Augustin Legardeur, Seigneur de Courtemanche, established, about 1704, the first permanent settlement in Labrador. From the governor of New France he had received a letter patent relating to the area lying between 52° and 53° N. A fort is supposed to have been situated here, together with about two hundred houses; some house-sites could still be seen.

It was a period entirely lacking in law and order; whalers, fishermen, traders and pirates had no consideration for others and merely tried to amass as much wealth as possible. The Indians and the Eskimoes were the worst off, for they were exploited and even arbitrarily killed. The natives retaliated with surprise attacks.

Seigneur de Courtemanche must have been an able man, for he managed to bring about comparatively peaceful conditions along the coast. He traded with the natives and even let Indian families enter his service as trappers.

We also made an overland trip to the village of Blanc-Sablon, which is situated close by the strait. There we were told that a polar bear had been shot in the neighbourhood the previous year. It is still fairly common for a few polar bears to be shot in these latitudes along the shores of Labrador and New-foundland. Old accounts indicate that in times past it was not at all unusual to encounter these animals quite far south.

The Strait of Belle Isle is rather unusual. As I have said before, the strait was of the greatest significance through the ages as a focal point of abundant hunting and fishing, and also as an artery of communication. The strait is about seventy-five miles long and about eleven miles wide at its narrowest point.

The strait was the natural route for fish, seal, walrus, whale, and polar bear to take during their annual migration. It is the gate to the Gulf of St Lawrence, where conditions of existence are very favourable for these animals. The cold Arctic current brings with it masses of plankton, and in addition there is a profusion of food-particles carried into the sea by the many rivers.

Traces of tented camps and other sites show that Indians and Eskimoes used to come there in the old days, and after the rediscovery of the country it was visited by fishermen and hunters from many lands. We can hardly conceive of the multitudes of marine animals that made their way through this strait, at a time when the whole region was virgin territory.

The harp-seal was of particular significance in this area. It migrates southward from Greenland and Baffin Island at about the end of September and arrives in the Strait of Belle Isle some time in November. At the beginning of March it calves at the breeding-grounds in the Gulf of St Lawrence, and in April–May it sets its course again for the north.

As the *Halten* entered the Strait of Belle Isle we kept a careful watch on the shore, for the specific reason that many scholars have thought that the Vinland voyagers sailed through this strait. As mentioned above, I could hardly believe that they would want to deviate from their natural course, which lay in the direction of the north coast of Newfoundland, and sail on instead along a coastline which they knew presented few opportunities. And we were to realize very clearly that if they had stayed on their course in a south-westerly direction until they could observe the land on both sides of the Strait of Belle Isle, the scenery would have had more of a frightening than a tempting effect on them. The coast was uninviting indeed, with hardly a patch of grass to be seen from the boat. When Cartier sailed past here in the early part of the sixteenth century he wrote: 'This is the land that God gave Cain.'

We passed through the Strait of Belle Isle and sailed towards the Atlantic Ocean, then turned eastward along the northern coast of Newfoundland. On a fine day at the beginning of June we anchored outside L'Anse aux Meadows. The grassy plain spread before us, and we could see cattle and sheep grazing— it was a far more fertile land than any we had seen during our long voyage.

Chapter Thirteen

L'Anse aux Meadows: the Excavations begin

L'Anse aux Meadows lay bathed in sunlight. Our dinghy was taking us into Épaves Bay. The tide was out, and we had to carry the boat for quite some distance up to the mouth of the river.

I had come back to the old marine terrace, and to the traces of ancient dwellings, hardly visible among the grass. In some places there were low protuberances, and I passed my hand over them. What would these old sites reveal? Who were the people who had lived here?

Black Duck Brook wound merrily along and even managed to create a miniature waterfall before it reached the sea. A stiff breeze came in from the ocean and made the tall grass wave. The air was clearer than it had been the last time I was here, and the islands appeared as a sharp outline against the horizon. Far out by Great Sacred Island an iceberg had grounded; it seemed to have reached the end of a long voyage. And far to the north I could make out Belle Isle and the coast of Labrador.

A flight of ducks came in low over the hills to the west of the river. They had probably come from one of the many lakes to the south, where the flat country extends far and wide.

The cows were grazing on the plain and the flock of sheep were in their accustomed place on the higher ground. Yes, L'Anse aux Meadows was a good and a beautiful place.

Before long we noticed someone coming towards us from the fishing village on the other side of the point. It was George Decker, of course, and his faithful dog Orvil, and he was followed by a flock of lively youngsters.

The work of excavation began, and the tension was great. There were three possibilities: the sites might have originated with Eskimoes or Indians, or with whalers or fishermen of the time following the rediscovery of the country in 1497, or with Norsemen belonging to a period long before Columbus.

We had begun our work at one of the smaller sites near the brook, where walls of turf were more or less visible; it was rectangular, and measured approximately thirteen by eleven feet. We were especially eager to find out whether there were any stone implements, or waste material left over when they were made, the usual indication that a site was originally Indian or

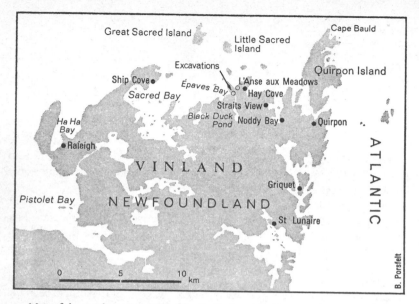

Map of the northern tip of Newfoundland, showing the situation of L'Anse aux Meadows, where the pre-Columbian house-sites were discovered and excavated.

Eskimo. As we slowly scraped our way down through the culture-layer, we were struck by the complete lack of any such material.

Towards the west wall there emerged, after a while, a fireplace; it had been carefully constructed, with a flat stone as a floor and vertical stones forming one side. Near by there was a pit, its bottom covered by a piece of slate, which contained a considerable amount of charcoal. This must have been a cooking pit.

Anne Stine then found the site of an open hearth in the eastern part of the room where the clay dirt was a reddish colour. Then a low elevation appeared along one of the two longer walls; it must have been the raised floor on which the people used to sit and lie down.

As she continued scraping near the spot where the open fire had been, she suddenly stopped, turned towards me, and said: 'I wonder if this is going to be anything like what we saw in Eirik the Red's farm in Greenland!'

She continued to scrape away very carefully and uncovered a small compartment in the ground next to the remains of the fireplace. It measured 6½ by 10 inches, and was very neatly lined with slate on the sides and bottom.

This could only be an ember pit, into which the embers were swept at night and covered with ashes, making it unnecessary to light another fire in the morning. Similar ember pits have been found in Iceland and in Greenland, at the big farms of Anavik, Herjolfsnes and Hvalsøy, and at Brattahlid, the home of Eirik the Red and his son Leif Eiriksson.

Having completed work on this particular dwelling-site, we started on the next, and throughout the long sunlit days we were slowly scraping our way into the ground. As far as we could see, there were traces of five buildings in all, the largest being about thirty-six feet long and thirteen feet wide. We were later to find several others.

One of the smaller sites was rather unusual. We noticed a small hollow near the edge of the terrace and were wondering what it could be. As Dr Martens was excavating it a small room appeared; it had been partly dug out of the terrace and faced the river. Between a large vertical slab and a boulder we found a fireplace. All around there were a number of brittle burnt stones, some about the size of a closed fist. Two rivets were also found.

It is possible that heated stones had been used for cooking the food, but the small dimensions of the room and its unusual position in the terrace with its entrance facing the river could indicate a different function: it could have been a bath-house! The facts are too few for any definite conclusion, but we do know that there were bath-houses in the Greenland settlements, and that a large number of brittle burnt stones was one of their very characteristic features.

Apart from that, it is of considerable interest to note that the C–14 dating of this site indicates that it goes back to the year A.D. 1080 ±70 – about the same time as the Vinland voyages.

There was nothing very grand about these sites; the traces we uncovered all indicated that the buildings had been plain and simple. Most of them were roughly rectangular. They had had an earthen floor; in some places there emerged low turf walls in which the layers could clearly be seen. Rocks and large stones had not been used to construct the buildings, and that is easily understood, since there is practically nothing in the vicinity but round stones, and these mostly on the beach or in the brook. The chief building materials were very likely turf and timber. The forests are all gone now, but a later chapter will show that even in historical times the forest must have come quite far down to the shore.

During subsequent excavations we still did not find any stone implements or any stone chippings indicating that Eskimoes or Indians used to live here. Nor did we find any fish-hooks, clay pipes, crockery, or any of the other things which one usually finds in places where whalers and fishermen have been staying. Our finds were, for the time being, rather sparse; among the more important I can mention some extremely rusty iron nails, and a lump of slag. This lump of slag was a curiosity indeed, to be unearthed in these wilds at the northern tip of Newfoundland, and it certainly provided food for thought.

Did the people living here produce iron from bog-iron? Later discoveries were to place this find in an extremely interesting light.

The fact that we made so few discoveries of artifacts has a reasonable explanation. Firstly, the preconditions for preserving objects for a long time were as bad as they could possibly be, because of the porous and acid terrace soil. We were to find that even bones had largely disintegrated or mouldered away, except in those cases where they had been exposed to fire. The nails appeared as a mass of rust almost without any iron core.

But this does not fully explain why we made so few finds. We must ask ourselves: what could the Vinland voyagers possibly have left behind? The implements and tools of a thousand years ago were simple, and the gear they could take along on a voyage across the ocean was limited. A number of implements were very probably made of wood, and would have disintegrated a long time ago. Their iron tools and weapons were valuable objects to these people coming from a country where iron was scarce. Swords, knives and hammers were things that they would take good care of and make sure of taking with them when they left.

And if the Norsemen had left a few things behind, it is very probable that the Indians or the Eskimoes would have picked them up. L'Anse aux Meadows was situated near the route which the natives followed on their voyage along the coast; if they had arrived at L'Anse aux Meadows from the seaward side, they could not easily have avoided seeing the buildings or the ruins of the Norsemen's dwellings. Anyone who is closely acquainted with Eskimoes or Indians knows that they are intensely curious whenever they come upon something new or strange in the wilderness. They possess a powerful urge to seek things out and their eyes are like hawks' when it comes to finding things. And the Norsemen's dwellings, or what was left of them, would present them with hitherto undreamed-of possibilities – they would look upon a piece of iron as we do on an ingot of gold. There is no doubt that they must have made a thorough investigation of the area.

Greenland provides us with striking examples of how thoroughly the Eskimoes have appropriated to themselves in the course of time any number of things from the ruins of Norse dwellings. Along the enormously long coastline from the southern point of Greenland to Thule and Ellesmere Island in the north, a number of finds of Norse implements have been made in Eskimo sites. And not only iron implements and other objects that might be of practical use, but also chessmen and other small objects that the Eskimo children might have used as playthings – or they may have taken them as strange and curious things worth saving.

A striking example of this practice is connected with the Norse farm Hvalsey, which must have been one of the largest and wealthiest in the Eastern

Settlement. People were living there for close on five hundred years; we know, at any rate, that a great number of people attended a wedding in Hvalsey church as late as 1408. But only very sparse finds have been made at the farm. Aage Roussell,[1] who was in charge of the excavations there, writes: 'It is strange, and indeed somewhat incomprehensible, that on excavating the large dwelling at Hvalsey we discovered only small finds of the poorest kind. With its geographical position, its fine church and many buildings, Hvalsey is one of the largest and richest farms in the settlement ... '

Facts like these must certainly be kept in mind during any future excavations of Eskimo and Indian sites in Newfoundland. It is indeed possible that at such sites one may come across objects that were originally among the possessions of the people who lived in the houses at L'Anse aux Meadows.

To help us in our work we had hired a number of men from the near-by fishing villages, and Anne Stine would gradually instruct them and make them into proficient scrapers. Among these were Carson Blake and Job Anderson, both of whom worked with us for some years. The latter, strange to say, was of Norwegian descent. His grandfather's name was Thorstein; he had been born in the district of Valdres in Norway, had emigrated to Canada, and had ended up in an Eskimo village called Makkovik in northern Labrador. There he had worked as a cooper for the Hudson Bay Company; he had married a Labrador woman and become the father of many children. In the course of the years I ran across a whole lot of Andersons along the coasts of Labrador and Newfoundland, and they were all descended from him!

We would hardly have started work in the morning before George Decker would come walking over towards us. He would be ramming his stick into the ground in order not to put too much weight on his bad leg; his dog would be jogging behind him. Even before he reached us he would give us the benefit of a new, humorous, and often risqué story, which usually ended with a loud guffaw. Full of life and good humour, this man had an inexhaustible supply not only of anecdotes but also of traditions and lore having to do with the people, with animals, and with the country as a whole. No one in that part of the country could rival him as a storehouse of information. Much of his knowledge originated from his great-grandfather, who had been the first man to settle in these parts.

After a while we began to call him 'Big Chief'; the name fitted him and he liked it. He was indeed a remarkable personality. The first time one met him one might easily get the wrong impression; for his face was rather dark and furrowed, and he had a strong chin and keen eyes. And he could be sharp enough when anyone crossed him, but we got to know him as a man who was kind and generous, tactful and gentle towards others. He was a 'gentleman' in the true sense of the word.

He was also an independent soul and never felt overawed by anything, not even when later on we had visits from cabinet ministers and members of Parliament. He had staked out his life in a remote spot on the northern point of Newfoundland. He had a small house that he had built himself, together with a fishing boat and fishing gear that he and his sons had made, he had his grandfather's old muzzle-loader with its powder-horn and a few other things, and was satisfied with life. He felt himself to be the equal of anyone. George Decker was one of the very finest examples of a free-born man that I have ever met.

I have written at such length about 'Big Chief' not only because he became our good friend but also because his help was to mean so much during the years when we worked in Newfoundland. 'Big Chief' is dead now; he passed on only a few years ago.

The weather was fine, often the sun shone, and it was so warm that we could work without a shirt on, and we bathed in the river. There were mosquitoes, but the swarms were modest compared to what they can be in other parts of Canada. The bogs directly behind the house-sites looked almost white from the cloudberry flowers, and along the terrace slopes there were beautiful strawberry flowers. We also kept our eyes on the irises whose buds had for some time been on the point of bursting into bloom. Then they unfolded their curiously spreading petals, and in certain places their great numbers made the ground look like a blue garden. The fishermen were happy, for the temperature of the sea was just right, and the waters between the islands were swarming with cod.

No drift-ice was to be seen, only a solitary iceberg once in a while. The huge iceberg that had run aground over by Great Sacred Island was slowly sinking into a watery grave. Every day about noon we would hear a loud crack; the iceberg had calved once again. Many pieces of ice were floating all round the gleaming colossus.

The *Halten* lay at anchor off shore, quite a distance from L'Anse aux Meadows, since the water was shallow very far out. The skipper was now the only man on board; he hardly ever went ashore. To him the sea was the natural abode of man, and the land was merely something that one had to tread on once in a while. But he kept in touch with things! He used to sit out on deck with his binoculars keeping tabs on us, and if any one of us had taken it just a little bit easy, he would not hesitate to belabour the sinner when he boarded ship in the evening.

We had pitched a tent down by the river, in the shelter of an elevated marine terrace; it was a snug place. This was where we had our meals and rested. Small boys would come by, eagerly fishing in all the pools. Usually they caught trout, but once in a while they would proudly show us a salmon.

We found that there were quite a few salmon in the river, especially in the autumn, and sometimes we even caught one with our bare hands. The fishermen also from time to time made excellent catches of salmon out at sea, and the fish were, on an average, larger than their relatives that we knew from Greenland. Our thoughts turned to the saga account of Leif Eiriksson's stay in Vinland and to this sentence in particular: 'There was no lack of salmon in the river or in the lake, and they were bigger salmon than they had ever seen before.'

Then came the capelin. This small fish swarmed by the million in towards the shallow waters in order to spawn. Down at the beach youngsters were running about with nets and pails, scooping up as many as they could handle. Masses of fish were washed ashore and looked like a glittering carpet covering the beach.

It was about this time that we noticed that Brunborg would once in a while take the dinghy and row out a short distance and then just lean over the edge and gaze into the water. We were used to him doing strange things, but at last we asked him what he was looking at down there. He replied: 'Flounder.'

We found out then that in the shallow bay, near the beach and for a fair distance out, there were small flounders hugging the sea bottom — hundreds of them. Fishermen maintain that the flounder comes close to shore in order to eat the roe of the capelin. This was of as great interest to me as to Brunborg, for I recalled the account of Thorfinn Karlsefni's voyage. At one point it says: 'They dug trenches where the land and the sea met at high tide, and when the tide went out there were halibut in the trenches.'

It couldn't possibly have been halibut, since that is a deep-water fish, but it might have been flounder, a fish that has a similar shape. This type of fishing in hollows which the saga mentions was formerly the custom in North Norway, and V. Tanner informs us that the Labrador Eskimoes were able to catch sea-trout in this manner.

The people who lived at L'Anse aux Meadows long ago must have had a huge supply of flounder right outside their door, and they were probably as amazed as we were. It would certainly have been advantageous for the Vinland voyagers if they could have caught fresh fish by merely digging trenches in the sand. But was it actually as simple as that? One day we tried to do what Karlsefni might have done. We dug three long trenches on the beach immediately below the house-sites. At the next ebb tide we found three flounder in the trenches.

Once in a while we were also visited by whales; they swam slowly into the bay to inspect the goings-on, then thought better of it and returned to their great ocean domain. Once again I would think of Thorfinn Karlsefni and the story in Eirik the Red's Saga of the whale that drifted ashore. Such an occurrence may not have been unusual in the old days when there were great quantities of whales off Newfoundland. It also happens today; in 1963, for instance, the drift-ice in the Strait of Belle Isle had forced a whale into a shallow bay, rendering it completely helpless. It was a rorqual, about thirty yards long. Thorhall the Hunter, who had been Eirik the Red's huntsman and was big, strong, swarthy, and looked like a troll, also talked about whales. He was disappointed that he had not got any wine and wanted to return to Greenland; as far as he was concerned, the others were free to 'boil whale' to their hearts' content.

From time to time we would put our scrapers aside in order to take a closer look at our surroundings. Below the terrace, whose height above sea level was about twelve feet, a wide depression opened up towards the river mouth, and we could not help wondering: long ago, when the sea level was higher, could there possibly have been a kind of lagoon or big pool here, a place where a ship might find shelter?

We found other traces of the people who had lived here. Among these were some large depressions. One of them looked especially interesting; it was curiously situated at the top of a terrace next to the river. 'That's the smithy,' Anne Stine said—we thought that she was only joking, but later on we did excavate a smithy there. We were searching for graves or burial places, but found no traces of that kind. We realized after a while that this first season merely marked the beginning of a long-drawn-out task.

On a trip to the source of Black Duck Brook we found currant, gooseberry and raspberry bushes, and the bogs were filled with cloudberries. The berries were just beginning to ripen, and it looked as if there would be a big crop that year. We came to a small lake, Black Duck Pond, about three miles from the sea. It had a beautiful situation, and was partly surrounded by willows. From here the brook ran out towards the ocean, and it was here that the salmon came to spawn. Not very far away there was another lake called Skin Lake, in which the fishermen used to immerse their seal-skins to get the hair to loosen and fall out.

One day we set out to make a thorough investigation of the ridge, about eighty feet high, that extended to the shoreline about three hundred yards west of the house-sites. The question was: should we find any cairns? After a time we did discover no less than four collapsed cairns. Curiously, two of them had been erected quite close to each other; there was only a distance of some fifteen feet between them.

About two feet of the cairns remained standing; the rest was a jumble of stones, most of them with a black covering of moss. There was an ancient look about it all, and we got a strong impression that the cairns must have been built a very long time ago.

Could there possibly be any runic inscriptions on these stones? In the far north, on the island of Kingigtorssuaq on the west coast of Greenland, there were found, as I have said before, three collapsed cairns, and in one of them a strange rune-stone. The names of three Norsemen were cut in the stone and also the time of year, as well as some magic runes, the runic inscription being very graceful. We investigated our stones carefully, but found no runes here.

But why had *two* cairns been put up so close together? On Kingigtorssuaq there were three cairns, and the rune-stone mentions three Norsemen, and we are thus tempted to believe that it was intended that there should be one cairn for each of them. Actually, two cairns near each other have also been found in two other places in the Western Hemisphere, and there is much to indicate that they were put up by Norsemen. One pair is situated at Jones Sound (76° 30′ N.) and the other is on Washington Irving Island east of Ellesmere Island (79° N.).[2]

What can have been the purpose of these cairns, and who were the people that built them? They were not placed on the highest point of the ridge or close to the sea, as one might expect if they were intended as seamarks. Strangely enough, they were placed on a lower level, and somewhat set back from the sea, which would make it very hard to sight them from any passing ship. But it is odd that when seen from the site of the dwellings they must have appeared sharply silhouetted against the sky in the west-south-west.

The cairns can hardly have been put up by fishermen from the village (which is quite a way to the east), that is to say, during the last hundred and seventy-five years or so. The people living there now have no knowledge of them, and the black moss indicates a very advanced age. It is also hard to understand what use the cairns can have been to the fishermen, since they cannot be seen from the village and only with difficulty from the sea. It is possible that they were erected by people who had visited the place for a time, such as Eskimoes or Indians, but such a surmise does not agree very well with the fact that the cairns seem to have been placed in spots specially selected for the purpose, and just where they are sharply silhouetted against the sky when looked at from the old sites. It is plausible to think that the cairns had a specific purpose for the people who long ago lived only some three hundred yards away from them.

It seems possible that the cairns had something to do with the various time-periods of their day. We know that the Norsemen would determine the time of day by taking a bearing of the sun and relating it to natural features, such as mountain peaks, mountain passes, rock piles, or cairns. For one thing it was necessary to determine when meals were to begin. It is of particular interest to note with regard to the two cairns built close together that, viewed from two of the largest house-sites, their position is approximately west-south-west. Furthermore, the sun would be above the cairns at about three p.m.

This fact recalls to mind the astronomical reference in the Greenlanders' Saga of Leif Eiriksson's stay in Vinland (see pp. 77–8). We are told about *eyktarstaðr* which must have been a mark on the horizon from which a bearing could be taken. This must have been somewhere between west-south-west and south-west, when the observation was made at nones, which in Iceland was about three o'clock in the afternoon.

There are no definite answers to the questions that arise in connection with the cairns at L'Anse aux Meadows, but it is an interesting fact, and one that we should keep in mind, that erecting cairns was a typically Norse custom. The custom was prevalent in Norway, Iceland and Greenland, where such cairns were placed on the high ground above the old farms.

We also visited the islands off the coast, the waters around them being shallow and full of skerries. We visited the tiny Flint Island, where pieces of brown flint were lying all over the beach, and Green Island, which is very flat indeed but where there is fine grass, yellow flowers and violets, and where a generation ago the eider duck used to hatch in great numbers. We finally sailed all the way out to Great Sacred Island; its north coast is steep, but to the south there are green hills with low vegetation. To the north there was nothing but sea as far as the coasts of Labrador, to the south we could see the low shore at L'Anse aux Meadows. Facing the fury of the ocean, this outermost island is an excellent mark for seamen. Anyone who set his course towards Great Sacred Island just could not help finding his way to L'Anse aux Meadows.

The excavations made slow progress. The lively youngsters from the fishing village were always with us, and they were a charming bunch indeed, and they behaved better than many city youngsters. On Sundays the people from the near-by villages would congregate round us, in their best clothes and wondering about the strangers who for weeks on end had been digging in the ground. Now and then, Lloyd, the son of 'Big Chief', would pass by, returning from the hunt, with a number of ducks over his shoulder, the old muzzle-loader in his hand, and a powder-horn hanging across his chest. We kept on digging and digging.

Chapter Fourteen

The Land and the People

L'Anse aux Meadows is situated at latitude 51° 36′ N. and longitude 55° 32′ W., that is, just about as far north as London. In relation to the Eastern Settlement in Greenland its position is about nine degrees farther south.

The climate is pronouncedly maritime and is to a great extent influenced by the cold, southward-flowing Labrador Current and also partly by the Gulf Stream. Summer temperatures will usually fluctuate between 10° and 20° C. (50° and 68° F.). Winters are relatively mild, and the fishermen have informed me that it seldom gets colder than − 15° C. (5° F.). The climate can vary a great deal from one year to another: one year will have a warm summer, another a much cooler one, and in the winter there may be long stretches of mild weather with very little snow.

The sea ice begins to form along the coastline some time in December. In the course of the winter it is usual for the ice to extend quite a long way out to sea, and it is then possible to walk or drive dogs to the islands or across the bays. The ice usually breaks up in May, and the coastline is often free of ice by the beginning of June. But there is no set rule; there are some years when the drift-ice heads for the coast at the beginning of June and even later.

A gently undulating landscape is typical of the entire north-eastern peninsula north of St Anthony. There are no hills more than about three hundred feet high. South of L'Anse aux Meadows an extensive open area spreads out, comprising small hills, bogs, and a number of lakes. There is an abundance of moss, lichens and willows, in some places a heavy growth of small wind-blown spruce trees, and grass in the sheltered areas. The limit of the forests is a line approximately eight miles from the shore, to the south-west and in the direction of Pistolet Bay. Somewhat to the south of this fjord rises White Mountain.

Walking along the shore in a westerly direction, not far from L'Anse aux Meadows one will come upon a beautiful grassy meadow, where the fishermen have built a barn. Farther to the west similar meadows are to be found along the coast of Sacred Bay. This bay cuts deeply into the land; at its head a forest of small spruce trees advances almost all the way down to the shore. Farther west, at Ship Cove and Raleigh on Pistolet Bay, there is also some good grass.

If you take a path south-east from L'Anse aux Meadows, you will soon come to a tiny fishing village called Hay Cove. The name is suggestive, indeed, for in the surrounding area there are many stretches of fine grass. From there it is about a fifteen-minute walk to Straits View, a fishing village situated on the deep indentation made by Noddy Bay. Farther east, there is only the small fishing village of Quirpon.

The preconditions for a fairly rich vegetation are much better in this area than in Labrador, a major reason being the fact that the topsoil has been created by the decomposition of palaeozoic rock formations. As for L'Anse aux Meadows and the neighbouring coastal areas, it is very difficult to estimate just how extensive the grass is, since in places it is interspersed with fields of lichen, but I should think that the grass here covers approximately forty acres. In this area, in the interior and along the coast, there should be fine grazing land for a number of cows and especially for sheep. The fact that the fishermen in the area keep only a small number of livestock is due to their being so busy with their main occupation that they have little time for other activities.

Another striking feature of the vegetation is the great amount of various kinds of berries.

Not so long ago, as has been mentioned before, the forest extended almost all the way down to the coast, but in the course of time it has been cut down by the fishermen, and there have also been forest fires. This has led to a retreat of the forest limit from many coastal areas of Newfoundland and Labrador.

George Decker told us that when he was a boy there was a wooded area a short distance behind the old house-sites and other places in the vicinity. His grandfather had told him that when he walked to the neighbouring village of Straits View, the path was cut through thick forest most of the way. Now there isn't a single tree to be seen, but the grass is thriving and grows tall. All of this agrees with our own experiences and observations. Scattered over the interior there are any number of tree stumps, and during our excavations we came upon stumps and large roots of trees.

The reduction of the forest must have had a number of different consequences. When the roots could no longer hold on to the moisture in the ground, it was so much easier for bogs to form, and there were areas where the grass could no longer maintain itself when the forest did not provide shelter. The landscape, in other words, was quite different in times gone by and offered man more favourable living conditions than it does today.

The men and women who lived at L'Anse aux Meadows in the Middle Ages also had another, more accessible, source of timber and fuel: driftwood. Every morning we would notice several eager youngsters from the village running along the beach picking up driftwood. In the course of the summer and autumn they would pick up such a great quantity that in the village the Colbourn family at least would have enough fuel for the entire winter. If

Plate 29. Squash-berries (probably *Viburnum pauciflorum*), of which there is an abundance in northern Newfoundland. They grow in clusters on bushes, and are somewhat larger than currants and are very tasty. At times, the local fishermen will make wine from them. Did the Vinland voyagers try to do the same? (Photograph: Erling Brunborg.)

Plate 30. There were many salmon in Black Duck Brook. Sometimes we even caught them with our bare hands. The saga account of Leif Eiriksson's Vinland voyage says that there were salmon in the river by which he built his houses. (Photograph: Hans Hvide Bang.)

there was a stiff breeze from the north or north-west, they would be able to bring home a magnificent haul, and the bay immediately below the dwelling-sites seems to be one of the best places for collecting such wood.

Some of the driftwood carried south by the Labrador Current was originally part of the large forests of Labrador. But some wood also comes drifting through the Strait of Belle Isle and was at one time big trees carried into the ocean by the St Lawrence and other rivers.

Beaches in northern regions far from human habitation, where the drift-wood has been piling up, are indeed something worth seeing. In the course of the centuries the drifting logs and pieces of wood have been piling up and form rampart-like mounds, which have been forced by the ice and the wind up on to land beyond the high-water mark. Such collections of driftwood may remain on the beach for hundreds of years in Arctic areas, and even in such relatively cool regions as L'Anse aux Meadows they will remain for some time. Another reason for the timber being preserved so long is the fact that it has a high salt content.

In other words, the people who lived at L'Anse aux Meadows long ago had a splendid supply of firewood and material for building right outside the door.

Today, the fauna of northern Newfoundland is rather restricted in size and variety, and there are many reasons for that: in many areas the forests have disappeared; hunting, without any regard to the size of the animal stock, has been common; and of no little importance is the fact that human civilization and the building of a road have prevented wild animals from entering the peninsula at its narrowest part.

The ocean presents an entirely different picture. Large shoals of cod press towards the shores, harp-seals have their seasonal run along the coast, and whales are a not infrequent sight. During the month of March the drift-ice carries the young seals to these more southerly climes, and they may be followed by white fox and even polar bear.

If we are to consider the possibilities of existence for the emigrants who lived long ago at the L'Anse aux Meadows sites, we must take into account conditions as they were at that time.

Was the climate different nearly a thousand years ago, at the time of the Vinland voyages and later? This difficult question has been and still is a controversial one. For Newfoundland and the adjacent areas there are, as far as I know, no data that throw light on the problem, but the studies that have been made with regard to Greenland may shed some light. Fridtjof Nansen[1] supposed that the climate of Greenland, by and large, has remained the same from the time of Eirik the Red to our day. The Swedish glaciologist Hans W. Ahlmann[2] is of the opinion that the climate around the year 1000 was not substantially different from what it is now, but that it began to worsen in the latter part of the thirteenth century and remained bad far into the fifteenth century. Of great importance in this respect are the pollen investigations that the Danish botanist Johannes Iversen[3] has carried out in the Western Settlement in Greenland. His investigations indicate that the climate of Greenland was relatively mild and moist in the eleventh and twelfth centuries. During the thirteenth and fourteenth centuries the climate became drier, more continental. But he thinks that summer temperatures have not changed much during the last thousand years. C. L. Vebæk[4] has given a résumé of the investigations made by various scientists and concludes as follows: A worsening of the climate seems to have taken place around the year 1500 and this continued until the beginning of the twentieth century, when the climate began to improve. But the changes of climate that took place between the years 1000 and 1600 were relatively small.

One would be inclined to believe that the climatological changes in Greenland and Newfoundland were somewhat parallel. The period of time of particular interest to us began around A.D. 1000 when the Vinland voyages took place, and lasted until about A.D. 1500, when the Greenland colony disappeared. According to the above-mentioned pollen analyses and other investigations we are led to believe that the climate of Newfoundland was not essentially different at that time from what it is today.

The fauna of Newfoundland must have been much more abundant in the past than it is at the present time. The old accounts corroborate this impression. Speaking of Gaspar Cortereal's expedition of 1501, his contemporary Pasqualigo[5] has this to say:

> ... No kinds of grain grow there, but the people in this country [the natives] say that they live only from fishing and hunting animals, of which there is an abundance in the country; there is thus a very large horned animal [caribou] covered with very long hair, and the hide of that animal they use for clothing and they also make houses and boats from it. Moreover, there are wolves, foxes, tigers [lynxes], and sable. They maintain, what I think is wonderful, that there are to be found as many falcons as there are sparrows in our country; I have seen some of them and they are exceptionally beautiful.

In other descriptions we are told about multitudes of salmon and cod and about an abundant bird life. In some islands there must have been numbers of the great auks, which were unable to fly and are now extinct. The great auks were killed with rocks and stones, and whole boatloads of dead birds were brought in from some of the islands. There were also many fur-bearing animals, but the mammal that was of greatest importance to the natives was the caribou. There must have been large herds of them grazing at L'Anse aux Meadows as well as in other parts of Newfoundland. As late as the end of the last century one of the British hunting clubs killed no less than two thousand animals.

But of even greater importance were the riches of the sea – the enormous shoals of cod, the numerous whales, seals, walruses, and so on.

We have mentioned some aspects of life in Newfoundland and how they must have affected life at L'Anse aux Meadows at the time when the Vinland voyagers arrived off these coasts. They came to a virgin land, in which only Eskimoes and Indians were roaming about. Although the natives were great hunters their only weapons were bow and arrow, spear and harpoon, and the reduction of wild life which they could effect was minimal compared to the annual increase. There were multitudes of all kinds of wild animals, and there was an equal abundance of marine life. At L'Anse aux Meadows the forest came all the way down to the shores, and the driftwood was piled up on the beaches. The grazing lands were much more abundant than they are today, since in many places the trees of the forest would provide shelter from the wind. And there were plenty of berries.

L'Anse aux Meadows must have been a very attractive region for men from a northern land who were experienced in utilizing just those possibilities that this northerly area had to offer.

The Neighbours of the Vinland Voyagers

As mentioned above, the sagas say that the Vinland voyagers encountered natives (Skraelings) in Markland and Vinland, and this account must have been a reliable one on the whole.

What was the distribution of natives along the coasts of Labrador and Newfoundland? What kind of people did the Vinland voyagers meet during their trip towards the south, and who were their neighbours in Vinland?

From the time of the rediscovery of the land in about A.D. 1500 and later, there have come down to us some scattered but highly interesting items of information. In Labrador there seem to have been a considerable number of Eskimoes along the far-flung coasts from Cape Chidley in the north to Mingan, on the north shore of the Gulf of St Lawrence, in the south. Very probably these people were Thule Eskimoes. Furthermore, there were a number of Indians in the country at that time, most probably the tribes that we know as Nascapi and Montaignais. They hunted the herds of caribou in the neighbourhood of the tundras in the winter and spring and followed the migrating herds down to the coast in the summer.

In Newfoundland, too, the explorers of the early sixteenth century encountered natives. At times the descriptions seem to refer to Eskimoes, but most often it appears that it was Indians who were meant. They were the Beotuk Indians,* or 'Red Indians' as they were called because they decorated themselves with ochre paint.

Alberto Cantino,[6] a contemporary of Gaspar Cortereal, writes as follows about the expedition of 1501 which reached the east coast of Newfoundland and about the natives who were brought back to Portugal as slaves:

> They forcibly kidnapped about fifty men and women of this country and brought them to the king. I have seen, touched, and examined these people, and, beginning with their stature, declare that they are somewhat taller than our average, with members corresponding and well formed. The hair of the men is long, just as we wear ours, and they wear it in curls, and have their face marked with great signs, these signs are like those of the [East] Indians. Their eyes are greenish and when they look at one, this gives an air of great boldness to their whole countenance. Their speech is unintelligible, but nevertheless is not harsh but rather human. Their manners and gestures are most gentle; they laugh considerably and manifest the greatest pleasure. So much for the men. The women have small breasts and most beautiful bodies, and rather pleasant faces. The colour of these women may be said to be more white than otherwise, but the men are considerably darker. In fine, except for the terrible harsh look of the men, they appear to me to be in all else of the same form and image as ourselves. They go quite naked except for their privy members, which they cover with a skin of the above-mentioned deer. They have no arms nor iron, but whatever they work or fashion, they cut with very sharp stones, with which they split in two the very hardest substance.†

Jacques Cartier[7] tells us, from his voyage of 1534, about an encounter with natives at Blanc Sablon in the Strait of Belle Isle, which was hardly a day's sail from L'Anse aux Meadows:

> There are people in this country with a splendid physique, but they are wild and barbarous. They wear their hair in a bun on top of their heads, like a bunch of hay tied fast; a nail or something similar is stuck right through it, and to it they fasten a few bird feathers. Both men and women are dressed in animal skins, but the women are wrapped up more closely and are more warmly dressed and have a belt about their waist. They paint themselves a kind of yellow-brown colour. They have canoes which they use on the sea; these are made from birch bark, and from them they catch many seals. After I had encountered them, I heard that they come from

* They, like the Indians of Labrador, are supposed to have belonged to the Algonquin tribe.

† Translation taken from Bernard G. Hoffman, *Cabot to Cartier* (University of Toronto Press, 1961).

warmer countries to catch these seals and to get other food for their sustenance.

Later items of information about the Beotuk Indians have come down to us but they are sparse indeed, and very little archaeological research has been carried out.

These Indians were to a great extent dependent on the hunting of the caribou, this being the reason that they would remain in the interior of the country during the winter — as, for instance, at Indian Lake and Exploit River. In all probability they also had camps farther to the north. In early summer the caribou would here, as in other regions, follow a definite migration route towards the coast in order to seek the earliest green vegetation and to calve. Later, the animals would seek higher ground. A very characteristic route, which is still used to a certain extent, follows the Long Range Mountains in a northerly direction; and at the time when there were large numbers of caribou, they must have spread out at L'Anse aux Meadows as well.

The Indians would follow the caribou down to the coasts. There they would also obtain fish, birds and eggs, as well as seals. In the autumn they would return to the interior, at the time of the caribou trek, and there they would stay through the winter.

Their weapons were bows and arrows, and spears; when hunting seals they would also make use of the harpoon. Their pyramid-shaped tent (tepee) was covered with birch bark. Their chief means of communication was a curious half-moon-shaped birch-bark canoe,* sewn together with the finest roots of spruce. They buried their dead in caves or on wooden scaffolds.

The Beotuk Indians were, from the very beginning, subjected to maltreatment and encroachment by the white man, assisted at times by the Mic-Mac Indians in Nova Scotia, who would for that and other purposes cross Cabot Strait. Some Beotuks were brought to Europe as slaves, others were just shot when they got in someone's way. The Indians tried to offer resistance, but this merely led to greater oppression and persecution. The Beotuk Indians were last seen at the beginning of the nineteenth century; when they died, an entire people had been extirpated.

How widely can the Indians and Eskimoes have been distributed in these areas five hundred years before the rediscovery — at the time when the Vinland voyagers set their course southward along the North American coasts? Which natives did they encounter?

As far as the Indians were concerned, we must suppose that the enormous

---

* There are extant older accounts to the effect that they used canoes made from skins, but these can hardly have been the common type.

herds of caribou in Labrador and Newfoundland had supplied man with meat and furs from far back in time. Whether it was Nascapi or Montaignais Indians who were living in Labrador at that time is uncertain, but their way of life, based on the caribou, must at any rate be ancient. Neither can we say anything very definite about the Beotuk Indians in Newfoundland. In the course of the centuries it is possible that tribes were displaced and moved about, but there is much to indicate that they have been living in Newfoundland for a very long time.

Then we have the Eskimoes, that strange people who in the course of time have wandered over huge Arctic areas, from Alaska to Greenland. By and large, their culture is divided into four stages:[8] Pre-Dorset, which in Alaska goes back to about 3500 B.C.;* Dorset, which takes in the period 800 B.C. to about A.D. 1300; the Thule culture, lasting from about A.D. 900 to about A.D. 1750; and finally the Eskimoes of our own time, descendants of the Thule people.

The Dorset period corresponds to the time when the Vinland voyages took place. The Dorset culture was unknown until the Canadian archaeologist Diamond Jennes discovered some sites at Cape Dorset on Baffin Island in 1925. It has subsequently been found in an extensive Arctic area from Melville Island in the west to Eastern Greenland. It is of interest in this connection to note that Dorset people also ranged south along the coasts of Labrador, and that their remains have been found in Newfoundland.

Their culture differs in many respects from that of the later Thule Eskimoes. We shall mention a few characteristics: Their implements were small and delicate, and of a special type. Their art was also distinctive. Moreover, they seem to have lacked certain tools and articles used by later Eskimoes, such as the bow drill and the ulu knife, and nothing has been found to indicate that they used dogs as a means of transport. Their dwellings, made of turf and stone, were not constructed with particular care. Some scholars assume that there was an Indian influence on their culture.

It has been maintained that the Tunnit people, about whom the Eskimoes had such strange legends, must have been the Dorset Eskimoes.

These people seem to have disappeared around the year 1300. They may have been absorbed by the Thule Eskimoes during their eastward migration, the latter being perhaps more numerous and more advanced. They reached the coasts of Greenland about A.D. 1100 and then proceeded slowly southward along the west coast. Before long the Norse Greenlanders were to encounter them.

The Greenlanders, in other words, met with two kinds of Eskimoes: the Dorset people in America, at the time of the Vinland expeditions; and later on

* Cape Denbigh Flint Complex.

the Thule people, on hunting expeditions north of the Norse settlements in Greenland and, some time later, even in the settled areas.

Taking a closer look at the extent of Dorset occupation of Newfoundland, in the area which the Vinland voyagers most probably reached, we find that relevant archaeological investigations have been sparse. But traces of the Dorset people have been found in a number of places,[9] especially in the more northerly areas — but, strangely enough, also as far south as on Cape Ray,[10] the south-western extremity of Newfoundland. Dr Elmer Harp[11] was in charge of the excavations at Port au Choix on the Strait of Belle Isle which revealed the first Dorset house-sites excavated in Newfoundland. At L'Anse aux Meadows we found Dorset implements. There is much to indicate that this people was widely scattered along these coasts and that the Vinland voyagers could not have avoided meeting them.

What, then, can L'Anse aux Meadows have meant to the wandering Indians and Eskimoes? They saw no value in the grazing lands, of course; they were in search of favourable spots for hunting and fishing. Such places they would have found at L'Anse aux Meadows. But natives who knew the country inside out would have discovered centuries before the places where hunting and fishing were the best, and that is where they would come every year. In Newfoundland several places might have been considered especially favourable, as, for example, the Strait of Belle Isle, through which seals swam in hundreds of thousands, the permanent crossings of the caribou, the rivers with the most salmon, or the islands where the great auk provided a never-failing food supply.

There is no doubt that the rich bird-life on the islands, the seal, the caribou and other attractions, would have tempted Indian or Eskimo families to pitch their tents at L'Anse aux Meadows on the green sward by the river, and they would probably have stayed there for a while. But not very long, perhaps, since they would know of hunting and fishing areas where there was a greater abundance of wild life and where it was easy to obtain the necessary food.

But how great the surprise would have been of the first Indians or Eskimoes who came paddling past L'Anse aux Meadows in their canoes or kayaks after the Vinland voyagers had settled there! There would be alarm and excited talk, and some would point eagerly towards the terrace by the river. Something entirely new was to be seen there: large curious-looking houses, and strange people walking about outside.

The Fishing Village

We often took a trip over to the little fishing village on the eastern side of the peninsula, and we soon became friends of the inhabitants. There were eleven families in all, almost sixty persons living in this remote spot, from where nothing but a narrow path leads to the next village, and where the coastal steamer is something that you can see in the distance once a week—if the weather is good.

George Decker told us that his great-grandfather William was the first man to settle in this area, having come from Conception Bay. He is supposed to have been of English descent. At that time there were no permanent residents on the northern peninsula, except in Noddy Bay, where an Englishman by the name of Henderson and his family had settled. One of William's sons was named Abel. He was the first permanent resident of Ship Cove, after having stayed some years in New Haven on the eastern shore of Sacred Bay. The other son, whose name was also William, was George's grandfather, and he continued to live at L'Anse aux Meadows.

George remembered his grandfather well; he was a giant of a man, and it was from him that George Decker had received all his information about the old days. In the time of his great-grandfather there were supposed to have been some Beotuk Indians left in the forests behind L'Anse aux Meadows; he thinks that this area must have been one of their last places of refuge after having been unceasingly hunted down by the whites. The Indians were always on the move, George Decker said. One day they might pitch their tents, and the next day they were nowhere to be seen. But they were a sly lot. Sometimes they lay down in the shallow water by the shore and covered themselves with seaweed, and then they would jump on a peaceful fisherman walking along the beach.

I asked Decker if he had any inkling of the origin of the name L'Anse aux Meadows, but he had no views about that. The first part of the name, L'Anse, is of course French. This word also appears in other place-names in Newfoundland and along the coasts of Labrador, its meaning being 'bay' or 'inlet'. The other part of the name, Meadows, means just what it says in English.

The name does not appear on old maps, a fact which may indicate that this particular spot lay outside the customary sphere of activity of the whalers and fishermen of the early days. According to Dr R. E. Seary,[12] the first time that the name appeared was in a French map of 1862, but it was in the form Anse à la Médée. Any possible interpretation of this word seems to be difficult, and I shall not attempt it here. But no matter how one can explain the origin of the French-English name L'Anse aux Meadows, it is exactly right as a descriptive name for the place involved: 'The bay with the grasslands'.

It is the cod that characterizes life in this area. The cod-fishing begins in the early part of June and lasts until some time in October. The people of L'Anse aux Meadows construct their own boats; these are so small—about thirty feet long—that all fishing has to take place inside the outer islands, or at least not too far from the coast. In the summer they use large, home-made traps, but later on in the season they will use long lines and tin-bait. Nets and lines of

Plate 31. Evening at the small fishing village at L'Anse aux Meadows. (Photograph: Erling Brunborg.)

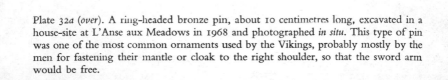

Plate 32a (*over*). A ring-headed bronze pin, about 10 centimetres long, excavated in a house-site at L'Anse aux Meadows in 1968 and photographed *in situ*. This type of pin was one of the most common ornaments used by the Vikings, probably mostly by the men for fastening their mantle or cloak to the right shoulder, so that the sword arm would be free.

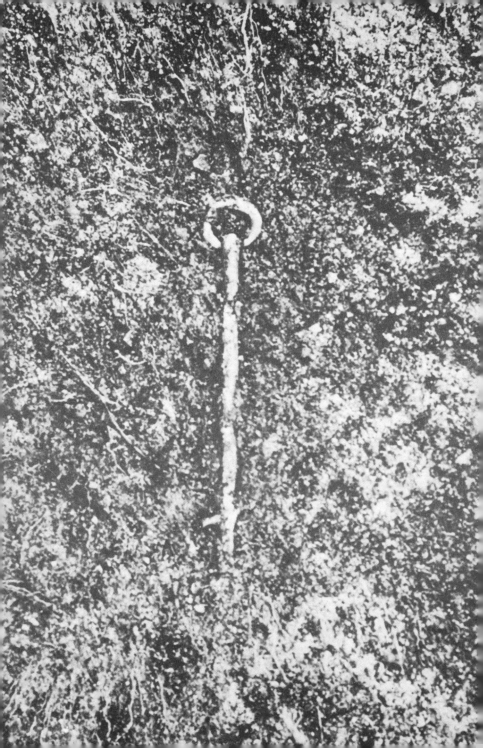

Plate 32*b*. The large house-site where the ring-headed pin was found close to the cooking pit (*centre*). The house-site is 27 metres long and 6 metres wide (outside measurements) and has four rooms. Several profiles have been made in the turf walls where a number of layers appear distinctly. Carbon analysis dates the building between 910 and 1090 A.D.

nylon were unknown at L'Anse aux Meadows when we came there. They moulded their tin-bait from lead, and they looked both astonished and pleased when we presented them with a number of gleaming Swedish steel baits.

The cod is salted down and wind-dried on long, low trellis-work, and the task is shared among the entire family, ranging from the smallest youngsters just learning to walk to their grandmothers. From time to time they also make excellent salmon catches. Often we would see large shoals of mackerel off shore, but no one wanted to fish mackerel or the multitudes of herring, which from time to time come churning in to the shore.

The yield from the fisheries varies greatly from year to year. It seems that the cod stays far out to sea whenever the summers are cold. The people also have their share of problems with regard to drift-ice or icebergs, which may pass too close and ruin the fisherman's gear. Then they set out in a terrible fury to tow large blocks of ice away from the traps.

Large numbers of squid will enter the bay and fjords at times; it is a favourite catch of the fishermen, primarily because they want to use it for bait, but it is also a much sought-after and appreciated delicacy. We experienced such a large influx of squid in Noddy Bay, where we had anchored the *Halten* because of the storm which ravaged the north coast. It was evening, the boats were lying in a long row in the bay, and everywhere they were pulling squid on board.

The most enthusiastic of all was Brunborg. He kept on fishing through half the night and returned to the *Halten* with the dinghy half filled with squid — which we had no use for. And he himself was so covered in liquid that he looked like an inkspot.

Sea birds are eagerly hunted at certain times of the year, and this has brought about a reduction in their numbers, or else the birds have become frightened and looked for a safer haven. Decker told us that when he was young there were large flocks of birds on each of the islands, and the low, flat Green Island was a permanent hatching-area for the eider ducks. He said: 'There were so many eider ducks that you couldn't put your foot down without stepping on an egg.' It was odd to hear this Newfoundland fisherman use exactly the same expression that appears in the saga account about Thorfinn Karlsefni, in the passage dealing with the host of breeding birds outside his headquarters at Straumfjord.

In the autumn a large curious-looking bird, soaring through the air without a sound, will arrive at L'Anse aux Meadows. It is the snowy owl, seeking its usual winter home after having spent the summer in Arctic areas. Whenever there has been a summer with a lot of mice or lemmings, there will be numerous snowy owls to be seen in this part of Newfoundland. The fishermen try to catch this bird, since its meat is considered a great delicacy. They catch them in steel-jawed traps put up on the top of the rocks and knolls.

The people, however, do not go in much for hunting animals on land, since fishing takes up so much of their time. In the forests to the south there are some solitary black bears, and once in a while a lynx may stray down to the coast. But the caribou do not pass by here any more. And for that reason there are no wolves to be seen either. George Decker told us that in the days of his grandfather there were quite a few about; in the night one might hear the wolves howl from the hills and knolls around L'Anse aux Meadows.

Nor do the inhabitants have much time for the keeping of livestock. No more than eight or nine head of cattle graze in the pastures at L'Anse aux Meadows, in addition to a score of sheep. In times past there might have been more, Decker told us, and he pointed out that it used to be the custom to let the animals stay outside throughout the winter, except on the days when the storms raged fiercest. The reason why it was possible to keep the cattle out of doors was that the wind from the ocean sweeps the coastal areas free of snow, and also winters are usually relatively mild over this whole area. During some winters there may be no frost for months on end, as for example in 1963, when there was hardly any snow until some time in February.

This makes our thoughts revert to the saga account of Leif Eiriksson's Vinland. Here we read: 'The land was so bountiful that it seemed to them that the cattle would not need fodder during the winter. There was no frost in winter, and the grass hardly withered.'

Here, as in other connections, we must make allowances for certain exaggerations, especially because today one has to travel a very great distance south to find conditions that are exactly like those described in the saga. But it may have been largely true, the explanation, perhaps, being as follows:

The Vinland voyagers came from an Arctic land, where sheep but not cattle could stay out in the open through the winter. In northern Newfoundland they may have experienced a mild winter without snow, like the one of 1963. They must have been struck by a fact that was both novel and of great significance, that the conditions in this new land were such that the cows could walk about in the open throughout the winter and that they would not have to do all the work connected with building insulated byres and gathering fodder. This new and surprising experience would have been kept fresh in mind and retold to succeeding generations, for it concerned the most important aspect of their livelihood.

Winter is the time of wood-gathering. The edge of the forest is, as mentioned above, only about seven miles away, and is a frequent goal of the men with their dog teams. Many trips have to be completed in order to collect enough material for a house, boats, and other things made from wood.

During especially cold winters, when the sea ice covers the ocean a long distance from shore, the men may go hunting for the baby seals (white-coats) that pass by on the drift-ice flowing south from the Labrador Sea. The fishermen will then set out with their dog teams. This is the time when, as I have said before, one may also encounter the Arctic fox and sometimes the polar bear. Three years ago a polar bear was killed at Ship Cove.

It should also be mentioned that wild berries are of considerable importance to the diet of the people at L'Anse aux Meadows. There are many varieties, and in the autumn one may see the women and the children working in the cloudberry bogs, the whortleberry tufts, and the sheltered places where the wild currants, raspberries, and squash-berries are to be found. The berries are preserved in jars, and until recent times they used to make wine from them also, more particularly from squash-berries.

The families and relatives of Decker and Anderson live on the shores of the bay, while Horvey Colbourn is the sole ruler of the area out on the headland. He is an energetic, hard-working fellow, quick and agile, and like a hawk when it comes to seeing to it that all chores are done the way they ought to be done. His wife's name is Maud; she is a hardworking woman with red hair, friendly and determined. They have eleven blond and lively children, and little Selma was the one who particularly stole our hearts.

Large families are fairly common both in Newfoundland and in Labrador. On our travels we would frequently come upon families with a dozen children, at times as many as twenty. They were raised according to old-fashioned methods. No psychiatrists have found their way to this community, with modern methods that permit the youngsters to do almost anything. The children help their parents from a very early age, and they look happy and satisfied.

At the tip of the promontory, not very far from Horvey's house, there are traces of an old fishing station, supposedly of French origin. In one place a number of bricks stick out of the ground; they are supposed to be the remnants of the baking oven. These ruins, however, do not give the impression of being very old. I found a few fish-hooks, a fragment of an old clay pipe and a few other odds and ends; in the village of L'Anse aux Meadows, fishermen have found many such articles in the course of time.

In the days of Decker's grandfather a three-masted French schooner used to cast anchor in Noddy Bay. Some of the French fishermen at that time had three small houses at L'Anse aux Meadows, just about where the people are living today. The schooner would return to France in October. As to whether the ruins on the promontory have any connection with the schooner and its crew, it is hard to say.

The people living out on the promontory do not have the benefit of running water. Colbourn discovered an old and very deep well on the sandy beach not far from the water's edge. It had probably been dug by French fishermen. The water is not very fresh, and has a very brackish taste to it. It is significant, though, that fishermen nevertheless settled down in that particular spot in the past, as they do today. And this in spite of the fact that if they had walked for fifteen minutes farther to the west, where we discovered the old house-sites, they would have had the benefit of the fresh water in Black Duck Brook right outside the house. But for fishermen it was not difficult to choose a site for living quarters: it was only on the eastern side of the promontory that the water was deep enough for boats to put in to shore, and that, of course, was of vital importance for the fishermen of that or any other time.

The people at L'Anse aux Meadows do not seem to live in a very tightly knit community. But at times one will become aware of certain aspects of their way of life that indicate that it is more consolidated than one had imagined. Common interests and customs, feelings *vis-à-vis* neighbouring villages, and other less concrete aspects of life and culture, create a web between human beings.

The world of ideas of the people at L'Anse aux Meadows is firmly rooted in the past. They speak the English of their forefathers, their dialect not being easy to understand until one is used to it. They also use many words which I should suppose are no longer current in the speech of their mother country.

At L'Anse aux Meadows there are also ghosts, as everybody knows. Decker told us about one of them that gave him a lot of trouble. To his house had been added a small annexe containing two rooms, and that was the place that a ghost had selected for raising a racket one night after another, making such a noise that no one could sleep. Time after time Decker would jump out of bed, seizing his muzzle-loader and rushing into the annexe—but all he saw was something white that immediately vanished. But at last he understood the reason for it all. The ghost refused to be chased away because Decker had placed the annexe right across the old path used by it every night, and ghosts are very particular about their routes. Thereupon Decker tore down the annexe, and since that time the house has been completely rid of ghosts.

Decker's home was a cosy place. He used to sit in a corner of the parlour, smoking a pipe, and glancing from time to time out across the sea. As a rule it would not take him very long to embark on the telling of some fascinating tale or recall the lore of the island.

Underneath the ceiling the muzzle-loader lay on a rack, and the powder-horn hung on the wall. The gun, the only one he ever used for hunting, was an heirloom from his grandfather. It was huge and very heavy. He would take it down once in a while, and handle it with the loving care of an old huntsman, and he would say: 'This is some gun, a great deal better than the puny things people are hunting with today. Once I got twenty ducks with one single shot.'

Decker, too, knew of a hidden treasure; he believed that it was an iron pot filled with golden ducats. He was not a little secretive about it, but I was given to understand that he had got his information from his great-grandfather, 'who saw it all with his own eyes'. In the dead of night a ship had steered into Sacred Bay, sailors had rowed ashore, and had begun to dig. The next morning the ship was gone. Many are those who have searched for the treasure, but Decker smiled indulgently and made it clear to us that no one but he knew all there was to know in this matter. One day, he said, he would take time off and unearth the treasure.

At times he would sing the old ballads and songs indigenous to this region. They are indeed many in number, and they usually deal with life at sea, about shipwrecks, pirates, love, and so on. The melodies are apt to be melancholy and the poems often very long. They tell of a time and a way of life that vanished long ago. And his wife Mae would sit there silently listening. A sweet and gentle woman!

Chapter Fifteen

To the 'Wonder Beaches' of the Saga

Skipper Sørnes smiled broadly when he was told that the *Halten* was to make another voyage. Labrador was to be our next destination. The previous summer I had made a preliminary trip by air over a part of that huge land; now the intention was for some of the participants of the current expedition to follow up with field investigations. Such a task would be of no little interest, we felt, since one objective would be to clarify and locate, if possible, the unique landmark mentioned in the sagas, namely 'Furdustrandir', or 'Wonder Beaches', the remarkably extensive beaches encountered by the Vinland voyagers. As mentioned before, it was also quite possible that the Norsemen had built houses in Labrador, where they probably fetched timber from the large forests.

It was decided that Anne Stine was to accompany us for a short time on this trip. Arrangements were made whereby she could return to Newfoundland on a Grenfell Mission plane, after which she would resume the excavations at L'Anse aux Meadows while we would continue our voyage.

First we sailed towards Belle Isle, the solitary island that seems to have been thrown by a supernatural power into the ocean at the mouth of the Strait of Belle Isle. It is situated about fourteen nautical miles north of L'Anse aux Meadows. What we saw of the south and west coasts was not very inviting, with steep mountainsides plunging into the sea, and the lofty plateau, reaching an altitude of about eight hundred feet, looking bleak and barren. We could detect no inlet that might serve as a harbour, and huge icebergs were drifting by along the coast. 'Devil's Isle' was the name given the island by sailors in the old days, and that is easily understandable. But the island makes a splendid seamark and aid to navigation, and as such it must have been equally helpful to the Vinland voyagers.

We then sailed across to Château Bay, situated at the western shores of the Strait of Belle Isle. The name is very descriptive indeed; on the heights facing the bay some curiously shaped basalt cliffs reach to the sky, and in some places they even look like columns of a temple set into the hill. Here was one of the most important harbours in this area in the heyday of the whalers and the fishermen. A great number of Eskimoes and Indians would also congregate here or in the neighbouring districts whenever they were at war with the white man.

On top of one of the heights we found the ruins of an old fort. It had been built by the British governor Palliser in 1767. The bay area must have had more than its share of violent and desperate acts in a period not noted for law and order. The harbour is good, but we did not see much grass, and it was difficult to believe that the Vinland voyagers would have been tempted to settle down here.

We continued our voyage northward along the coast of Labrador, passing on the way a number of fjords which cut deeply into the country, and we decided to investigate them further on the return trip. The previous year I had seen the coasts and forest lands from the air; now I was observing the land from the sea and received quite a different impression, one chiefly of bleakness and desolation. There was an abundance of rocky, weather-beaten islets and skerries, with a grey coastline in the background. We could only guess that conditions were different inland when the mouth of a fjord revealed some vegetation or when we glimpsed forest-clad hills in the far distance. There were no real mountains to be seen anywhere, nothing but a rolling country extending far into the west.

We set our course against the Labrador Current, which flows at a speed of about ten nautical miles per day. I became even more aware than before of the great significance the currents must have had to the Vinland voyagers, who from their homes in Greenland selected a route that gave them the benefit of a favourable current all the way to America.

Huge icebergs were drifting slowly past, the tallest being about a hundred and fifty feet in height; in the distance they looked like strange, bluish-white ships. Once they had led a quiet life as part of a glacier in Baffin Island or perhaps in an area farther north. Then the glacier had calved—a splash in the ocean, with such force that the fish were killed from the pressure miles around. An iceberg had been born! From then on it led a life of its own, drifting southward—the ocean would wash up against it, storms would sweep over it, the sun would begin to consume the masses of ice. Some icebergs would founder, others would enjoy a long journey into warmer climes, but their common destiny was obliteration.

It was an iceberg originating in this region that sank the *Titanic*, and many a fishing vessel has suffered the same fate in the course of time, particularly when fog has blanketed the sea. Fog is a characteristic feature of the Labrador coast; it is apt to appear when the warm air from the south is mixed with the cool air above the cold water of the ocean. We were enveloped in the fog several times; it seemed as impenetrable as a wall, and at such times it gave us little enjoyment to think of icebergs and skerries. Adam of Bremen's description from 1070, a generation or so after the Vinland voyages had occurred, is rather to the point: 'Beyond this island [Vinland] there is to be found no inhabitable land, but everything beyond is filled with intolerable ice and terrible fog.'

North-east of Sandwich Bay, and some distance out at sea, lie the Gannet Islands. We made a detour in their direction in order to observe the islands' bird life, which is supposed to be something quite out of the ordinary. Low-lying islands rose out of the sea, there was brilliant sunshine, and the air was clear.

We steered the dinghy into a small bay. There were birds everywhere, on the tops of rocks and in rock-ledges they were sitting close together; there were razorbills, guillemots, and puffins with their red parrot-like beaks and white shirt-fronts. As we approached, thousands of birds rose into the sky with a rush. We went ashore and walked about among the birds; they looked at us with some amazement and did not fly away until we were right on top of them. Cracks and crevices in the rock were filled to overflowing with chattering and hatching guillemots, and when we walked across the dark green carpet of stiff grass, so well fertilized by the birds, the puffins jumped up from almost under our feet, from their nests underneath the turf.

I also glimpsed an Arctic fox in its shabby summer attire; it must have come to the islands with the drift-ice. It had certainly managed to carve out a good life for itself. Here it could gorge itself on eggs and birds; it could lie down for a nap without a worry as to the future, like someone who has retired with a big bank account.

After a while we left the island and set out in the dinghy in order to find the *Halten*; the skipper had been asked to stand by and merely proceed at slow speed from where we had left her. But where was she? At last we discovered her far out at sea, with a billowing sail and her course set for Europe. Had the skipper gone mad? We went out quite a way from the shore but felt uneasy, since there was a heavy swell and a plastic dinghy is not very well suited for an ocean-going voyage. At last the *Halten* turned about and set her course towards us. The skipper gave us a big grin from the deck, his face black as coal, tell-tale evidence of another bout with his arch-enemy, the engine. It had played up, and exploded in an entirely novel manner, and he had had to hoist the sail and hover far off shore in order not to be flung on to one of the islands.

We needed to replenish our supply of fish, and it was not long before the skipper, with the aid of the echo-sounder, detected an entire shoal. He got hold of his tin-bait, and then got busy! It was no sooner overboard than the cod bit, and the skipper pulled in the line. One large cod after another was thrown on the deck, and very soon there was a fairly large heap.

Anne Stine had been watching the proceedings with an expression of womanly disapprobation as the heap grew. She hinted at something that

Plate 34. Which one is the bigger? Erling Brunborg and Dr Odd Martens photographed with the trout they caught during just a few hours' fishing in Hawke's Bay, Labrador. (Photograph: Helge Ingstad.)

Plate 35. Anne Stine measuring one of the turf walls at the largest of the dwelling-sites; the various layers may be distinctly seen. (Photograph: Hans Hvide Bang.)

Plate 36. Anne Stine uncovers a hearth in the first site to be excavated. (Photograph: Erling Brunborg.)

sounded like 'rapaciousness' and made it clear to us that now we had caught enough. We thought that her view was not at all justified by the circumstances, since we always used to take the best care of the fish – we salted it or dried it, and gave away all that we did not use ourselves. I said to her, 'Try it yourself.' Hesitatingly she grasped the line, but when the cod began to bite she became a changed person. She became almost ecstatic and gazed with rapture at each open-mouthed fish as it cleared the gunwale and landed on the deck. It was hard to say which looked the more surprised, she or the cod. In the end I had to remind her gently that unfortunately we had to continue our voyage. But after that I never heard her use the word 'rapaciousness' in connection with fishing.

We arrived at Cartwright, one of the most beautiful spots along the entire coastline. Here we met Louise Greenfield, who supervises the clinic and the boarding-school at the Grenfell Mission. She is a charming Englishwoman, who of her own choice has settled in this lonely Arctic village, where for a great number of years she has helped the sick and has taken care of Eskimo and Indian children. We enjoyed the privilege of her marvellous hospitality, and she provided us with much valuable information about the country and the people.

Cartwright is situated at the mouth of Sandwich Bay, a large fjord indenting the land in a southward direction. The village was named after an Englishman, Captain George Cartwright, who in 1775 established a trading post in this locality. He was one of the first white men to settle permanently in Labrador. He must have had a forceful personality; he was also one of the few men who at that time showed some understanding of the Eskimoes and the Indians, and, in contrast to so many others at that time, he got along very well with them.

But Cartwright had his problems. One night he was awakened by some armed men who had entered his house by force. They were the crew of an infamous American pirate captain, Grimes, who hailed from Boston and had moored his ship, the *Minerva*, off shore in the dead of night. Cartwright was robbed of everything he owned; they even took his boat. In his diary he wrote laconically: 'May the devil go with them!'

Cartwright was an enthusiastic hunter, and the plain and unembellished prose of his diary testifies to the abundance of animal life in Labrador in times gone by, a fact that is of importance in relation to the Vinland voyages. Thus he relates his experiences on a hunting trip which took him up the White Bear River. The river was so full of salmon that he could not even shoot into the water without hitting a gleaming fish. And he observed no less than thirty-two polar bears which were also 'fishing', some standing on shore while others were swimming about in the shoals of fish and feasting on salmon. He shot six polar bears. This account is probably basically true; there are records from other

Arctic areas of numbers of polar bears gathering at spots where there was an abundance of food.

William Hovgaard[1] thought that Thorfinn Karlsefni had his headquarters at Sandwich Bay. I did not meet anyone who had ever heard about old house-sites in the area, but we sailed into the fjord in order to explore its shores. We steered between the mainland and the big Earle Island, the current here being very strong. As far as that is concerned, both the island and the current fit the description of Straumfjord. This is not very significant, however, as such geographical features are comparatively common along these coasts. It was a beautiful fjord; its shores were more fertile and appealing than most parts of Labrador. The forest in most places came down all the way to the beach. We went ashore in a few places that were all rather inviting, but everywhere there was so little grass that I found it difficult to believe that the Vinland voyagers would have wanted to settle down here with their livestock.

At the head of the fjord was the lagoon-like estuary of Paradise River, the gleaming river and the green forest adding up to a pretty picture. The *Halten* lay to some distance from the shore, and while we were admiring our surroundings a small rowing-boat made its way towards us. The oarsman was an old man, straight as a ramrod, with a grey beard and a pipe in his mouth. He had two fellow-passengers, two very small children. We asked him to come aboard, and invited him to have a cup of coffee and a brandy. Our guest's occupation was fur-trapping and salmon-fishing, and his cabin was not very far away. Anne Stine, who was getting acquainted with the children, turned to the old man and said, 'You've really got some fine-looking grandchildren.'

'Pooh,' he replied. 'They are my very own children.'

'How old are you, then?' she asked.

'Seventy-eight.'

'Have you any other children?' she asked.

'Twenty-one,' the trapper replied and lit his pipe.

We visited his cabin, a rickety wooden hut with cracks through which the wind whistled. Inside there were only a table, a bench, a few stools, and a pile of old clothes. His wife—his second—was young and looked Indian. Round about the house there swarmed children of all ages: most of them would appear and then as suddenly slip away among the bushes, looking like frightened animals at the sight of strangers. But the old trapper seemed to be infused with a spirit of calm and quiet; he was one of those who were content with life. His possessions were almost nil, but there were salmon in the river and fur-bearing animals in the forest, and far into the distance extended the wilderness in which he was his own lord and master, a free man.

We arrived at North River at the western mouth of Sandwich Bay. From this spot a wide beach extends about thirty-five miles in a northerly direction.

We went ashore and looked round. The land was flat and open, the wide river flowed slowly from out of the forest and seemed to be navigable for quite a distance. In the past there had been quite a few Eskimoes living here, and later there had been a number of 'settlers'. Now we could see only one house and a small dilapidated cemetery. On the grave of a small boy was a stone with the following words: 'Killed by dogs'. We replenished our supply of fish, and that was an easy task in the river estuary, the big trout biting with great enthusiasm.

We continued our voyage northward along the coast; to the west there was a wide, white beach, bordered on the other side by the forest. After some hours we approached a promontory which was probably a few miles in length; from the sandy beaches it seemed to jut out like a spear into the ocean. It had a curious shape; in the middle it could have been as much as three hundred feet in height, and from that central point the terrain sloped down evenly on both sides. This was Cape Porcupine.

At first we sailed round the promontory, keeping some way from the shore, in order to be able to see the entire landscape the way the Vinland voyagers must have seen it when they came sailing from the north. No islands protected the mainland from the ocean. There were similar extensive beaches along the shores north of Cape Porcupine, these being perhaps even more prominent and distinctive, the white border continuing on as far as the eye could see. From the character of the waves we could tell that there were shallows far out from the shore. The spruce forest came all the way down to the beach, and the large straight trees combined to form what looked like a green wall. The forest extended westward far into the distance, and the land seemed to be very flat.

This type of landscape—the long and curiously formed promontory, the extensive and wide beaches below the forest which faced the sea—would have been sure to impress itself on the minds of passing sailors. It should be added that nowhere else have I seen beaches to compare with these as regards extent and distinctiveness—and I have travelled along the entire coast of Labrador, the north shore of the Gulf of St Lawrence, and much of the coast of Newfoundland and Nova Scotia.

Let us take another look at some of the information contained in the sagas regarding the voyages of the Norsemen along the coasts of Markland:

Bjarni sailed in a direction opposite to that of the others, that is, he sailed from south to north. In the Greenlanders' Saga it says that after two days he came to the second land, 'and noticed that it was flat and covered with forests'.

The Greenlanders' Saga says about Leif Eiriksson's southward voyage along the coast of Markland: 'They put to sea and found the second land. This time too they sailed in to the coast and cast anchor, lowered a boat and went ashore. The country was flat and covered with forests, and wherever they went there were white sandy beaches sloping gently down to the sea. Then Leif said:

"We shall give this land a name according to its natural resources, and call it Markland [Forest Land]." ... They then sailed out to sea before a north-east wind and were at sea two days before sighting land.' And that land was Vinland.

Eirik the Red's Saga says about Thorfinn Karlsefni's southward voyage along the coasts of Markland: 'After two days they sighted land again and sailed in towards the coast. There they arrived at a cape; they sailed along the land and had it on their starboard side. It was an open harbourless shore with long sandy beaches. They rowed in to the shore and found the keel of a ship and called the place Kjalarnes. They also gave a name to the beaches, calling them Furdustrandir [Wonder Beaches] because it took them so long to sail past them.'

In the saga accounts there is so much that agrees with the actual geographical features seen when sailing along the beaches south of Hamilton Inlet that there can be little doubt that these are the identical Furdustrandir. Cape Porcupine was probably given the name Kjalarnes (Keelness) not because the Norsemen ever found a piece of a keel there but because it has the shape of an overturned boat. I have pointed out above (see page 63) that when the Greenlanders' Saga says that Leif Eiriksson took two days to cover the distance from the beaches of Markland to Vinland, this agrees very well with the actual distance from Cape Porcupine to the northern coast of Newfoundland.

We did as Leif Eiriksson had done in his day – we lowered the dinghy and set out for the shore. We did not see any harbours along this coast, and it was impossible to land on the beach because of the huge breakers. We hove to at the outermost point of Cape Porcupine and then proceeded along the coast for about half an hour until we reached the beaches, which extended in a northward direction.

They were indeed marvellous beaches! They might have been about eighty yards wide, the sand was white and very fine-grained, and the beach sloped gradually down to the sea. The waves were cascading up on the beach, making intricate white foamy patterns all over the sand. Beyond the beach a sandy terrace covered with stiff grass rose up to the edge of the forest. We followed a creek for some distance inland and found nothing but trees and bushes, an almost impenetrable forest of alder, aspen, and birch trees along the creek, but spruce everywhere else. The spruce trees were surprisingly tall and thick; in many places huge trunks were lying prostrate on the ground. A primeval forest.

On the white beach we detected something else that fascinated us: bear tracks. They were very recent, and in the fine, moist sand the impressions of the paws and claws were as distinct as if they had been cast in a mould.

We stayed at Cape Porcupine a few days and investigated the long promontory. It was a beautiful place, with dense, wind-swept spruce forests that climbed almost to the top of the hill in the centre of the promontory, but there were also treeless areas where ducks were swimming about in ponds.

Along the coast we encountered, from time to time, old traces of man—as, for instance, large stones placed against one another to serve as a store room, a cairn, and traces of a house-site, the character of which we could not determine.

We soon realized that this promontory sticking out into the sea was a favourite place for animals of many kinds. We met that strange character that has given its name to the promontory, the porcupine. The Labrador porcupine, incidentally, is much larger than its Scandinavian cousin. Ptarmigans swooped past us and alighted on the rocks along the beach. We also saw two Arctic foxes; they were shabby and greyish-looking, not yet having been given the benefit of their beautiful white winter coats. Brunborg, of course, found their lair, got into a good position during the course of the night and took films of the young ones at sunrise.

But first and foremost the black bear was to be found here, and in considerable numbers. One might almost think that these animals had congregated at Cape Porcupine from all over the forest in order to discuss the bear problems of Labrador. But the explanation is simple: the capelin comes in to these shores in droves. And huge numbers of this salmon-like fish are thrown up on the beach to the great joy of the bears. Behind the capelin come shoals of cod, racing in among the capelin, churning up the water, and gulping down the smaller fish in no time at all. The masses of capelin, panic-stricken, try to escape by hugging the shore, but the beasts of prey are following with open jaws. We stood there for a long time watching this remarkable drama staged by Nature.

The first time I met a bear was during a walk among the hills, where there were only small spruce trees here and there. Suddenly a huge monster jumped up from the thicket right in front of me and fled at full speed. The black rump disappeared in the direction of the coast, just about where Anne Stine was supposed to be at the time. I ran down to look for her—she is not used to being called on by bears, she might get the fright of her life—and even if a bear is not usually malicious, one never knows.

I found her at last, and it was quite clear that she was in high spirits. Out of breath from running so fast and filled with anxiety and husbandly worry, I asked her whether she had seen the bear that I had disturbed. 'Not yours,' she replied in a tone of voice which I thought was rather flippant and surprising under the circumstances, as if she was referring to another bear and regarded it as her own property. Then she ecstatically told me that when she and Dr Martens had been standing by a rock on the beach, two bears had come padding along—the wind was blowing in her direction. They had not stopped until they were twenty feet or so away, but then they had made a fast about-turn and had vanished from sight. 'They were the funniest things, and they came so close, and imagine, one of them had something white on his nose,' she added, her eyes sparkling. You never can tell with a woman!

That evening we saw ten bears; they suddenly emerged from the dense forest, ambled along the beach, and gobbled up capelin. When they got wind of us, they ran away, but soon returned. They were indeed delightful creatures, these black brutes, padding along in their inimitable way, seriously intent on many different matters. We did not shoot any of them.

We lit a huge bonfire from driftwood on the outermost point of Cape Porcupine, and we sat there for a long while, just looking out across the ocean. Once again our thoughts reverted to the Norse sailors who, like us, had gone ashore here in wonder—about a thousand years ago. Perhaps they too had seen bears jumping out of the forest.

Chapter Sixteen

Along the coast of Labrador — a large House-site discovered

Leaving the extensive beaches at Cape Porcupine behind, the *Halten* continued northward, and before long we were about to cross the wide Hamilton Inlet, a fjord which cuts into the mainland to a depth of about one hundred and fifty miles. The head of the fjord, which is quite wide, is known as Lake Melville.

It was a quiet and serene day; an almost unnoticeable swell was the only movement in the sea, the light of the sun was filtered through haze, and the islands in the distance looked as if they were floating on the horizon. A multitude of birds — razorbills, ducks, gulls, guillemots and puffins — were bobbing on the surface of the ocean or flew past us in every direction. Immediately in front of the *Halten* two dolphins had been gambolling ever since the early hours of the morning.

We sailed past several islands, and then the inlet narrowed and became a constricted sound, the Narrows, through which flowed a strong current. At its narrowest it is scarcely more than six hundred and fifty yards wide, and the tide sometimes rushes past at six or seven knots.

We made a stop at Rigolet, a tiny and very beautiful place near the mouth of the Narrows, and were supplied with some useful information by a man who was living there. At the present time only a few families reside on the shores of the fjord itself — not including, however, the area at the head of the fjord. These settlers are usually of mixed blood.

Things were different in the old days. A large part of Hamilton Inlet was in the distant past the Eskimoes' very own fjord. Place-names testify to the same thing, and they indicate that they once lived as far inland as Hamilton River. In 1824 about a hundred and sixty Eskimoes were living along this fjord, and before that there were undoubtedly an even larger number. They went in not only for fishing and seal hunting, but also for hunting caribou. But the whites and the Indians pushed the Eskimoes northward, in this area as in so many others in Labrador. This hardy race, which in times past lived in great numbers along these coasts and roamed as far south as the mouth of the St Lawrence

River and Newfoundland, was forced northward step by step, until at the present time they are represented by only a few small groups in the northernmost part of Labrador. But how could a people using only bows and arrows possibly prevail over well-armed fishermen and whalers? The missionary Jens Haven wrote as late as 1764: 'No kayak was tolerated within the range of the guns of a European ship.' In addition, the white man's diseases mowed down hundreds of Eskimoes and decimated their settlements.

On the other side of the Narrows there was an idyllic bay, and we paid a visit to the two families living there. First to meet the eye were a few cabins, a number of beautiful Eskimo dogs tied to a tree at the edge of the forest, and a huge bear-skin stretched out to be dried. We met a few people, with Eskimo facial characteristics and a friendly disposition that will long be remembered. They invited us to eat some newly boiled salmon and other dishes, the best that they could offer a stranger.

The name of the eldest was Williams, and he provided us with much information about the big fjord and its environs. On the other side of the bay I had noticed a few small grassy plots that seemed to have been the sites of old houses.

'Oh, yes,' Williams replied, 'those are the remains of the homes of Palliser, Puneak, and Maku, and they had many children. But the houses collapsed, there were no people any more to live in them.'

'Did they leave for the north?' I asked.

'They disappeared. A man came once and persuaded them to go with him to a strange country, and then they disappeared, almost all of them. The women and the children too.'

The small grassy plots on the old sites tell of a great tragedy, of the misfortunes that some white men in our own day brought on people living in the wilderness—in order to make money.[1] Hagenbeck, the proprietor of a zoo and a circus, came to Labrador in 1880, and on the strength of all kinds of promises succeeded in bringing eight Eskimo families back with him to Europe. At first he put them on exhibition in his zoo and then he displayed them all round Germany and in Paris. Soon all of them died. In 1893 and 1894 an American businessman tried something similar; once he enticed fifty-two Eskimoes to accompany him, at another time he succeeded in getting thirty to come with him to civilization, among them women and children. He operated on an even larger scale than Hagenbeck; he displayed the Eskimoes in America as well as in Europe. Most of them succumbed before long, a very few returned to Labrador broken in health and in spirit. Some of these Eskimoes had come from Hamilton Inlet.

'Were there many that had come from here?' I asked Williams.

'Oh, yes, there were Palliser, Puneak, Maku, Shuglues, and others. And then the women and all the children. They took all their belongings with them, their dogs and their tents.'

'How many of them came back?'

'Only a few. They returned wearing white men's clothes. They were ill and drank a lot.'

On the other side of the bay the last rays of the evening sun touched the grass-covered sites where the houses had collapsed. There were no children playing any more round their homes.

Not very far away lies Eskimo Island, and Williams told us about fights that had taken place in the old days between Eskimoes and Indians. First the Eskimoes carried out a surprise attack on the Indians staying on the point close by, and they then withdrew to their own island. But the Indians' revenge was not long in coming. In the dead of night they paddled out to the island, attacked the Eskimoes unawares, and killed many of them. When Williams was a young boy, he had seen graves on the island, and there had been quite a few of them.

We paid Eskimo Island a visit. It was a beautiful and rather small island, with piles of blue shells on the beach, yellow flowers in the cracks in the rocks sloping down to the sea, and a few wooded areas. We found the former sites of four rather large Eskimo houses, a considerable part of the walls, made of stones and turf, still standing, in addition to traces of even older habitation.

Then we set our course across the wide expanse of Lake Melville. From the boat we had a splendid view of the lake and the wilderness surrounding it, with dense forests in most directions advancing close to the beach. The Meady Mountains were silhouetted against the sky to the south; it is said that hunters visiting that area kill many caribou each year.

Could it be possible that the earliest of the Vinland voyagers had sailed through this fjord? Some scholars have thought so. And they have based their views on the account in Eirik the Red's Saga telling how Thorhall the Hunter left the headquarters at Straumfjord and travelled north to Furdustrandir in order to search for Vinland in that region. They also base them on the account of Thorfinn Karlsefni's voyage from that very same place for the purpose of finding Thorhall. We are told that Thorvald came too and that a uniped killed him with an arrow. This is supposed to have occurred near a river running from east to west.

As mentioned before (see pp. 67-8), these parts of the saga accounts do not seem reliable. It would indeed have been very strange if the Vinland voyagers were looking for Vinland two days' sailing away in a northward direction, along a coast which on their southward trip they must have already found to be unfavourable in many ways and not least because it lacked grassland.

The scholars who favour Hamilton Inlet suppose that Karlsefni came as far as one of the rivers emptying into Lake Melville, English River seeming to some the most plausible in this respect.

The question ought to be the object of further investigation, at least. Someone who knew the locality well told me a great deal about English River. It was supposed to have received its name from three Englishmen who had settled somewhere along its banks after having taken part in the battle of Waterloo. By this river they lived as trappers for the rest of their lives – being through with war and civilization. There was something appealing about this story. I have myself lived in the wilds of northern Canada in the company of a Frenchman who had fought in the First World War and had been gassed. For the rest of his life he wanted to be close to nature, and there he found happiness; he had no intention of ever returning to civilization.

We set our course for English River. It cascaded down the sides of the slopes of the Meady Mountains and then ran more quietly through the dense forests and into the fjord. By the estuary there were shallow reefs far out into the lake; even the dinghy had to make a zigzag course to approach the shore. The saga says that Karlsefni steered into the river-mouth and hove to by the south shore, but that was not possible in this estuary.

By the mouth of the river there were sandbars covered with sandwort, and large areas with purple pea blossoms, but hardly any grass at all. We proceeded in the boat a short distance up river, where we landed some fine trout. It was indeed a unique voyage through a veritable jungle of spruce trees, so dense that it was almost impossible to make one's way through it on foot. We glided along over the dark and quiet surface, now underneath a canopy of branches and trunks, now making a detour round trees that had plunged into the water when the banks had caved in. A brace of ducks took to the air, their wings making a clattering noise.

At the edge of the forest and near the river estuary lay an old cabin of the type trappers would put up; I was later told that it belonged to an Eskimo. On the outer walls hung a number of steel traps. The door was unlocked, and we went in. There was a small table by the window, two narrow bunks with hay and part of a bearskin in them, and a tree stump to be used as a chair. Part of a caribou's antlers were nailed to the wall, on them hung a pair of snow-shoes, and in the corner lay the shrivelled carcase of a duck. I recognized it all from the years that I had lived as a trapper in northern Canada. It was a long time ago, but everything in that little trapper's cabin was familiar to me.

Even though the first Vinland voyagers may not have got to Hamilton Inlet, it is possible that Norsemen arrived in this particular region during subsequent voyages. At any rate, the country offered an abundant supply of timber and valuable furs of various kinds. In times past there was a great number of marten, whose fur, perhaps because of the dense forests, could become so dark and beautiful that it was called 'Labrador Sable'.

We continued our explorations and in due course reached the head of the fjord at North-West River, a village that I had visited the year before in a seaplane. Benedicte and I greeted our friends among the Indians, we gave them photographs that we had taken of them, and the pictures created something of a sensation.

And so the *Halten* set her course back to L'Anse aux Meadows. On the way back we would have a lot to do, since on the way north, as mentioned before, we had passed the more southerly coast of Labrador, with a number of deep fjords that were now to be investigated.

When we arrived at Pikes Run at the mouth of Hamilton Inlet, we heard some shots fired not far away and steered in the direction of the sound. We came upon a bay, at the head of which there was a small cabin. By the rocks sloping down to the sea was standing a short man skinning a seal. John Palliser was his name, and he was a friendly type, whose face exhibited strong Eskimo features. His entire family was grouped round him, all of them watching him work with very serious expressions. The group consisted of his wife, his mother, and five attractive barefoot youngsters.

This scene afforded a glimpse into something essential in the world of the people living in the wilderness: the long wait of the family for the hunter and the food, the joy after a successful chase, and then the great event — to see the killed animal outside one's home — fresh meat into which to bury one's teeth. The dead seal was lying there on the rock, its dark blood flowing down the rocky slope, streaking the bluish-green water.

On the homeward voyage we had a closer look at several fjords — Black Bear Bay, Hawke's Bay, White Bear Arm, Gilbert Bay, Alexis Bay, St Lewis Inlet, and others. Many of them cut pretty far into the mainland. To sail from the desolate coast into the fjords was like arriving in an entirely different country. We came to the forest, which became ever more thick and abundant the farther we travelled into the interior; the spruce trees, especially, could reach a great size, and there were larch, birch, aspen, and alder besides. But there was very little grass.

We did not see many human beings, but we would at times come across some small houses at the heads of the fjords. At this time of the year the inhabitants would stay on the coast, fishing, and in the autumn they would return to these houses and spend the winter there. That was the time when they would start their trapping.

We had the wilderness to ourselves. Once in a while a bear would pad past on the beach, black as coal; in a quiet bay, mother ducks would swim about with long streamers of enthusiastic youngsters following in their wake; an osprey would come sailing, then plunge suddenly into the sea, and rise into the air with a wriggling fish in its beak. Sometimes a round black head would emerge from the water right in front of the *Halten*; it was the harbour seal (*Phoca vitulina*), always bursting with curiosity at these new and strange things that had invaded its domain. Farther inland were to be seen the tracks of the caribou, and we came upon old beaver dams. Of the lemming, also a denizen of this region, we found no trace; on the other hand, we saw innumerable forest mice, and they represented, indeed, a year's continual feasting to many kinds of animals and birds, not least the hawk. I have hardly ever before seen so many hawks. They had built their nests far up along the steep mountainside above the fjord, and when the *Halten* continued on her way they circled the ship, emitting their characteristic shrieks.

One of the most beautiful of the fjords visited was Hawke's Bay. This bay branches off into many smaller sounds and bays, and to the south-west there was a narrow sound through which we sailed in the dinghy into a completely isolated part of the fjord. A small river emptied into the fjord, softly rippling over polished rocks and pebbles. We walked a short distance up stream and came upon a nice little lake surrounded by reeds and trees, where an otter suddenly dived with a splash. We needed fresh fish on board and threw out the tin-bait, without any great faith that we would get much of a haul in such a small lake. But we had no sooner tossed out the hook when the fish bit, and this went on for a long time. Our catch were gleaming fat trout, the largest weighing about nine pounds, and they put up a valiant fight. After a few hours we had loaded the dinghy with a large supply of fresh fish.

On cleaning the fish after we had got back to the *Halten* we discovered that these trout were meat-eaters. In every one we found mice, usually three or four, the record being eight. The Indians' name for a certain kind of trout is *kokomesh*, which means 'the fish that eats everything'. The name certainly fitted the trout that we had caught. But they provided us with some sumptuous meals—and didn't taste of mice.

The trip into Alexis Fjord, the longest of the fjords in this region, was also an absorbing experience. Once more we set off in the dinghy and travelled as far as the big river entering the fjord. Here we saw large areas where forest fires had been raging and had left their tell-tale evidence: bare standing trunks without number, the ground black everywhere. It was a sad but at the same time very picturesque sight. The only living thing we noticed was an owl. We found a few pieces of the hide and some bones of a bear—what an unspeakable tragedy it is when the raging fires cover an entire forest and the animals flee in terror or run panic-stricken right into the flames.

Forest fires are a scourge to large parts of Labrador, the most frequent cause being lightning. Afterwards the region will seem dead for a long time, until lichens and moss begin to grow. Then deciduous trees will slowly appear and after a long while the spruce.

At the head of the fjord we went ashore on an island rich in vegetation. The birch trees were so large that one could hardly get one's arms round them, and there were big currant bushes with ripe berries. It was the first time we had noticed the droppings of moose. Strangely enough, this animal is not indigenous in this part of the country, a number of individual animals having been introduced into Labrador some time ago. This area is indeed well suited to the moose, and if more animals could be brought in so that there would be a sizable stock, they would be a great boon to the people in these parts.

The *Halten*'s voyage along the enormous wilderness of Labrador – the Markland of the sagas – was nearing its end. We had seen the 'Wonder Beaches' and other extensive shores, and had gained much insight into many of the things that may have been of significance to the Vinland voyagers when sailing and taking stock of the country. We had also found a number of old house-sites, but they had originated from Eskimoes, trappers, fishermen or whalers. Even though the sites were low and overgrown it was not difficult to identify them; stone implements, ceramic objects, fragments of clay pipes, large rusty nails, fish-hooks, whalebones, and so on, provided us with sufficient information.

As we sailed south we kept quite a distance away from the shore, outside the skerries, and I think that we were probably just about following the route of the Vinland voyagers. What might these people have thought about the land that emerged from the ocean, especially as they were interested in good grazing lands? The desolate islands and the forbidding coasts of Labrador would not seem very tempting to them; if they sailed into one of the big fjords in order to take a closer look at the country, they would find forests but very poor grazing lands. My guess is that they would reason like this: 'Let us keep on sailing south; then we shall probably get to a land that is better than that unpleasant Markland, to a place where there is grass for our livestock.'

Like us, they would pass Battle Harbour, but then they had to decide whether to continue along the whole Labrador coast in the direction of the Strait of Belle Isle, changing course to the south-west. As we looked searchingly at the barren coastline, it struck us that the Vinland voyagers would not have been very eager to sail farther along a land they already knew had very little to offer – if they had a choice. And this they had. Straight ahead of us a new land came into sight – the northern coast of Newfoundland. And far out into the ocean, north of Newfoundland, an island was sharply etched against the horizon – Belle Isle. The Vinland voyagers would no doubt have thought: 'Let us take our bearings by that island and keep the same course towards that new land; it might offer better opportunities.'

When we approached the north coast of Newfoundland, I asked our experienced skipper towards what point he would set his course. 'Towards *that* one, of course,' Sørnes replied, pointing at Great Sacred Island, the big island lying farthest out in the ocean. And he added: 'Every sailor would do the same thing.'

We passed the island, and we could now see the level country round L'Anse aux Meadows and the black Noddy Hill in the background. We were filled with suspense, for it had been a long time since Anne Stine had left us to fly back to the excavation site, and during this whole time she and her assistants would have been busy digging. What could she have found in all this time?

The anchor was lowered, and before long the dinghy scraped against the beach at the mouth of Black Duck Brook. Anne Stine, 'Big Chief', Job Lloyd, and a flock of girls and smiling children, were there to greet us. It was like coming home.

'How have the excavations been going?' I just had to blurt out.

'Well, we haven't found Leif Eiriksson's slippers yet,' Anne Stine replied with a smile that might mean anything, 'but come and see for yourself.'

We walked up to the north-east section of the old marine terrace, and there we saw something new: a house-site that was larger than any we had seen before and where the work of excavation was well advanced. Much was still unclear, but the site seemed to be about sixty feet long and to comprise several rooms. Here and there we could see remains of turf walls as well as fireplaces with a good deal of charcoal.

The ground in this particular spot had been flat, only a bit uneven here and there, and we had had no idea that there might be the remains of a house underneath the turf. Anne Stine told us that one evening, when the sun was low in the sky, its oblique light had thrown into relief the faint contours of something that looked like the corner of a site. She had begun to dig and discovered the culture-layer.

There was still much work to be done, but the part that was excavated indicated that the large house-site would divulge something of significance. Anne Stine was standing there by her discovery, rather tired but beaming, and this was understandable.

We all concentrated our efforts on the excavation of the large house-site and continued to work at it until far into the autumn. The air in time became much cooler and the wind quite a bit stronger, but most often the sun would be shining and there was no reason to complain.

Silently the snowy owl came flying in from the north and the migratory birds at L'Anse aux Meadows began to get ready for their trip to the south. The wild berries were now ripe, and I have never before seen such a multitude and so many varieties of berries in a small area. Beyond the site the bogs had turned yellow from the great quantities of cloudberries. The slopes around were partly red from cranberries, and there was no shortage of crawberries and blueberries. In more sheltered spots we would find red and black currants, gooseberries, raspberries, and squash-berries. One day, when we had decided to have raspberries for dinner, Brunborg picked several pounds in no time at all. There were more than enough berries for anyone who wanted to put by a supply for the winter or to make wine.

Icy winds came racing in from the sea and announced that a new winter was on the way. It was time for us to finish our work for this year and go back to Norway. We had by then discovered six house-sites in all along the old marine terrace, in addition to the large, curiously shaped pits. Some of this had been excavated, but much work remained to be done, and it would be necessary to return with expeditions during many summers to come in order to bring the work to completion.

All aboard, the *Halten* set a southward course along the west coast of New-foundland, and it was indeed interesting to have a look at that part of the island as well. In the northern part of the Strait of Belle Isle the coastline was almost straight, and there were few harbours. Farther to the south there was no shortage of fjords or harbours. In the background there were forests, and far inland we glimpsed the heights of the Long Range Mountains.

At last we had put Newfoundland behind us and our position was some-where out at sea quite a long way north of Nova Scotia when we suddenly heard a muffled sound from the engine-room. Then all was silent. The *Halten* was lying there helplessly drifting.

One of the cylinders had burst. We stood looking silently at the ruins of the engine as if we were at the sick-bed of a patient who had just died.

The skipper and the old engine had been arch-enemies for months. It had tried almost everything to make life intolerable for him, by having any number of its parts either wearing out or just refusing to work any longer; at times it would sputter and even burst into strange-sounding explosions. But the skipper was not the type to be intimidated. Every time the engine began to show its bad temper he would tackle it with his usual never-say-die spirit, and he always managed to make it mend its ways. But this time the old motor had played its ace of trumps: it had just gone and died.

But it had miscalculated just a tiny bit. As a surgeon once in a while is able to revive a heart that has stopped beating, our skipper and Brunborg managed to inject a spark of life into the other cylinder. We hobbled along with only one cylinder working, and the speed was lamentable.

We sniffed at the wind and the weather — the atmosphere seemed heavy and strange, and we wondered whether there might not be a storm brewing. During the last few days we had tried to get weather forecasts on the radio, but all in vain, the reason being either atmospheric disturbances or the fact that the radio had been drenched in too much salt water.

When we got out into the open ocean east of Nova Scotia, the waves began to behave in a curious manner. Time and again they would sweep over the gunwales and after a while there would be a great deal of water inside the ship. Our dinners were floating about on the floor, to the indignation of our cook, Dr Martens, who was an orderly person. One night I was thrown from the upper bunk, smashing our fine dining-table in the process; but I could not complain since my own injury amounted to no more than a few bruised ribs.

We had previously been at sea in all kinds of weather, so we did not take this too seriously. The important thing was that the one cylinder kept working, that we were moving forward, no matter how slowly. But there was one thing that we thought rather strange: for some days there had been no ships, not even a solitary fishing-boat, anywhere to be seen.

At last, one evening we saw the lights of Halifax in the distance, and eventually we tied up at one of the quays. The harbour-master came over to us and asked us where we came from. When we replied, he gave us a strange look and said: 'You weren't worried about Esther?'

That, we thought, was a curious remark. On board our ship someone or other might have had a woman on his mind – but why Esther?

'It was damn lucky that she changed her course south of Halifax,' he continued, and told us that she had been reported to be on the way to this particular area. Pretty dangerous things, these hurricanes, and this Esther was supposed to move about at a tremendous speed.

This, then, was the explanation of the curiously behaving waves and the ocean devoid of ships. We noticed that the harbour was crowded with ships, all of them securely lashed to the quays. Hurricane Esther was on the rampage.

And here old *Halten* had come hobbling in from the ocean on one cylinder!

Plate 37 (*previous page*). The largest of the house-sites has been almost completely excavated. The great hall is on the left with a long fireplace in the central part. The turf has been put back on top of the foundation walls so that the contours of the building may be clearly seen. (Photograph: Hans Hvide Bang.)

Plate 38 (*previous page*). Dr Kristján Eldjárn (*right*) and Gísli Gestson begin the excavation of a curious hollow in the ground next to Black Duck Brook. It was here that they were to find the smithy. (Photograph: Hans Hvide Bang.)

Plate 39. The smithy is here fully excavated. In the centre is the anvil, a long smooth stone embedded in the ground. In the background, to the left of the smithy, a hollow in which charcoal was produced for the use of the smith. (Photograph: Hans Hvide Bang.)

Plate 40. Anne Stine at work near one of the ember pits. (Photograph: Erling Brunborg.)

Chapter Seventeen

To Northernmost Labrador

During subsequent summers, five archaeological expeditions were made to L'Anse aux Meadows. Before I deal with these in some detail I wish to tell about the exploratory journeys we made to *northernmost* Labrador. These took place in late autumn, in the course of two consecutive seasons, after the excavations at L'Anse aux Meadows had been completed for the year.

Up to that time I had got to know Labrador as far north as Nain. I was greatly interested, however, in becoming more closely acquainted with the most northerly parts of the country, as far as its northernmost point, Cape Chidley. It was there that the Vinland voyagers would have sighted land after they had crossed Davis Strait and sailed south from Baffin Island, and on a visit there one might have a better impression of which course it would have been natural for them to have chosen. In the account of Leif Eiriksson's Vinland voyage in the Greenlanders' Saga it says that in the first land he came to there were 'large glaciers' and he called it Helluland. Like A. W. Brøgger[1] I believed that this land must be identical with Baffin Island, but many others, among them Gustav Storm,[2] have thought that it was Labrador. It would be meaningful, then, to ascertain whether there actually are glaciers in northern Labrador and if they may be seen from the sea.

It was also important to take into consideration the fact that whenever the Norse Greenlanders wanted to get a shipload of timber, the northernmost areas of Labrador would be ideal, since the distance from Greenland was not too great. But the question was: Would the forests in this area have been large enough and were the trees big enough to use for shipbuilding, etc.? A trip to the most northerly parts of Labrador could, in other words, provide me with much valuable information of different kinds. We were also to search for actual traces of the Norsemen and I had been given some leads by Eskimoes, but we knew full well what a needle-in-a-haystack task that would be.

Erling Brunborg and I climbed aboard an Otter, which the Royal Canadian Air Force had very kindly placed at our disposal. Our course took us northward along the Labrador coast. As we crossed Davis Inlet, where the Nascapi Indians live, it struck me that this area had been favoured with extensive, sheltered forests nearer to the ocean than at most other places along the coast.

Would Norse sailors have thought it a natural thing to seek land and shelter here, I asked myself? Later on I was to have the opportunity of investigating this region more closely.

At Nain I met my friend of the year before, the old Eskimo Isaac. He knew the coast well, as far as the northernmost point, and he gave me much useful information. But he was first and foremost interested in the seals. 'Lots of seal up north,' he would say, and there would be a far-away look in his eyes.

We took to the air again, passed over rows of skerries, and I asked the pilot to try to set his course for Sculpin Island. On that island there were supposed to be some ruins that had been discovered long ago by Herrnhuter missionaries, and they were thought to be of Norse origin. The ruins had been written about by various scholars, and V. Tanner investigated them in 1939. His conclusion was that they must be remains of former Eskimo habitation.

We saw Sculpin Island below us. It was a tiny island with hardly any vegetation. We circled above it at a low altitude and got a good look at its scattered stone ruins. It would have been contrary to everything we know about the dwellings of the Norse Greenlanders to conjecture that these houses, built in such a desolate spot far out at sea, might be of Norse origin. For the Eskimoes, however, the situation would be ideal, since in all probability there would be an abundance of seal in the surrounding seas.

We continued our flight, the vegetation below us becoming ever more sparse; only in the inland areas could we detect patches of wooded areas – the Arctic landscape was making its appearance. But then we were in for a great surprise: around the fjords south and west of Okak Island there were amazingly dense and extensive forests. These areas, too, I was later to explore in greater detail. There was also a small forest somewhat farther north, around the Napaktok Fjord, situated at about 58° N., but the trees seemed to be only small.

Suddenly there was a change of scenery, and below us the immense Torngat Mountains rose into the sky, stretching northward all the way to Cape Chidley. This mountain world was naked, wild and picturesque. Peaks reaching an altitude of three thousand feet, some of them curiously shaped, plunged into the sea. Several islands off the coast also had peaks that reached to the sky, but there were no rows of smaller islands and skerries protecting the coast, which was exposed to the ocean.

I looked for glaciers, but in vain. All I saw were some white spots in among the mountains, a few miles long at the most. They were probably small glaciers, but they would hardly have been visible from a ship sailing along the coast. The description of the saga as to 'large glaciers' does not fit northern Labrador at all. The Helluland of the sagas must be Baffin Island.

While we were flying over these mountains, clouds were closing in on

Hudson Strait far to the north, so that the area round the strait opening into the sea could not be seen. Some scholars, like H. R. Holand, hold the view that Norse sailors ventured into Hudson Strait and continued as far as the James River. This is not very probable. First of all, the waters of Hudson Strait are very difficult to negotiate, owing to the ice and powerful currents — the difference between high and low tide is about sixty feet. Moreover, such a western route would have given every appearance of leading into the Arctic regions and not away from them. Ice and cold weather were among the things that the Norse Greenlanders had had enough of where they came from — their minds were set on more southerly and favourable countries.

The highest peaks of the Torngat Mountains rise to about five thousand feet; in the far north they slope down towards Cape Chidley, where the average altitude is about twelve hundred feet. The Vinland voyagers must have been able to see this conspicuous region of high mountains from away out at sea, and it struck me much more forcefully than before how simple their route actually was. After having crossed Davis Strait in the course of two days (*døgr*), they would never be out of sight of land the rest of the way. First there would be Baffin Island, with its high snow-covered peaks, then Resolution Island, and then the northernmost point of Labrador. From then on it was only necessary to follow the coast of Labrador in a southward direction until the north of Newfoundland emerged before the ship's bow.

On the return trip we landed at Nain, and once again I paid a visit to my Eskimo friend Isaac. His eyes lit up when he heard that I had seen the coasts along which he had roamed in his kayak when he was young. But nothing that I could relate about flying, mountains, and ruins registered with him. All he said was: 'Did you see any seals?'

During a subsequent autumn I and the photographer Hans Hvide Bang flew north in order to explore in greater detail a forest region that had caught my attention, at Tasiuyak Bay, a bit to the south of Okak Island. If these forests measured up to my first impression, this would be the most northerly forest area in Labrador that could be utilized and would also be the forest nearest to the Norse settlements in Greenland for anyone following the traditional Vinland route.

We landed at one end of a lake a mile or two away from Tasiuyak Bay. The plane took off again, and we were alone in the wilderness. The scenery was enchanting: to the west we could see one lake after another in among the wooded hills; in the background rose a massive mountain, with a white cap of newly fallen snow. The night frost had left its mark on the hillsides, and there was a riot of colours — the lichen-covered slopes were rusty brown or fiery red, the birches had put on a new coat of yellow leaves.

We pitched our tent and walked over to the river to catch some fish for our evening meal. The river was the sort that most fishermen can only dream of, with rushing rapids and broad lagoons in which some real big fellows were swimming about. E. P. Wheeler had told me that the Eskimoes called this river Augut-tausuvik, which means 'The place where he thought he was a big man'. This name is an ironic reference to an Eskimo who was foolish enough to brag and say that he could run his kayak down the very hazardous rapids to be found in this river. He did try it, but he lost his life in the attempt.

When we came down to the river bank, we discovered another fisherman on the other side – a black bear. When he saw us, he got up on his hind legs, and then slowly ambled up the cranberry-covered slope.

One is usually disappointed when the fish does not bite; in this river it was the fish that was disappointed if it did not get the opportunity to bite. After only about twenty minutes of fishing we had a goodly supply of char, some trout, and one salmon. The largest fish was about fifteen pounds.

The following days were spent exploring the forests and the coast. We found traces of the activities of Eskimoes; for centuries they have hunted and fished in this area. In the old days there must have been an abundance of seal, fish, birds, and also caribou. We saw large flocks of ducks, and in the forests we would often encounter 'bushpatrick', which is of the size of the Scandinavian black grouse and sits quietly on a branch until one is right on top of it.

One of our main objectives was to ascertain whether the forest corresponded to the impression I had got from the air. And this it did, especially at the head of Tasiuyak Bay, where the trunks of the spruces were as much as fourteen inches thick. On a subsequent occasion I visited the forests around the neighbouring fjord, Okak Bay, and they consisted of equally fine specimens.

The Norsemen in Greenland would, in other words, have been able to obtain in these northerly areas satisfactory materials for the building of ships and for other purposes. But could they easily have discovered these forests? Out beyond the coast there are scattered islands, but they do not lie so close together that the Norse explorers would not have got a glimpse of the forests inside. If the men were searching for timber, one would think it natural that such experienced sailors would have sailed into the fjords and investigated further.

All this does not mean that I claim that the Greenlanders fetched timber in this particular area. But it is of considerable interest to point out that this is the most northerly region in Labrador where they could obtain timber for ship-building, etc. The distance from this point to Greenland is shorter than from any other afforested area of any consequence. Along the route of the Vinland voyagers the distance from the Western Settlement to the area around Okak

Bay is about eight hundred nautical miles, and that means a voyage of no more than five days or so.

However, in the course of the five centuries their society survived, the Norse Greenlanders might also have had other objectives than fetching timber when voyaging to North America, and for that reason they would continue southward along the coast of Labrador. Like Leif Eiriksson in Vinland, they may very well have fetched timber from the particular places where they had settled down for a longer or a shorter time.

We were roaming about in a wilderness completely uninhabited by man. It was a beautiful autumn, with cool days and brilliant sunshine. A great quiet infused the forests, the river, the hills, and the lakes as far as the big mountain in the west. When in the evening we had tossed a few fish on to the bank and were sitting by the fire waiting for the kettle to boil, we would also keep on the lookout for our neighbour—the black bear. All day long he would be eating berries up on the slope on the other side of the river. He paid no attention to us, he was much too busy eating. And that was quite understandable, for winter was drawing near, and to him there was nothing so important as accumulating a good layer of fat before creeping into his winter lair and beginning his long hibernation.

Chapter Eighteen

A visit to the Nascapi Indians

During my earlier trip by air across the whole of Labrador I had taken especial notice of another forest region, at Davis Inlet. In this particular area, as I have already said, large forests advance closer to the sea than in most places along the coast. It seemed to me quite possible that Norse seamen would have been tempted to sail in past the big island called Ukasiksalik to the sheltered and inviting region inside. It would be well worth our while to investigate this beautiful district in somewhat greater detail. At Davis Strait I would also meet with the Nascapi Indians, who live farther north in Labrador than any other Indians. Perhaps these people, who knew the country better than anyone else, would give me some valuable information.

It was late September, and the excavations at L'Anse aux Meadows had ceased, to be resumed the following year. The other members of the expedition returned to their homes; Hans Hvide Bang and I flew north to the Nascapi Indians.

Davis Inlet did not disappoint us. It was a sheltered sound with wooded hills on both sides, a friendly contrast to the rest of the weather-beaten and rather desolate Labrador coast.

A few tents were to be seen among the trees up on the hillside. A flock of children scurried into the tents at the sight of us; they remained standing behind the closed flap and regarding us quizzically through a little opening at the top. Some women, returning from the forest with big loads on their backs, threw us a quick glance and quickly disappeared into the tents. A few men continued with what they were doing, and ignored us completely. There was an air of stiff-necked independence about these people, as if they were saying: What are you doing on our territory?

We pitched our tents not far from them, and after a few days we were on speaking terms, but they still kept their distance. These Indians—a little over a hundred in number—are something out of the ordinary among all the Indians of Labrador. There is an air of the wilderness about them, and even though they now have the benefit of certain modern implements and conveniences, they are still primitive in their thinking. The Finnish scholar V. Tanner wrote as late as the summer of 1937: 'Never before have I had such an overwhelming impression of standing face to face with Stone Age people, with veritable cavemen.'

The Nascapi Indians are caribou hunters, their way of life having been intimately connected with that animal since ancient times. They are divided into several groups, one being concentrated around White Whale River near Hudson Bay, a second group living in the Ungava region (the Chimo Indians), and the third branch of the tribe the one that we encountered. Their hunting grounds extended over an enormous area bordering the Labrador tundras. They would pitch their tents by a number of lakes such as Mistastin, Mistinibi, Indian House Lake, and so forth. This is the land of the caribou, and in the past there were hundreds of thousands of them here. The Indians hunted them with bow and arrow, later on with rifles, caught them with snares, or killed them with spears from canoes when the herds swam across the rivers. But the ways of the caribou were inscrutable, and sometimes the herds just disappeared for a time, in which case the lot of the Indian was hunger and a fight for survival through a hard winter. Not seldom it would happen that some would starve to death. The fierce struggle for existence hardened the people and taught them to act quickly and skilfully. In situations where others would have succumbed, they were able to survive.

We know that with the arrival of the white man in this region, as soon as the ice broke the Nascapi Indians would travel by canoe down the rivers to the northern coast of Labrador — to Voiseys Bay, Davis Inlet, and other places. Before the coming of autumn they would paddle up the Natakwanon and other rivers back to the hunting grounds next to the tundra. Some Indians lived in this region all the year round.

True, the trading post down by the coast would exert a great attraction, and the means of barter would generally be the Arctic fox, but the rhythm of their existence — the journey to the coast and the return to the inland areas — was primarily dependent upon the trek of the caribou. In early summer the caribou would seek the coast, to get a taste of the first growth of the sweet grasses and to calve, and the Indians would follow them. The migration of the caribou has always been something like this whenever they moved in large numbers and wherever nothing blocked the movement of the herds — on the Canadian tundra north of the Great Slave Lake, in Alaska, and in Siberia. Even the domesticated reindeer in Norway sets out for the coastal areas in the summertime. Finds involving stone implements near Davis Inlet also point to the old migratory routes of the Indians.

Some scholars take the line that the Nascapi Indians reached all the way to northern Labrador until relatively late, that it was the pressure exerted by the hostile Iroquois that drove them, as well as the related Montaignais Indians, towards the east and the north. It may not necessarily have happened that way;

at any rate, other Indian tribes may, in the distant past, have lived off the enormous stock of caribou in the interior of Labrador. It is difficult to imagine that primitive peoples would not find them and want to make use of them in very ancient times. No matter who they may have been, they would have followed the caribou down to the coasts in the spring. To put it another way: when the Norsemen came sailing past, some of the 'Skraelings' that they encountered may well have been Indian caribou hunters.

The numbers of caribou have lately been greatly reduced; and the possibility of living by caribou hunting in the wilds is much poorer than it used to be. Consequently, the Nascapi Indians do not migrate over such great distances as they used to, but basically they continue to live the way their forefathers did. They are nomads, and the caribou is the important fact of life, even though they also go in for hunting small game and fishing in rivers and lakes. They live in tents and do not own any more property than can be loaded into a canoe. 'Economically and socially they must be regarded as being among the most primitive people on the globe,' V. Tanner has said.

The fact that the Nascapi Indians have preserved so much of the old and traditional in their way of life, both physical and mental, is grounded in their always having lived in such isolation. Very little of what we call civilization has reached them, and its harmful effects have been relatively slight. It is very significant that Father Peters, who has lived for many years at Davis Inlet, has always placed great stress on their being given the opportunity to continue their nomadic way of life in conjunction with the hunting of the caribou. If that way of life cannot be maintained, the people will decline.

They are a dynamic people, they have slender bodies and beautifully shaped limbs, their gait is supple and springy. Their faces are characteristically Indian, their hair pitch-black, and their flashing brown eyes are typical of the tribe. The appearance of the men is keen, sometimes even arrogant.

The first friends that we made among the Indians were three boys between six and ten years old. Machim, Patni and Achetai were their names, and they were three real rascals who managed to upset our tent and everything in it as soon as they saw their chance. Before long, however, we became better acquainted with some of the adults, especially with a great hunter named Cenis, who was marvellously proficient at shooting birds with bow and arrow. We were also told a few things of interest, such as about a battle between Indians and Eskimoes in the old days on an island that is situated directly south of Davis Inlet and is called Massacre Island. But about old ruins they knew very little. We managed to get a few Indians to accompany us to some places that sounded promising, and we also investigated other places on our own, but without any result.

Suddenly one day the Indians began to strike camp. Tents were taken down

Plate 41 (*previous page*). Two little girls from L'Anse aux Meadows, who could almost hide in a hollow next to the largest of the dwelling-sites. (Photograph: Erling Brunborg.)

Plate 42 (*previous page*). The hollow shown in Plate 41 proved to be a large cooking pit, in which we found soot, charcoal, and stones that had been exposed to fire. (Photograph: Hans Hvide Bang.)

Plate 43 (*below*). The largest of the dwelling-sites, comprising five or six rooms. Where the man is sitting is the position of the long-fire in the great hall. The dark elevated areas are what is left of the turf walls. Some of the hollows are believed to have been cooking pits. (Photograph: Hans Hvide Bang.)

Plate 44a. A spindle-whorl made from soapstone, found in a Norse ruin in Greenland. This type of spindle-whorl is well known from Viking Age and Late Medieval finds in Sweden, Norway, and Iceland. (Photograph: National Museum of Copenhagen.)

Plate 44b. The spindle-whorl made from soapstone that was found at L'Anse aux Meadows. (Photograph: Per Maurtvedt.)

and their few pieces of property were packed and brought down to the shore. One by one, canoes and a few motor-boats disappeared in a westerly direction. And we followed them, in order to participate in their nomadic life. I knew full well how relations between an Indian and a white man become quite different when they are on an equal footing in the wilderness. Perhaps they would then become more voluble and give me information about ruins and other things of interest to us. Perhaps they would relate to us their old legends and these might contain something that could throw light on the problem that we were interested in. But I will admit that my expectations of learning something relating to the Vinland voyagers were modest indeed, and that I was by no means adverse to participating once more in a nomadic life with Indian caribou hunters, just as I had done years ago. It was curious to meet a people who not only in their way of life but in their way of behaving were so similar to the Indian caribou hunters that I had lived with for four years in northern Canada (north-east of the Great Slave Lake). It would also be interesting for me now to compare these two cultures, both of them based on the hunting of the caribou.

Father Peters took us along in his motor-boat to the head of Sango Bay. We met the trapper and fisherman Albert Edmund, who was living in this neck of the woods together with his wife Charlotte and the ninety-four-year-old David. She had originally come from Chimo on Ungava Bay. They invited us to stay for the night, and we had a very pleasant time.

A motor-boat loaded to the gunwales with Indians, equipment and dogs arrived in the late afternoon. There was a rather stiff wind blowing, and the waves were pretty rough. While still a distance from shore the Indians threw their dogs overboard; one of them was almost drowned while swimming for the shore, but no one paid any attention. After a while the skinny dishevelled animal crawled up on the beach, and just lay there.

As usual, all of the dogs belonging to the Indians were small and skinny, living on the edge of starvation, and they were now facing a long winter during which they would be mercilessly whipped in order to pull the sled the harder. Albert's dog team was a great contrast to this; they were big, well-fed animals with curled up, bushy tails. But there is no one like the Indian to get dogs to pull, even when one was convinced that there was no strength left in the animals. There is a strange rapport between an Indian and a dog, Albert told us. An Indian can get any kind of dog to pull, and not only because it is afraid of the whip—there is something more to it.

Albert lent us an old canoe. He told us that navigation was very difficult in many places along the rivers farther inland, and on his insistent advice we took the Indian Jerome along with us as guide. Thereupon we set off in the wake of the Indian families up the Sango River; at times we could paddle the canoes, at other times we had to pull them up the rapids. Then the country broadened out, and ahead of us lay the large Lake Sango, surrounded by forests and with hazy blue mountains in the background.

Some of the Indian families had put up their tents on an idyllic bay near the outlet of the river, and in order to stay away from the thieving Indian dogs we pitched our tent on the other side of the river. A storm was brewing, and the waves were capped with white; we should no doubt have to stay here a few days.

We used the time to visit the Indians in order to become better acquainted, but that was no easy task. Our guide Jerome blurted out one evening, in his halting English: 'Women they don't like you.' We were cut to the quick, for if there is anything any man is loath to hear it is that he is not being looked upon with favour by the women. But it was useful advice, for in the northern wilds as in most other places it is the women who have the deciding voice in so very much in life. We made a special effort to get into their good graces, and in this we succeeded after a while.

Jerome became more and more silent, and I realized that it had to do with his wife, whom he had left behind in the camp by Sango Bay, in the company of some young men. On the third day he slung his cartridge-pouch and his gun over his shoulder, set off in the direction of the forest, and disappeared. Just left us, without a word.

The sunny weather came, and the beautiful Lake Sango resembled a shining mirror. The Indian families loaded their canoes and departed, the dog packs jumped into the river and swam to the other side, and then trotted in a long single file along the shore. We followed them.

We travelled for several days, first as far as the other end of the lake and then up another river. The current became so strong that it was impossible to paddle; we made ourselves long poles, and punted the canoe up stream from early in the morning till late at night. Hans displayed a talent for punting, an art which is not very easy to come by. But then again, he had lived in North Norway among the Lapps, many of whom are past masters in punting their craft up the rivers.

The canoes of the Indians were loaded with heavy and strange cargoes. There was a colourful mixture of women, children, puppies, and equipment. The canoes were loaded down nearly to the gunwales, but the Indian standing in the stern pushed the long pole into the river bottom with unerring skill and steered the craft through the powerful current without a drop of water coming in over the side.

The air was cold, and in many places the banks of the river were fringed with ice. The mosquitoes had, on the whole, put an end to their blood-sucking feasts, but the sandflies were still active. The forest spread out all round us; at times we would pass through steep gorges and cut through sandy moraines. Now and then a flock of wild geese would take to the wing. Every turn in the river offered something exciting—what would come up next?

On the last day we had fallen a bit behind the Indians. The brittle canvas covering our old canoe had been ripped by one of the many trees lying in the river. We had to go ashore and patch it up with resin, and that could not be done in a moment. It turned out to be a long day, for we had been punting for twelve hours; darkness set in and we had still not seen any trace of the Indians ahead of us. Was it their intention to travel on all night?

Coming round a bend in the river, we heard the barking of dogs, and we could make out the outlines of tents at the edge of the forest. Dark shadows emerged from the black of night—Indians came running and greeted us with a smile. The atmosphere was suddenly completely different; it seemed as if we belonged. They helped us carry our equipment ashore and put our canoe on dry land; afterwards they showed us where the best camping-ground was and gave us a hand in putting up the tent. When that was done, Nabon offered us a present—a cut of delicious caribou meat. We lost no time in putting it in a pot on the fire, and the tent was filled with the most wonderful aroma!

We had arrived at the place where the Indians had been fishing from time immemorial. Here they were to stay for some time, in order to fish and not least to give sufficient and proper nourishment to their dogs, all of whom were in a miserable condition. Some of the hunters had come upon the caribou in the mountains, only a day's walk away in a westerly direction.

There was an abundance of fish. The Indians placed their nets in a part of the river right above the camp where the waters were especially still; they would pull them in a few times a day, and every time they would be completely filled with fish. When the canoes were paddled back to shore the women and the dogs would be standing on the beach, showing the greatest interest in the catch. Some of the catch would be thrown to the dogs, the whole pack in that case joining in a vicious brawl, in spite of the fact that there would be fish lying all around and they were just too full to swallow any more. The fish the Indians caught was the Arctic char, which just at that time was on the way up the rivers of Labrador; it would weigh up to twenty-four pounds. Big fish like this are no exception in this part of the world; trout caught in the big lakes far inland may weigh as much as fifty pounds.

Soon we felt at home in the Indian camp; we visited the various tents as we had a mind to, and always met with smiles. There was a certain peaceful atmosphere about the little community on the bank of the river far in the interior of the wilderness. Here the Indians were relaxed and happy. The men set off on hunting expeditions; some looked for smaller game, others roamed for days into the mountains in the west in search of the caribou. And we would benefit to the extent that we would have fresh caribou meat in our pot or strips of dried meat—the Indians consider meat to be the only decent food. Everyone talked about 'Atéuk', the caribou, and they discussed where the main part of the herd might be keeping itself, but they would not strike camp and move into the mountains until all the fishing was done. Even though the stock of caribou has been greatly reduced during recent years, there is a sufficient number left for these Nascapi Indians to subsist on.

The women were fully occupied with work from morning till evening. They sewed, tanned hides, cooked meals, fetched firewood, and did other chores. Since times of old it has been their destiny to work hard. In the distant past when the Indians did not have dogs, they used a smaller type of sled (*otasenágask*), and when the tribe departed for a new camp it was the women who would pull the sleds. The man was only a hunter—and the lord of creation.

Their young girls had fine features, and their brown eyes gave them an aura of softness. They were full of vitality, especially the graceful Maniata. A group of girls would from time to time disappear into the woods, where they would use their axes with a very experienced touch and then return to camp with large bundles on their backs supported partly by a strap over the forehead. So that it would not cut into the skin, they had placed spruce twigs underneath the strap, the twigs looking like a green adornment bordering their pitch-black hair.

To live among these caribou hunters was very much like my life with the hunters at the edge of the tundra north-east of the Great Slave Lake. It was not so easy to put one's finger on the differences between the two tribes. Their ways of thinking and looking at things as well as their culture seemed to be closely related. There were differences, of course. The snowshoe of the Nascapi Indians, for instance, is not bent up in front, and there may be other differences; there is a limit to what one may learn about a hunting people during a short stay with them. But it was a curious experience, indeed, here in the wilds of Labrador to listen to the legend of 'The man who lassoed the Sun', a legend that was told me many years ago in an Indian tent somewhere on the tundra east of the Great Slave Lake.

Only one of the Indians knew some English, but he was a wise and competent interpreter. The Nascapi Indians speak a language that is related to that of the Montaignais Indians; the two people understand each other even though their dialects are different. Both groups represent, as I have said, branches of the Algonquin tribe. It struck me as being very curious that the Nascapi Indians' word for 'Indian' was *innu*, plural *innuits*, this being very similar to *innuit*, which the Eskimoes call themselves. But I dare not express any opinion about this linguistic problem.

'Méteoaté!' ('people are coming'); the shout went up over the camp. A canoe appeared, and a tall, sinewy man went ashore with his family. He had a narrow, oriental-type face, a tiny patch of hair protruding from his chin. He must have been about fifty years old, but was agile and quick in his reactions. This was Thomas Nor. He was a gentleman of the old school, and it was immediately evident that he was highly respected by all. In his younger days he had roamed far and wide across the tundra and the borderlands to the west, from Chimo on Ungava Bay in the north to Seven Islands in the south, to North-West River and many other far-away places.

Such great journeys were more or less commonplace in the old days to these nomads, who moved about with great ease. Indians belonging to other groups along the Labrador coast used to roam about in the same manner. In this way they got to know each other, and contacts were established. And in the vast interior, the habitat of the caribou, many hunters and their families would meet every year.

Thomas Nor was steeped in the traditions of his forefathers, and he knew the old skills well. He could describe in great detail how a birch-bark canoe, a bow and arrow, and a spear should be made. Every little piece had its own name, and there were a great number of them. I have no doubt that if Thomas were ever robbed of his gun and knife, he could go out into the forest and manage just as well as did his primitive ancestors.

In his conversation he would often revert to the caribou. He told us about the great numbers of caribou there had been in Labrador in the past, but he spoke also of years when the caribou disappeared and people starved to death. To me it was also of great interest to be told how the Indians in the old days, in the same way as the Nunamiut Eskimoes in northern Alaska, had made big enclosures (*menekén*) into which the caribou were chased and then killed with arrows and spears. Like the Nunamiuts, they too had legends about the mammoth (*achiotásk*).

One evening when the green and purple northern lights were flickering and sparkling far above the hills, he remained standing as if spellbound outside our tent and just stared into the sky. Then he said, 'vestevegábo' ('northern lights'), and it was said in such a way that I got the impression that it meant something important to him. That was all he said, and I don't know what he was thinking, but according to the old beliefs of the Nascapi Indians the northern lights were the spirits of the dead dancing and feasting.

I asked the Indians numerous questions about aspects or details of their traditions which might be in any way connected with a meeting with Norse people a very long time ago. Nothing very significant emerged from all this, but the following detail may be of some interest in this connection: In the Greenlanders' Saga's account of Thorvald's Vinland voyage we are told that he met 'Skraelings' who slept under their overturned boat. The Nascapi Indians told me that it was customary in the old days to sleep under one's birch-bark canoe. In the account in Eirik the Red's Saga of Thorfinn Karlsefni's Vinland voyage we are told about natives who carried with them fat and blood in containers. This was a dish which the Nascapi Indians used to prepare in the past and was called *monapón*.

The weather turned much colder, the ice along the bank extended ever farther into the river. We were now past mid-October, and there was a danger that one night the ice would completely bridge the river and cut off our return route. Some of the Indians had already set out on the westward trek into the mountains, looking for the caribou, and we would have liked very much to join them — but our time was limited.

'Sitapmok' ('watch where you're going'), Thomas said as we stepped into our canoe to begin the trip down river. Off we went, and the Indian camp disappeared round a bend. One must indeed have exerted every ounce of energy in punting up river in order to be able to enjoy to the full a trip down through the rapids. But it was essential to keep one's eyes open, for there were a lot of tree-trunks with pointed branches immersed in the water. We scared up a fox, came upon a bear, and had a grand voyage down to Lake Sango.

There was quite a wind blowing when we got down to the lake, but it was not bad enough to make it a hazardous crossing. On our starboard side some distance ahead there was a diminutive island, and if the wind were to get much worse we could find shelter there. Just as we were paddling across the lake, we suddenly saw a pitch-black cloud formation rise into the sky behind the mountain, and then a gale hit us as if shot from a gun. The waves were suddenly high and white with foam, our little craft was bobbing up and down, and we were drenched every time the waves came splashing against the sides of the canoe.

It was rather a tense situation; a small error in manoeuvring would be sufficient for the canoe to fill with water. It was a question of whether we could tack a bit in the face of the wind and waves and try to reach the little island; if not, we should be swept along over the expanse of the great lake, now whipped into a frenzy, and our chances did not look very good. We paddled and paddled — and made it.

We stayed on the island for four days while the storm was raging, and we felt like Robinson Crusoe. This turned out to be an unexpected addition to our itinerary, and after a while we were a bit short of food, especially since it was impossible to do any fishing in that kind of weather. We walked about on the tiny spruce-clad island and searched for something edible; after a time we found some bushes with currants that tasted marvellous. Then we heard a clucking sound from a tree—our joy was great on discovering 'bushpatricks' even on this speck of an island. We shot three of them, made a fire from driftwood on the beach, broiled them on a spit, and agreed that a more enjoyable existence could not be found.

When after some time we reached Davis Inlet, there were only a very few Indians left in the settlement, among them the chief, Joe Rich, who was too old to set out on a long trek in search of the caribou. He possessed a greater store of information than most about the traditions of his race, and there was no end to his knowledge of the old myths and legends. Night after night I would sit with him listening to his stories and jotting them down.

He led me into the Indians' strange world of superstition, in which the whole of Nature plays a part, and where every form of life is imbued with its own spirit. The caribou, the bear, the wolf, the wolverine, the otter, the sparrow, the louse, and other animals would speak and act like human beings. And human beings would be transformed into animals. Then there were the dreams; they were of very great significance. Of not least significance was everything to be found above the abode of man—the sun, the moon, the northern lights, the stars, and the icy winds that swept across the tundra. Here too spirits were present, and some of them were evil spirits, *matséno*. A great deal of this body of beliefs and superstition had been incorporated into their highly imaginative legends. One of their leitmotifs was the caribou and man's perennial struggle with evil powers who always try to prevent a successful hunt. But one of the most elevated places in their world of superstition was held by the god of the caribou, Katipenimitawk.

Sitting there and listening to the old Indian, I had a feeling of the same curious atmosphere that I had experienced when I lived among the Eskimo caribou hunters—Nunamiut—in the Brooks Range in northern Alaska, and the Eskimo Paneak had told me the legends of his people. The legends of these inland Eskimoes seemed to be very closely related to the stories told me by the Indian chief—revealing better than anything else the essence of the primitive mind—centring as they did on the struggle for existence and the fear of death.

In this chapter I have dwelt on some of the experiences connected with our visit to the Nascapi Indians, the northernmost Indian tribe in Labrador, great caribou hunters who spend the summer at Davis Inlet. In the distant past there must, as I have said, have been other hunters who voyaged down the rivers from the land of the caribou to this part of the coast. This heavily forested, sheltered coastal district is so situated that in the course of time it could have been a natural thing for the Norsemen to seek harbour here, in order to fetch timber, to hunt, or perhaps to barter goods with the natives. Our exploration of this particular area did not result in any proofs that this was the case, but I did get more closely acquainted with the most primitive tribe in Labrador, and I got a deeper understanding of what the people might have been like that the Vinland voyagers called 'Skraelings'.

Chapter Nineteen

A New Expedition — a Smithy discovered

The preliminary excavations at L'Anse aux Meadows had shown great promise. There were many circumstances that indicated that the sites were of Norse origin, and nothing had come to light that made us believe that they had originated with Eskimoes, Indians, fishermen or whalers. But there was much work still to be done, and we looked forward with no little anticipation to the search for additional traces of these early settlers.

There was a strong indication, in other words, that we were about to find the solution to that age-old problem regarding the discovery of North America. For that reason I thought it right that a number of well-known scientists from several countries should be invited to participate in my next expedition, the one carried out in 1962. The participants were: from Iceland, Dr Kristján Eldjárn, Professor Thórhallur Vilmundarson, and Gísli Gestson; from Sweden, *phil. cand.* Rolf Petré; from Canada, Dr William Taylor and Dr Ian Whitaker; from Norway, beside my wife and myself, State Geologist Kari Henningsmoen, Hans Hvide Bang, and Benedicte Ingstad. Anne Stine was in charge of the archaeological work, as she had been before and was to continue to be until the work was completed.

The Norwegian group arrived in North America some time ahead of the others, Halifax being the actual point of departure for the expedition. The Royal Canadian Navy had shown us the courtesy of placing the ship *Eastore* with a full crew at our disposal for the voyage north to L'Anse aux Meadows. Then as well as later we met with the greatest interest and helpfulness from the men of the Navy, including Rear Admiral K. L. Dyer and many others.

We set our course in a northerly direction, Captain Sam Lillington being in command of the ship. It was a grand feeling just for once to be merely guests on board and to be waited on instead of having to struggle against wind and weather in our own small boat. For a time we made our way through the very same waters that we had crossed in a southerly direction the year before. As the *Eastore* sped with such great ease over the great expanse of ocean, our thoughts reverted to the *Halten*, our little ship which in this very same locality had come limping along at three knots with only one cylinder working, and only just missing hurricane Esther.

This voyage would not take very long, we thought. But when we approached the northern part of the east coast of Newfoundland, we felt less certain of that, for we met with masses of rough drift-ice, moving before the ever stronger north wind. This was in the middle of June, and we were at about the same latitude as London.

There was no question of trying to get round the northern tip of Newfoundland and over to L'Anse aux Meadows; we just had to get the ship in to St Anthony as fast as possible before the ice blocked our route. Very slowly the *Eastore* forged her way through the ice to the west. Captain Lillington was a typical, phlegmatic mariner, but the ship had not been built to make her way through Arctic ice, and when the ice-floes crashed loudly against the side of the ship, or swung over in the direction of the propeller, I should imagine that the captain was not as unaffected as he seemed.

We finally reached St Anthony. All we could do now was to make our way across the peninsula and try to reach L'Anse aux Meadows from the west coast. We transported our equipment over to Pistolet Bay, where we got hold of two men and three fishing boats, which proved to have just about enough room for the equipment and ourselves. Thereupon we embarked on a voyage that would take us in an easterly direction along the north coast of Newfoundland.

Could we manage to get through the drift-ice from this direction? For a long time it looked far from hopeful, but we slithered through the open channels, and whenever we thought we were completely stuck, our experienced crew would always manage to find an escape route. Off ship Cove we discovered to our amazement a small boat in the middle of the drift-ice: its crew, a man, his wife, and two children, were busily engaged in fishing, as if being surrounded by dangerous ice-floes was an everyday occurrence. And they were hauling in plenty of cod.

At dusk we at last saw L'Anse aux Meadows straight ahead, and we thought we could relax. Then we suddenly collided with a dense and solid ribbon of drift-ice, and it seemed as if we should be forced to come to a full stop not very far from our destination. We leaped out on to the ice, used our axes, poled the ice-floes to the side, and managed to force our way through. All this happened on Midsummer Eve. This proves how the local ice conditions can vary from year to year. When our previous expedition had been there we had seen practically no ice at all.

The tents were pitched, and the excavating began. Slowly the drift-ice disappeared; only a few solitary icebergs were to be seen in between the islands.

One day a seaplane landed on the waters of the bay; the passenger was Dr William Taylor, archaeologist at the National Museum of Canada. It was of great value to us to be joined by a scientist who was an expert in Eskimo and

Indian archaeology and, in addition, was familiar with Canadian history and culture subsequent to the rediscovery of the country. Dr Ian Whitaker of the University of Newfoundland at St John's arrived somewhat later. They were the right kind of men, with that cheerful disposition that often characterizes those who are accustomed to living in tents in far-away places.

Every morning our geologist, Kari Henningsmoen, would set out on a hunting expedition for favourable bogs in which to drill for pollen. She was bubbling over with energy and never allowed wind or rain to daunt her. It was certain types of bogs that she was searching for, and whenever she found the right one she would use the large drill she had brought along and extract layers from below. These layers contained pollen from the vegetation that had covered the land in past ages. The tiny seeds in the pollen have an outer wall which is very resistant as long as it is not exposed to the air, and they keep for thousands of years. These seeds may vary in appearance, in accordance with the different species, and by closely examining them one can determine from which kinds of plants or trees they originated.

Consequently, such a pollen analysis may provide information about the vegetation in a certain area down through the ages, on the basis of which one may get an idea of the prevailing climate. To us it was of great importance to get an idea of what the climate in Newfoundland was like about a thousand years ago, at the time when Leif Eiriksson and other Norsemen sailed to North America.

It was also quite possible that her investigations might tell us something about the extent to which the land had been elevated. The geologists know very little about the elevation of the land in Newfoundland. If it was true that a thousand years ago the surface of the ocean was higher than now in relation to the land, it would probably have been easier for ships to get into the bay at L'Anse aux Meadows, which is very shallow at the present time. It is also possible that in those days a ship might be able to enter a short distance into a pool formed by the brook.

Our excavation of the large house-site that Anne Stine had discovered the year before became a hard but very interesting task. Additional rooms, hearths, cooking holes, and curious trenches were unearthed. Since the comprehensive investigation and excavation of this site were not to be completed until a later summer, I shall discuss it in greater detail in another chapter. I shall only mention here that the house-site proved to be about seventy feet long and fifty-five feet wide and comprised six rooms.

'Tent ahoy!' was the shout that we heard early every morning outside our tent. And 'Big Chief' 's bearded countenance would appear in the tent opening; we weren't properly awake before George Decker was in full swing telling us his strange tales, as for instance about the butcher who dug up corpses and sold the meat, about the pirates who abducted a beautiful girl engaged to a local swain, and about a Newfoundland woman who used to beat up her husband with a stick and who had such a 'wonderful miserable temper'.

In order to provide ourselves with some variety in our diet I set out one day for a fishing village where lobster was supposed to be more easily available. I got an unbelievably large number of lobsters, a whole sackful, for only about four dollars. Then I walked across bogs and hills and returned with my load, which was very much alive, emptying my sack on the grass in front of the tents. The lobsters were greeted with great joy, and it did not take us long to arrange a feast, happy in the thought that we had a supply of such regal food for a long time to come. But a whole sackful of lobster long outlasted our desire for shellfish, and our appetite declined as the days passed by. It was a long time before we wanted to look a lobster in the eye again.

The weather was quite different from what it had been the previous summer, which had been sunny and warm. Not infrequently cold winds and rains would drive in from the sea. The mosquitoes were few, and the flowers were late in blooming. The bad weather finished them to a great extent, and when autumn arrived hardly any berries were to be found in areas which the year before had had an abundance of them. Fishing, too, was poor; it is probable that the cod found the coastal waters too chilly and retreated to the ocean. The ice conditions are probably one of the underlying causes of such a great change in the climate.

In these regions where the weather conditions may vary so much from year to year, it is probable that anyone who came upon these coasts might get quite different impressions of the land, depending on whether they happened to meet with favourable or cold and unpleasant weather. The account in the Greenlanders' Saga about Leif Eiriksson's headquarters is full of the praise of Vinland. In the account of Eirik the Red's Saga dealing with Thorfinn Karlsefni's headquarters, which must also have been situated in Vinland, we are told of a severe winter, and that it was difficult to obtain food. This may well be reconcilable with the fact that both expeditions had their headquarters at L'Anse aux Meadows, where both the climate and the fishing may vary so greatly from year to year.

When the bad weather set in, our womenfolk sometimes had a rough time of it. One night the rain was pouring down so heavily that even Black Duck Brook showed its less pleasant side and rose up as high as the floor of the women's tent. And the rain was whipping through every tiny tear in the canvas. Inside, practically everything was afloat. The two women spent the night on camp chairs with their feet in the water and their heads resting on their arms on the table. But they never complained.

*

The three Icelandic scientists, Dr Kristján Eldjárn, Professor Thórhallur Vilmundarson, and Gísli Gestson, arrived, together with the Swedish archaeologist *phil:cand*. Rolf Petré. It seemed to get quite crowded by Black Duck Brook. The Icelanders were assigned an excavation project of their own, and so was the Swede, both of these projects being situated in an area that we had left untouched and had planned to assign to visiting archaeologists. In this particular area there were distinct traces of human activity in some parts, and in other parts there were no such traces; but for several reasons there seemed to be good possibilities of new discoveries.

Along the old marine terrace, extending in an arch from Black Duck Brook in a north-easterly direction towards the sea, we had so far uncovered six house-sites. But there might be more underneath the turf, even though the terrain seemed to be comparatively even. We felt that there was one spot especially that was very likely to be the site of a house. Rolf Petré began to dig in this spot, and it did not take him very long to come upon a culture-layer containing a great deal of charcoal. After a lot more work he unearthed quite a large house-site, about thirty-three feet by fifteen. In its centre he found a hearth, and next to it he unearthed a small box-shaped ember pit, made of slate and of the same type that we had found earlier and that had also been found in Greenland and Iceland.

Petré made some important finds, among them a fragment of a bone needle of the type used by the Norsemen. No less interesting was a narrow piece of copper, about two inches long, on which some cross-stripes had been made. It was found inside the hearth. Laboratory tests have shown that it is not composed of pure copper, but has been produced by a primitive smelting process and contains a number of minerals. For that reason it cannot have originated with Eskimoes or Indians, who would have used the natural ore — almost one hundred per cent pure — and hammered it into the desired shape while it was cold. The smelting process was unknown to them. It is hard to say what this particular piece of copper was used for; perhaps it was part of a belt and just dropped into the hearth while its wearer was working.

To us it was of particular interest that the fragment of copper was found in the hearth, since that fact afforded us the possibility of C-14 carbon dating of the charcoal among which it was lying. The charcoal probably originated from the time at which the fragment of copper was lost. The carbon dating showed this to be A.D. 900 ±70 years. This is just about the time of the Vinland voyages.

Not very far from the large house-site, in a northerly direction, there was a curious round depression in the ground, wide enough for two small girls to sit in out of the wind (see Plate 41). A similar one had been discovered on the other side of the brook, down towards the sea. Dr Petré and the party of Icelandic scientists excavated one each.

These hollows proved to be just over two feet deep. The one by the brook was about seven feet long and three feet wide at its upper edge; the hollow by the large house-site had a diameter of about nine feet. In the hollows they found soot and charcoal, in addition to a considerable number of stones which had probably been picked up on the beach. They were about the size of a man's fist and had obviously been exposed to fire.

These hollows must have been cooking pits, in which the stones had been heated, the food placed on them and covered up with earth or something else. Cooking pits were used in the Stone Age and have been found in different countries. The excavations in Greenland showed that the Norse Greenlanders frequently made use of such pits and very probably in more recent times than in other areas. Most often they were found inside the houses, but also out in the open. The probable reason why cooking pits were used in Greenland to such a great extent is the fact that the people found it difficult to obtain pots big enough for large households.

In other words, the Vinland voyagers were familiar with the use of cooking pits in Greenland. During an extended voyage to a strange land, on which it was possible to take only limited equipment, such a method would have been a great help to them. Every day it was necessary to cook for a large crew; Leif Eiriksson's expedition numbered thirty-five men, Thorvald brought along thirty men, Thorfinn Karlsefni had about one hundred and sixty, and Freydis about seventy. The large pits at L'Anse aux Meadows could hold considerable quantities of seal and whale meat; even a caribou could be put into them if cut into sections. Our thoughts reverted to the poem recited by Thorhall the Hunter, who says that they 'boiled' whale meat in the place where Thorfinn Karlsefni's expedition had made its headquarters in Vinland.

In order not to anticipate the archaeological report to be published later, I shall not attempt here to discuss in greater detail whether the cooking pits must be considered to be of Norse origin. I shall merely say that it seems very likely that the pits are a part of the old settlement on the terrace. Also, the carbon datings obtained from the charcoal in the two cooking pits agree very well with those that we have obtained from the house-sites.

Petré also investigated a considerable area somewhat away from the sites, where it was possible that the middens were located. Here, too, the conditions for preserving organic materials were very poor; bone, for instance, was very often found to have completely disintegrated or crumbled into dust. The finds were few in this area.

During the excavations carried out in the previous year we had found several lumps of iron slag in one of the house-sites. It was a curious find, and it made us wonder. The slag indicated that the people who had lived on this old terrace had extracted iron from bog-iron.

Before I proceed, I wish to dwell briefly on the most important characteristic of this process of iron extraction as it was carried out in the Viking Age and in the later Middle Ages in the mother-country, Norway. The first step was to produce charcoal in a kiln. Bog-iron was found underneath the turf in or near bogs. It was first crushed and roasted over a fire in order to remove organic materials and moisture. Then a pit was dug in the ground and lined with rocks or clay. In this pit bog-iron and charcoal were mixed well together, then a fire was lit, and a bellows used to supply sufficient air. The content of iron oxide was thus reduced, and in the pit there would after a while be produced slag and a lump of iron. This part of the process was both important and difficult: the temperature had to be greater than the melting-point of the slag, about 1,100° C., but below the melting-point of the iron, which lies between 1,250° and 1,400° C. If the heat was excessive, the iron would turn into pig-iron, and could not be used to make important objects such as swords and knives. How they managed to keep the temperature so exactly within these limits is not quite clear; at any rate, it must have required a great deal of experience.

The lump of iron was then picked up with tongs, placed on an anvil, and the slag was hammered out of it. Then came the tempering, which was quite a process in its own right: the iron had to be heated up to a certain temperature and then it had to be cooled suddenly by immersion in water. Not until then could the iron be shaped into knives, axes, and weapons.

Iron extraction from bog-iron was, in other words, a difficult art. It presupposed a trained specialist who knew every step in the process. If a sailor had gone ashore at L'Anse aux Meadows and had been lucky enough to find some bog-iron, he would have been incapable of extracting iron from it unless he was a smith and had had special training in this field.

We had found lumps of slag in the dwelling-sites in L'Anse aux Meadows, but the questions now were: Was there any bog-iron here? Where was the kiln, the pit in which the smelting process had taken place? And where was the smithy?

The bog-iron was discovered close to the brook and not far from the house-sites and the large bog behind them. There was a great deal of it; when we turned up the turf with a shovel there was a layer of bog-iron nodules right underneath. Their size varied, but some were as large as a hen's egg. Their colour was rust-red, but when we cut into the nodules, a delicate blue lustre appeared.

On the other side of the brook and not very far from it there was, as mentioned previously, a fairly large hollow in the upper part of the marine terrace. There was no doubt that it had been made by human beings. We were wondering what it might possibly be — except Anne Stine, who with womanly stubbornness remained firm in her contention that this was the smithy.

The excavations in that spot had been reserved for the Icelanders. Right underneath the turf they made a curious find, namely, a beautiful oval lamp made of soapstone, no doubt of Dorset Eskimo origin. Once upon a time they must have visited this old site. The Icelanders continued digging, down through a culture-layer.

One day we heard that something had happened up on the terrace where the Icelanders were working. We all rushed up to see. The men were on hands and knees, carefully picking up small objects with eagerness and care, as if they had found gold.

It was iron slag. A whole lot of nodules, some small, others as large as a hen's egg. As they dug farther down into the culture-layer, the number of nodules rose to many hundreds, their total weight being about thirty pounds. They also found small, thin pieces of iron, which reacted easily to a magnet, and some bog-iron. On the slope towards the river they also found slag and bog-iron.

It was a plain but fascinating scene that greeted us when the little room by the brook on the upper part of the marine terrace had been fully excavated. It measured nine feet by twelve. The earthen floor was black from the coal. In the centre of the room, about three inches above the floor, there was a rock embedded in the earth. It was flat on top, quite level, and about ten inches long, but it had evidently been longer, one end having been broken off. Not very far away there was a hearth.

There can be no doubt that this room had been a smithy. The flat stone in the centre must have been the anvil, the hearth close by would probably have been the forge. I have confined myself here to mentioning a few main features; the excavations did offer other highly interesting details, but it seems preferable to defer discussion of them until the publication of our scientific report.

It seems likely that the lump of iron that had been extracted from the bog-iron had been brought into the smithy, and the slag hammered out of it. But in order to smelt bog-iron and do the work in the smithy, charcoal was needed, and where had that been produced?

About eight yards away from the smithy there was another depression in the ground on the top of the marine terrace. The Icelanders dug here as well. Directly underneath the turf appeared a layer of charcoal, and deeper down there was more, one of the layers being about eight inches thick. The depth of the pit from the surface of the terrain to the lower layer of charcoal was about two feet six inches; the hollow widened out towards the surface and was about eight feet by seven at the top. This must have been the charcoal kiln.

The smith at work with sledge-hammer and tongs, and his assistant working the bellows. Detail from a wood-carving from Hylestad in Setesdal, Norway, from about A.D. 1100. The iron was produced from bog-iron. This art was continued in Iceland, Greenland and North America, where a smithy has been excavated at L'Anse aux Meadows.

All we needed to find now was the pit in which the smelting of the bog-iron had taken place. Archaeologists have never had an easy time of it finding such pits; in Greenland, for instance, they have found both a smithy and slag, but not the smelting pits, and in Iceland it seems that only one such has ever been found. Nor did we find any at L'Anse aux Meadows, but during a subsequent summer there was discovered a concentration of slag a short distance away from the smithy, at the top of the terrace and near the steep slope going down to the brook. It is possible that the smelting pit was located somewhere near that spot, and that in the course of time part of the terrace slid down into the brook.

These finds contributed in a very significant way to our insight and understanding of the old settlement at L'Anse aux Meadows and of the people who lived there. We shall now take a look at the extraction of iron from bog-iron from a historical point of view. The art was known in Europe at least as far back as 2000 B.C., and in Norway at least from 400 B.C. In the Viking Age and in the Middle Ages production of iron was on the increase in Norway, becoming an important factor in the economy of the country. Many slag heaps, lumps of iron, kilns and some smelting pits, especially in the remote mountain valleys, tell the story. Iron extraction became not only a permanent part of the work on the farms, but a real vocation for many. During the Viking Age Norway was self-sufficient as far as iron was concerned, and it is quite possible that some of it was exported. In Iceland, which was settled around the middle of the ninth century, the extraction of iron from bog-iron was common in the Viking Age and probably continued until the fifteenth century. In most parts of Iceland slag has been found; but only one smelting pit, as well as pieces of iron produced from bog-iron. The anvils were usually made of iron, but could also be of stone, like the one found at L'Anse aux Meadows. The process was undoubtedly the same as it was in Norway.

It appears that the smith's trade was very highly regarded. There was a Norwegian by the name of Skallagrim who emigrated to Iceland during the reign of King Harald Hårfagre and was thus one of the earliest settlers in Iceland; we read in the saga that he was an excellent smith and very busy with the smelting of bog-iron in the winter. We are also told that he raised a large stone from the sea bottom and used it as an anvil. He started work so early in the morning that the farmhands began to grumble. Skallagrim then made this song:

> Early must the blacksmith
> who will silver earn
> start at bellows, blowing
> fire in blue-black coal.
> Singing sledge I swing,
> beating hard the steel
> which red-hot gleams and sparkles,
> while greedy bellows blow.

As mentioned above, slag and smithies have also been found in the Norse settlements in Greenland. Dr Niels Nielsen, who has made a thorough study of this matter, considers it proved that the Norse Greenlanders produced iron from bog-iron, and that they did so from the earliest time of the colonization. Icelanders and Norwegians brought the knowledge with them to Greenland.

Thus, the fact that we found a smithy, bog-iron, slag, small pieces of iron, and a charcoal kiln at L'Anse aux Meadows agrees with everything we know about past iron extraction from bog-iron in Norway, Iceland and Greenland, that is, the countries in which the Vinland voyagers and their families had their roots.

To the North American natives, Eskimoes and Indians, iron extraction was an unknown process; they might put to use natural copper or metal derived from meteorites, but they would always hammer the metal while in a cold state.

It is also very improbable that fishermen or whalers in the period immediately following the rediscovery of North America, that is, around A.D. 1500 and later, extracted iron at L'Anse aux Meadows—in an area which they must have regarded as a remote wilderness. This would imply that they brought with them a smith who had special insight and experience regarding the difficult art of extracting iron from bog-iron, at a time when extracting iron from ore had become prevalent in Europe. It is clear, furthermore, that neither fishermen nor whalers lived at the old house-sites excavated. No find originating from them has been made and carbon datings from the hearth in the smithy give a reading of A.D. 1090 ± 90 years and A.D. 890 ± 70 years.

To the Vinland voyagers it would have been of great importance to take a smith along with them. They set out for a strange and unknown land in order to found a settlement, and without a smith who knew the elaborate art of iron extraction they would be in a very difficult situation—they might even revert to a Stone-Age state.

One day then, about a thousand years ago, a smith must have stood inside the small room excavated at the top of the marine terrace above the brook, swinging his sledge-hammer and beating the molten iron, making the sparks fly. And the din of his rhythmic beating would reach the people of the turf-covered houses and reverberate across the wide expanse of the meadows.

Chapter Twenty

The Excavations continue–a Journey to White Bay

In 1963 we set out on another expedition to L'Anse aux Meadows in order to continue the excavations. Besides Anne Stine and myself, the participants were Charles Bareis and John Winston from the University of Illinois, Hans Hvide Bang, Nicolay Eckhoff, and Benedicte Ingstad from Norway. Somewhat later during the summer we were joined by Dr Henry Collins from the Smithsonian Institution and Dr Junius Bird from the American Museum of Natural History.

The previous year I had suggested to the Prime Minister of Newfoundland, Mr Joseph Smallwood, that shelters should be built over the most important of the house-sites so that they might be preserved for posterity. If that were not done, they would soon be obliterated by the wind and the weather. My suggestion and plans were accepted, and a builder was sent up to see us and given detailed instructions.

When we returned to L'Anse aux Meadows the next summer we were very anxious to see what had been done. Would the new buildings spoil the beautiful landscape? It made us happy to see that the buildings looked attractive; they harmonized very well with their surroundings. With their sloping roofs and dark-brown walls they reminded us very much of chalets in the mountains of Norway.

Anne Stine continued her work at the house-sites and discovered new and interesting details. The work on the largest house-site and the surrounding area proved to be a big and very time-consuming job, but we knew that it would soon be finished.

Among the important tasks still to be accomplished was the digging of a great number of test trenches in the area. We already knew that there could be house-sites below a surface that showed no trace of what was hidden underneath. There was also a possibility that we might unearth scattered artifacts of various kinds. We were also hoping that we might find remains of graves, or traces indicating that ships might have been pulled ashore.

Our many test trenches ran far out into the surrounding meadows; but as so much was uncertain, we could not set our sights too high. However, this task was to yield interesting results, even though we did not learn much that was new with regard to the Norsemen.

We found some very rusty fragments of iron, some of them in deep layers, but most of the finds were of native origin, such as the head of an Eskimo harpoon (Dorset) and some Indian stone implements. Most of these were found a short distance away from the largest house-site in the direction of the beach, in an area where Rolf Petré had made similar finds the year before. In the same area two open hearths were uncovered, probably used by tent-dwellers, and the coal provided us with an opportunity for carbon dating. As mentioned before, the Icelanders had already found a beautiful Eskimo lamp (Dorset) made from soapstone, and other scattered stone implements had also been unearthed.

What we had found added up to a small but fine collection of Eskimo and Indian stone implements. There is much to indicate that they will provide an interesting contribution to our knowledge of the archaeology of Newfoundland, about which not very much is known at the present time. They also shed light on life at L'Anse aux Meadows in the distant past. Eskimoes and Indians must occasionally have pitched their tents in the meadows; however, the scattered finds seem to indicate no more than temporary sojourns. The traces of natives in this area agree well with the account in the saga about the Norsemen's meeting with 'Skraelings' in Vinland.

That year there was more salmon in Black Duck Brook than previously, and at times we made very fine catches. But something else about the brook interested me more. It was possible that the people living near the brook a long time ago might have lost something in the water. I started a rather large undertaking, one that did not yield any results but was nevertheless a task that we could not afford not to try: Black Duck Brook was diverted from its bed. It was the smith whom I especially had in mind. How easily might it not have happened that one of his tools or something else could have slid down the steep slope at the smithy and into the brook? Or he might have lost something when he had to jump from rock to rock across the brook, on his way to or from the smithy. Thus, one day Black Duck Brook churned through another part of the meadow. Its old bed, through which it formerly had snaked in long curves between the willows and down to a little waterfall, now lay there dried out and sad. We dug a long time in the dry river bed, but the good smith who jumped across the river a thousand years ago must have had a firm grip on his tools.

It was obvious that people to the south had heard about our discoveries at L'Anse aux Meadows. It became a frequent occurrence to have visitors flying in. George Decker was amazed when yet another plane landed on the bay, and said: 'No plane ever landed here before in my lifetime, and now they are as thick as mosquitoes.'

One day a few private tourists arrived, having come all the way from the United States; then we were paid a visit by a bishop, some clergymen, and a member of the Newfoundland Parliament; our visitors had increased in rank to government ministers when the Governor of Newfoundland sent a message announcing that he too would pay us a vist. He was to arrive on a destroyer on a certain day and at a certain time. Soon afterwards a man by the name of White turned up; he was the Magistrate from Bonne Bay, on the south-west coast of the island. He was a very pleasant fellow, and was accompanied by an unusually powerful-looking representative of the Royal Mounted Police in full regalia. In his official capacity White was to receive the Governor, and I was asked to act as host and show our honoured guest the excavations.

All the inhabitants of L'Anse aux Meadows were not a little excited at the prospect of a visit to their small village by not only a warship but also the Governor himself—all, that is, except George Decker, who was never impressed by anything. The first task was to look round for a flag, for there was general agreement that there could be no reception without a flag. At last a small rumpled British flag was found—the only one in L'Anse aux Meadows. It was nailed to a stick.

The great day arrived, and from the lowest strata of my equipment I extricated a tie—this was one time I had to look respectable. As the hour approached, I walked over to one of the houses in the village from which there was a splendid view of the wide expanse of ocean. I stood next to the Magistrate, who obviously felt the solemnity of the occasion, and a little girl in her Sunday best, who held on tight to the stick with the British flag. We looked at our watches; the Navy was usually on time.

There was a howling gale, and the wind was whipping up the white-capped waves that pounded high against the skerries. I could not make myself believe that the Governor would want to make the hazardous trip from the ship to the quay in a small motor-boat in such terrible weather.

The ship came into sight. A grey hulk, it passed the islands in the far distance, and seemed to reduce its speed somewhat. The Magistrate, who had come a long way in order to be present at this solemn occasion, remarked anxiously: 'I think His Excellency will make it all right, don't you?' But the grey ship increased its speed—and steamed due south. 'Perhaps it will stop in the lee of one of the islands,' the Magistrate suggested gloomily. But the warship did not stop at all; it vanished in the storm.

And the reception committee was left standing by the window—the Magistrate from the south-west coast, the little girl in her Sunday best carrying the flag, and I, wearing my tie.

I would like to insert here a few words about the interest and helpfulness shown my expeditions by various Canadian authorities and government bodies. The Government of Newfoundland was very accommodating in many ways. This was also the case with regard to the Department of Northern Affairs and National Resources, which among other things had new maps made of L'Anse aux Meadows by the National Historic Sites Division. Dave Alexander and his staff did splendid work in mapping the area. The Royal Canadian Air Force photographed the site and the Royal Canadian Navy placed a ship at our disposal.

The most surprising development in this respect occurred one day in early autumn. A boy came running across the fields with a telegram in his hand. It said that the Royal Navy offered to send a destroyer to pick up the expedition at a certain time and transport it to Halifax. I turned a friendly thought to the men of the Canadian Navy, who wanted to be so helpful, but there was still much work to be done and I had to decline with thanks. Through the years one is sometimes obliged to decline an offer, but that was the first time I had to decline the offer of a destroyer.

I shall now say a little about a reconnaissance trip made by plane and boat to a neighbouring area of L'Anse aux Meadows — along the eastern coast of the long northern peninsula and southward into White Bay. I set out on this trip accompanied by Hans Hvide Bang and Nicolay Eckhoff.

There was not enough time for us to make any intensive search for ruins; the important thing was to get an impression of the area and its overall possibilities. We were wondering whether the area might prove favourable from the Norsemen's point of view, as the people who in ancient times lived at L'Anse aux Meadows would probably have thought it natural to sail along this coast for the purpose of exploration and hunting. The account in Eirik the Red's Saga seems to indicate that Thorfinn Karlsefni sailed along this coast on the occasion when he reached 'Hop', and Thorvald Eiriksson, too, appears to have sailed in this direction when he found the place where he wanted to build his new home, where he encountered the natives and was killed in the ensuing battle. These eastern shores of the peninsula were not only located not far from L'Anse aux Meadows but, according to the Skálholt map, they seemed to be a part of *Promontorium Winlandiae*. If the natural conditions proved favourable, it was possible that Norsemen had also settled in that area during the five-hundred-year history of the Greenland settlements.

The east coast proved to be quite fertile. The forests in many places came down to the shore, and from the air they looked like a green carpet extending all the way to the Long Range Mountains. There were a number of fjords and bays as well as rivers, which in the past must have abounded in trout and salmon. We also saw grassy meadows in several localities; none of them, however, covered as wide an area as the fields at L'Anse aux Meadows.

Our investigations were concentrated around Sops Arm, where the conditions seemed to be especially favourable. At the mouth of the bay lay the large Sops Island, which displayed a fairly rich vegetation, including spruce trees and deciduous trees, colourful flowers, and wild berries, such as raspberries, currants, and gooseberries. We also noticed tall grass growing in a number of open fields near abandoned fishermen's cottages.

On the north-east promontory of Sops Island we found several ancient sites, partly obliterated by potato fields. Arlington H. Mallery[1] thinks that these sites are of Norse origin, but the stone implements found here make it clear that they are Eskimo (Dorset). The people who lived here had selected a beautiful position, on a terrace about fifteen feet above sea level and surrounded by woods. The harp-seal is supposed to come past here on its annual migration, and two polar bears were shot here a few years ago.

Additional traces of the Dorset Eskimoes have been found in the White Bay area and I believe that further investigations will reveal more. This indicates that if the Norsemen had sailed southward along the east coast of Newfoundland, they would probably have met with Dorset Eskimoes.

We searched this fjord and the surrounding area in a motor-boat, and found that conditions in general were quite favourable. Only a few people live in this remote area; we met a number of friendly and hospitable people, such as Arthur Budden and his wife, and Watson Budden, who gave us valuable assistance. The latter told us that he knew of two deep pits, in the forests to the west, that he thought had been used for trapping caribou a long time ago. We started out to take a look at them.

It was about two hours' trek, largely uphill and traversing beautiful spruce forests and areas with deciduous trees — tall birches, aspens, and alders. Then we arrived at the pits. Nicolay Eckhoff, ever alert and enthusiastic, immediately discovered two more, which meant that there had been at least four in all. Their size was amazingly large; they were about twelve feet in depth, about twenty-five feet long at their upper edges, and almost as wide. They were about a hundred to a hundred and fifty feet apart. There was no doubt that they were very old; a large spruce tree was growing inside one of the pits, and at the bottom we found charcoal, the remains of a forest fire.

Watson told us that the pits were situated in the exact area where the caribou used to have their migratory route. It was here that the animals would turn northward in the springtime, to graze on the slopes of the Long Range Mountains, and in November they would pass through here when going south towards the great lakes in the forests, Indian Lake and others. The stock has been greatly reduced, but in earlier times there used to be a great number of caribou in this area.

Who, then, had dug these pits? In the first place, it was natural to think of the Beotuk Indians, who must have frequented this region and were also great caribou hunters. In the various accounts dealing with these Indians there is no information about pitfalls, but they do mention fences that were put up in order to guide the animals in the direction of the hunter. I know of no other Indian caribou hunters in North America who have made use of such pitfalls, and digging deep ditches is a task that does not fit in with the nature of the Indian. It is also improbable that the typical coastal people, the Eskimoes, made these pits in the heart of the great forest, and it is hard to believe that white people, whose main livelihood was fishing, would bother with digging these deep pits so far away from their homes. We know that pitfalls dug to trap caribou have been widely used in Norway since ancient times, and there were frequently several dug next to each other, but we dare not draw any conclusions in this matter.

The chief impression gained from the trip to the northern part of the east coast, the area adjacent to L'Anse aux Meadows, was that in quite a few places it offered good possibilities for settlement. In an age when everything was virgin territory, the Norsemen might have found here what they were in need of: grazing lands, forests, seal, cod, salmon, caribou, fur-bearing animals, and much else. It will not surprise me if traces of the Norsemen are found in this area also, some time in the future.

The work of excavation went steadily ahead along the shore of Newfoundland's most northerly promontory. New finds were similar to the previous ones, and there could hardly be any doubt that the sites were Norse and pre-Columbian. This all agreed with the theory that I had advanced earlier on the basis of historical sources and old maps.

One day we visited Dr Elmer Harp at Porte au Choix, a cape on the west coast situated at the southern entrance to the Strait of Belle Isle. For several years he had been there excavating a number of sites, remains of turf and stone houses made by the Dorset Eskimoes — the first unearthed in Newfoundland.

It was a beautiful place; the ruins were situated on a grassy plain near the sea. Here there must have been excellent opportunities for hunting, with the harp-seal migrating through the Strait of Belle Isle. It was interesting to compare these houses with ours; they were entirely different, being fairly small round or rectangular house-pits which may have been covered with tents of skins. This difference Dr Harp had occasion to confirm when he visited us later on. Furthermore, he had made numerous flint finds, as many as several thousand in one house-site. We could not help thinking of our largest house, where we had found only one small fragment of flint in a sterile layer.

One of the most important tasks at L'Anse aux Meadows was nearing completion – the excavation of the large site which Anne Stine had discovered two years ago. This excavation had given rise to a great deal of expectation from the very beginning. It was discovered, surprisingly, in a spot where there was hardly any trace of it on the surface of the ground. When the first excavation revealed the existence of the culture-layer we were long kept in the dark as to the shape and the dimensions of the site. We had to scrape and scrape, while wondering what it all would lead to.

Slowly the shape of the site emerged. A turf wall and a large hall with a long fireplace appeared, then additional rooms with hearths, pits in the floor, curious trenches, slates and other kinds of stones, extremely rusty nails, lumps of slag, and other material. The main part of the work had been completed – a place where human beings had lived long ago saw the light of day once more.

The dwelling was about seventy feet long, and its greatest width was about fifty-five feet; it consisted of five or six rooms. The floor was of hard-packed sand. The low walls were more or less sharply delineated as elevations of turf or of earth and sand. In some places the layers of turf were very distinct.

The biggest room was a large hall about twenty-six feet long and about fourteen feet wide. At each end there were two smaller rooms, this making the whole structure appear as a typical long-house.

In the centre part of the hall the place of the long fire was indicated by a number of stones; it was about ten feet long. In its centre there was a small stone chamber – like those ember pits we had found at two other sites. There was also a cooking pit and a flat stone. On each side of the long fire and over towards the walls the layer of earth rose somewhat, an indication of earth benches. They had probably been covered with twigs, skins or boards, and the people might have used them not only for sitting but also for sleeping.

In the other rooms there were also hearths; the one in the north-east room was especially well made. Near it was discovered a circular impression in the earthen floor; this seemed to signify that a pot or other vessel used to stand there. Similar impressions have been found in Norse dwellings in Greenland, and it has been concluded that they have been caused by barrels which contained milk.

In the hall itself, as well as in the other rooms, there were several pits in the floor. Without going into details I will only say that some of them must have been cooking pits.

The room facing south had a curious feature: two grooves in the floor. There was a distance of about ten feet between them and they were more or less parallel. What purpose can they have had?

From Norse farm-buildings in Greenland, and also from Leif Eiriksson's home at Brattahlid, we know of grooves or channels in the floor inside the houses. Their purpose may have been drainage, and partly providing fresh water indoors. Bits of information in the Icelandic sagas also point to the fact that it was important to have water available in case enemies set the house on fire. In *Hardar Saga Grimkelssonar* we read, for instance, that Thorbjorg of Indridastad changed the course of a river and made it flow right through her house when the enemy approached. And the Vinland voyagers had probably good reason to fear attacks from Indians or Eskimoes.

Actually, however, such explanations do not fit the circumstances. Decomposed wood was found in the trenches and it is probable that timbers had lain in the grooves and provided support for an interior wall. This feature is known from Scandinavia during the early Middle Ages.

Various interesting finds were made in the largest house. We found lumps of slag, very rusty nails, a needle whetstone, a stone lamp, which made us think of a similar find in Iceland, and a few other things. But we found nothing pointing to Eskimoes, Indians, whalers or fishermen. Scattered over the floor was a lot of charcoal, indicating that the house had been burned down.

How the largest house and the other buildings were constructed cannot be determined on the basis of the excavations. There is much to indicate that the houses were to a great extent built of turf, but it is probable that wood had been used as well for the roof, posts and doors, etc. It was not difficult to obtain timber; there were probably forests in the vicinity, and on the beach there were always piles of driftwood. But there are few stones to be found in the neighbourhood that could have been useful as building material.

This site is so large that it must have comprised several houses, which were probably constructed as one unit, as was the case in Iceland in the old days. This fact makes our thoughts turn again to the various Vinland expeditions. The Greenlanders' Saga says that everybody stayed at Leifsbudir. Leif Eiriksson's expedition numbered thirty-five, there were thirty men in Thorvald's party, Karlsefni had sixty besides women and livestock, and Freydis took about seventy persons, of whom about half settled in the neighbourhood of Leifsbudir. According to Eirik the Red's Saga Karlsefni's expedition included a hundred and sixty men in addition to women and livestock and, as mentioned previously, this saga seems to indicate that the people settled in the same place as Leif. In such circumstances it is probable that in time they built several additional houses, and the easiest way to do that would be to make extensions to old ones.

We cannot say anything definite about this, and we have no detailed information whatsoever about the actual building of these houses. However, it is tempting to believe that the leader of the expedition and others of high rank lived in the big house, which dominated its surroundings and was situated closest to the shore. As in other Norse settlements in the eleventh century, the communities in Greenland must have been aristocratic in structure—the old families were the powerful ones. Such conditions might have altered somewhat during a voyage to far-away lands, but the fundamental principles underlying an aristocratic society would hardly have diminished much in importance.

We often thought about all the charcoal that had been found on the earthen floor of the large building, which indicated that the house had been burned down. This is also the case with several Norse dwellings and churches in Greenland. What had happened at L'Anse aux Meadows? Had Indians or Eskimoes set fire to the house after the Vinland voyagers had left? Had it been their fear of evil spirits which had impelled them to do so? Or had a bloody and tragic episode occurred during a subsequent landfall in Vinland, one of which we have no knowledge? Had there been an attack by the Indians, arson, and a bloody battle? We do not know, but at one time in the distant past the great house must have been a blazing fire, lighting up the wide plains of L'Anse aux Meadows.

One day a small plane appeared in the southern sky and landed on the bay. We were wondering who it might be; we dispatched the dinghy and it returned with two men who came towards us smiling. The taller one shook my hand, and with his other hand he presented me with a bottle of old brandy —not a bad way to greet a stranger. The two newcomers were Dr Henry Collins and Dr Junius Bird, two well-known American archaeologists. Dr Collins had been sent up by the National Geographic Society, which was the main sponsor of my expedition this year, and he was to study the site and give his opinion of it. They both joined our expedition and took part in the excavations. This was indeed a refreshing development, since they were both not only deeply interested in the task on hand but also possessed that good humour which often characterizes men who for years have travelled far and lived close to Nature.

As mentioned above, the material from our excavations at this time was of such a character that there was no doubt that the site at L'Anse aux Meadows was of Norse origin. But we were of course very interested to hear what conclusions Dr Collins and Dr Bird might come to. They were both considered to be among the most highly respected archaeologists in the United States; Dr Bird had also made excavations in Labrador. But I did not ask them anything.

One day it so happened that Dr Bird and I were sitting next to each other on the slope, digging like moles in one of the test trenches. Suddenly he stopped, looked out over the site, and then he said: 'You got it all right.' That was all. Later on they sent in their reports, in which they put down detailed reasons why the sites must be Norse and pre-Columbian.

Chapter Twenty-one

A Norse Spindle-whorl

We soon found that there was not enough time to complete all the work that had to be done at L'Anse aux Meadows, and a new expedition would be needed. In the 1964 expedition the participants were, in addition to Anne Stine, Dr Junius Bird and his wife Peggy, Birgitta Wallace from the Carnegie Museum in Pittsburgh, who was Swedish-born and had trained as an archaeologist in Sweden, and the Canadian Tony Beardsley.

At that time we knew that the site was Norse, but there was one thing which we had secretly been hoping for during the entire work: to find an article so obviously and conspicuously of Norse origin that even to those who were not archaeologists it would be clear that Norsemen had lived at L'Anse aux Meadows in the distant past.

During my various expeditions I sometimes dreamed of a sword appearing in the earth—it was a large and very fine sword. But would a Viking ever leave his sword behind? And he would have lavished equal care and concern on his hunting-knife, perhaps the only one he had in the strange new country. And if anything of value had been left lying about, it is more than likely, as mentioned previously, that it would have been picked up by Eskimoes or Indians.

Then it happened! Anne Stine decided to make a test trench right by the southernmost room of the largest house-site. During the excavation Tony suddenly saw something strange—a small ring made of stone. He gave out a yell, and Anne Stine, Birgitta Wallace and Junius Bird all had a look at his find and then joyfully hugged each other. Anyone with a knowledge of Scandinavian archaeology would know what a ring of this type was—it was a Norse spindle-whorl.

It was made of soapstone, and was about an inch and a half in diameter. The back was somewhat curved and black from soot and it is probable that it had been made from an old cooking pot or an oil lamp. Since we did not find any other soapstone pieces at the sites, it is likely that the people had either brought the spindle-whorl with them or had found a piece of soapstone left by Eskimoes or Indians.

This type of spindle-whorl is well known from Viking times and later in

Sweden, Norway, Iceland, and Greenland. If we place the spindle-whorl from L'Anse aux Meadows next to one of those dug up somewhere in the Norse area the similarity is as close as it can possibly be. (See the illustrations facing page 185.) It was a very important tool for the spinning of wool, and women in the north made good use of it. To the Indians and Eskimoes of Newfoundland and Labrador, primarily hunting people, a spindle-whorl would be a strange object.

This find provided us with more than we had dared to hope for. Yes, it was even more significant than a sword would have been. It told us that among the people who lived at L'Anse aux Meadows a long time ago there were also women. It also revealed that they must have had wool from which to spin thread.

It is also remarkable that this find tallies so well with the information embodied in the saga. Eirik the Red's Saga tells us that Thorfinn Karlsefni took women on his great land-taking expedition, among them his wife Gudrid. In addition, he had livestock, which must have included sheep. These animals would have been essential to people from Greenland about to establish a new colony in a far-away place, where it would be necessary to weave cloth, sails, and other things. On Freydis's expedition to Vinland there were also women, but we are not told anything about livestock.

The small room which was next to the spot where the spindle-whorl was found lay by itself, being the only room on the south side of the great hall. Could this have been the women's quarters? Immediately outside this room must have been the most sheltered and sunny spot at the time the large house was standing here. A woman may have sat in the sun there, and spun, a thousand years ago.

After the completion of seven archaeological expeditions to L'Anse aux Meadows, the result may be briefly summarized as follows:

Eight larger or smaller house-sites have been excavated, one of them a smithy; also four boat-sheds, and three large outdoor pits, of which two must have been cooking pits, and in the third of which charcoal must have been produced, probably for the use of the smith in his work. Various finds have been made at the sites and in the many test trenches.

How may we interpret these finds? Without going into details I shall mention some of the features of special significance:

The house-sites display characteristics which are very similar to the way of building known from the Norse area during the Viking Age. At L'Anse aux Meadows we find house plans of the 'long-house' type, as have been found in Greenland and not least in Iceland, where several similar house-sites from the early Middle Ages have been excavated in Thjorsádalur.

An attempt at a pictorial reconstruction of the houses that once stood at L'Anse aux Meadows. Some large rooms discovered recently are not included in this drawing. Far to the right is the charcoal kiln, from which smoke is rising; the smithy is close by but cannot be seen, as it nestles into the marine terrace round the bend of the brook. (Drawing by the architect and archaeologist Håkon Christie.)

With regard to the hearths, Norse parallels are also to be found in Greenland and Iceland, as for example the long fire and the ember pits.

Among the objects found we might mention: a few stone tools, some very rusty nails, fragments of iron, a small piece of smelted copper, a stone lamp like those known from Iceland in the Middle Ages, a whetstone for needles, a fragment of bone needle of Norse type. In addition, we have the most important find, the soapstone spindle-whorl of unquestionable Norse type.

An evaluation of the archaeological material can hardly lead to any other conclusion than that the sites at L'Anse aux Meadows must be Norse and pre-Columbian.

This conclusion is corroborated by twelve carbon datings (C–14) from the different sites. All these date back to a time somewhat before or a little after A.D. 1000. The latest date indicated by the C–14 method is A.D. 1080 ± 70 years. The datings agree well with the conclusions based on the archaeological material.

Even though our findings leave little room for doubt, it may nevertheless be of interest to look a little more closely at the other possibilities which we constantly had in mind during the excavations.

Was it possible that the people who lived here were Eskimoes or Indians? The type of houses, the hearths and the smithy, the finding of iron and a melted-down piece of copper, viewed in conjunction with the carbon datings, the needle and the spindle-whorl of Norse type, etc., all indicate that the sites cannot have been of native origin. As mentioned before, some finds of stone implements of Indian and Dorset Eskimo origin have been made largely in the many test trenches. These finds are of great interest not only from an archaeological point of view, but also for the reason that the sagas describe the meeting of the Vinland voyagers with the Skraelings and the subsequent barter and fighting. The Greenlanders' Saga says that this happened at Leifsbudir when the men of the Thorfinn Karlsefni expedition were staying there. The number of stone tools and fragments that have been found is so limited that it is improbable that natives can have had permanent settlements at L'Anse aux Meadows. It is likely that, from time to time, they pitched their tents for briefer stays in the area.

What about fishermen or whalers? The archaeological material also excludes them. In addition, we have the carbon–14 datings, according to which the settlements go back to about A.D. 1000, that is, more than four hundred years before North America was rediscovered.

A few significant items may be added. The bay below the sites is, as previously mentioned, so shallow that it would have been of no use to fishermen and whalers, even if we take into consideration the possibility that there may have been a slight elevation of the land since the sixteenth century. The Norsemen, on the other hand, could pull their ships ashore in shallow water and even pull them quite a distance over land.

We have pointed out before that the fishermen of later times have elected to settle on the other side of the promontory, where it is possible for them to land their boats, and where there are traces of an older fishing hamlet. This in spite of the fact that the area of the Norse sites provided fresh water from Black Duck Brook and was also more inviting in other respects.

If we postulate then that whalers and fishermen may have stayed at L'Anse aux Meadows, there is every reason to believe that here, as in other places in Newfoundland and Labrador, they would have left behind at least some small traces of their activity. While the Vinland voyagers brought with them simple tools and implements in comparatively small ships, the whalers and fishermen came from Europe with larger ships and all kinds of equipment. Theirs were expeditions fitted out as large-scale business projects. A number of things would have been left behind at their shore stations, and we should have come upon something at least having to do with their activity during our excavations of

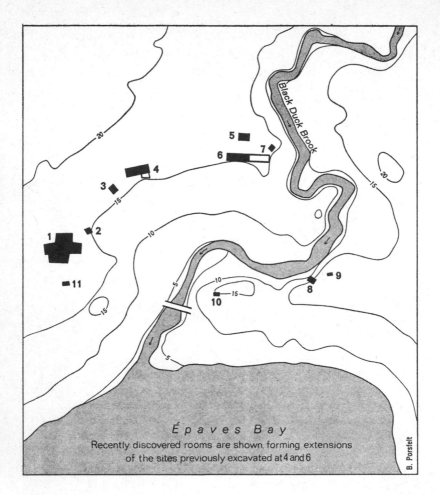

Épaves Bay

Recently discovered rooms are shown, forming extensions
of the sites previously excavated at 4 and 6

B. Porsfelt

Outline map of the L'Anse aux Meadows area, showing the position of all the excavated sites. The contour lines indicate elevations in feet. 1: The large house-site.
The Norse spindle-whorl was found close by the south wall of this site. 2–7: Other sites,
some with hearths, ember pits, and cooking pits. 8: The smithy. 9: Large pit with
charcoal, probably the charcoal kiln. 10–11: Large cooking pits. — Since this book was
written other finds have been made and excavated: a large and a small room connected
with site 4, a large room connected with site 6, and four (possibly five) boat sheds.

such a large area, especially since our excavations were not confined to the sites—a number of long test trenches were made in various directions. But nothing at all was found that might be related to fishermen or whalers, not a single fragment of clay pipe, of ceramic and similar objects, of hooks, tools, etc. There was a *total* lack of such finds.

Who were the Norsemen who lived at L'Anse aux Meadows about five hundred years before Columbus? It is not possible to answer this question with any certainty, but there are some interesting indications.

On this question we must revert to the available historical information, and first of all to what the sagas say about the matter. I must refer to my account given earlier in this book. According to my interpretation of the saga text and other sources I concluded that Leif Eiriksson probably built his 'big houses' in northern Newfoundland and I believed part of this area to be Vinland. This theory was the underlying reason for my expeditions—and a group of Norse house-sites, some surprisingly large, were actually discovered at the northern tip of Newfoundland.

The Greenlanders' Saga says that the expeditions led by Thorvald Eiriksson, Thorfinn Karlsefni and Freydis all made their headquarters in the houses that Leif Eiriksson had built in Vinland. At L'Anse aux Meadows there has been found a Norse spindle-whorl which indicates the presence of women and of wool. Thorfinn Karlsefni had both women and livestock with him, very probably including sheep.

This agrees with other aspects of the saga, which, however, may seem difficult to understand if one does not know the region to the west and south-west of Greenland in detail. How is it that the Greenlanders' Saga, which is based on what experienced sailors have told, offers such a very brief description of the route to Vinland and Leif Eiriksson's houses there? And we are here concerned with navigation along strange and very extensive coasts, with innumerable fjords, bays, and islands, where sailors familiar with the locality may lose their way even today. How was it possible for subsequent voyagers to Vinland to find Leifsbudir—a mere speck in a huge area—on the basis of the sketchy information about the route given in the sagas?

The Greenlanders' Saga tells us that Leif did not want to give the houses in Vinland to Thorfinn Karlsefni and Freydis, but he was willing to let them use them. This indicates that he looked upon them as something of value and that it would not be difficult to find them.

In this case, as in so many others, we find that the saga makes sense. The route is actually just as uncomplicated as the description indicates. I have mentioned that, after the Vinland voyagers had made the short crossing of Davis Strait, there was only one thing for them to keep in mind on the southward journey:

namely, not to lose sight of land to the west. They had first to sail along the coast of southern Baffin Island and then only steer due south along the extensive coast of Labrador until the northern part of Newfoundland appeared straight ahead. Great Sacred Island would then be an unmistakable landmark, and L'Anse aux Meadows lay just behind that island.

It was as simple as that. By enlarging only a little upon the terse statement in the saga, Leif Eiriksson could sit in his large hall in Greenland and give others sailing directions which could not be misunderstood.

The saga contains some information about that part of Vinland in which Leif built his houses. This information, especially the geographical descriptions, must be evaluated with great care, since the details may be made to fit several places along the coast.

Leif Eiriksson and his men must have been filled with joy and anticipation on arriving in the new land, and they praised it, perhaps in rather too strong terms, as was frequently to be the case in respect of North American discoveries. If they saw L'Anse aux Meadows on a sunny summer day, as we did, it is understandable that it made a deep impression on men coming from an Arctic island. It should be recalled that the forest formerly grew close to the shore.

The saga also indicates the great importance Leif Eiriksson attached to the possibilities of grazing for livestock. At L'Anse aux Meadows there are in fact grassy fields which are unique in the northern area facing the North Atlantic. The Vinland voyagers believed that the livestock could stay out of doors the entire winter at Leifsbudir, and, as previously pointed out, it is a fact that some time ago the livestock did just that at L'Anse aux Meadows. There was also salmon to be had, and they were larger than those in Greenland, as the saga emphasizes. Moreover, there were plenty of wild berries, from which they could make wine.

About Leif Eiriksson's arrival in Vinland the saga relates:

They sailed in towards it [the land] and came to an island which lay north of the land. There they went ashore and looked around, and the weather was fine. They saw that there was dew on the grass, and it came about that they got some of it on their hands and put it to their lips, and they thought that they had never before tasted anything so sweet.

They then returned to their ship and sailed into the sound which lay between the island and the cape projecting northward from the mainland. They sailed westward past the cape. It was very shallow there at low tide. Their ship went aground, and it was a long way from the ship to the sea. But they were so impatient to get to land that they did not want to wait for the tide to rise under their ship but ran ashore at a place where a river flowed out of a lake ...

This beautiful and vivid account mentions several physical features that agree with those at L'Anse aux Meadows. Here there is a very pronounced cape pointing north, and there is an island north of it. And the bay directly below the Norse sites is so shallow that the sea-bed lies exposed for a great distance at low tide.

The saga, moreover, says that Leif Eiriksson built 'large houses' in Vinland, and several of the buildings that stood at L'Anse aux Meadows were surprisingly big, especially in view of the fact that they were situated in a remote wilderness area at the northernmost tip of Newfoundland. There must have been accommodation for a considerable number of people.

It is also of interest to see what the result would be if we suppose that another, and to us completely unknown, Norse expedition made L'Anse aux Meadows its headquarters. The size of the house-sites indicates that it must have been quite a large-scale expedition. This expedition, then, would have reached the very same area in which, according to the historical sources, Leif Eiriksson probably built his houses. In addition, as in Karlsefni's expedition, there must have been women (cf. the spindle-whorl). In such a case, a strange thing must have occurred, namely that this to us unknown expedition, in accordance with the carbon datings and archaeological reckoning of time, must have taken place at about the same time as the Vinland expeditions that are mentioned in the sagas. And the saga-writers must, furthermore, have overlooked a contemporary expedition of such a large size and confined themselves to relating the others. This seems hard to believe, indeed.

In this, as in other instances, it is not possible to submit strictly scientific proofs that house-sites can be associated with known historical figures. But it may be said that a number of circumstances indicate that it was at L'Anse aux Meadows that Leif Eiriksson built his 'large houses' and that northern Newfoundland is the Vinland of the sagas.

But whether they were actually Leif's houses is not the important thing. What is of importance is the fact that, given the archaeological assessment and carbon datings, the house-sites at L'Anse aux Meadows are Norse, pre-Columbian, and date from about A.D. 1000.

Chapter Twenty-two

The Far Wanderers

Many questions arise, and they are far from easy to answer. How far south did the Vinland voyagers sail from their headquarters at the northern tip of Newfoundland? Eirik the Red's Saga relates that Thorfinn Karlsefni undertook an extended voyage of exploration in a southward direction. The Greenlanders' Saga tells us that both Leif Eiriksson and Thorvald set out on exploratory trips from Leifsbudir, and it seems quite probable that men with such inquisitive minds would sail quite far to the south. We do not know anything certain in this matter, but Vinland voyagers had fast ships.

Nor do we know anything as to whether Norse sailors reached more southerly areas, such as Massachusetts, Rhode Island, New York, and so on. But it is quite possible that they did. The settlements in Greenland continued as viable societies for almost five hundred years; the people did experience increasing difficulties, but throughout this period the fairly simple way to a fertile neighbouring country was well known. And the shores of the North American continent could guide them farther south.

Our knowledge of voyages later than about the year A.D. 1000 is, as mentioned previously (see page 93), very limited. One of these voyages was the one organized by Bishop Eirik, who, in 1121, set out from Greenland 'to search for Vinland'. From as late as 1347 there is an account of the small storm-tossed ship that arrived in Iceland and Norway after having been to Markland.

An important reason for Norsemen down through the centuries continuing the voyages to North America may have been their need for timber and a desire to hunt walrus, and fur-bearing and other animals; it is also quite possible that they wanted to make iron of bog-iron where fuel was easy to find, or trade with the natives.

As conditions in Greenland became ever more difficult, it is also possible, as mentioned before, that some of the inhabitants emigrated to the neighbouring region. In fact, a few of the sources indicate that this was the case (see page 94). It is also probable that after a while the Norsemen would change their attitude towards the natives, and this in turn would make it easier to settle in the new country. To the very first Vinland voyagers the natives were an unknown race who inspired fear; later on, however, when the Eskimoes had emigrated southward along the west coast of Greenland and even settled in areas adjacent to those where the Norsemen were living, they became a familiar sight to the Norsemen and probably even carried on barter with them. Thus the Norsemen of later times would have entirely different premises for associating with the North American Eskimoes and Indians than did the very first voyagers to Vinland.

If a migration actually took place, what can have been the fate of these people in the New World?

It is possible that the Eskimoes or the Indians killed the Norsemen. The settlers did not have firearms, as did Columbus's men, and they had to fight on even terms as far as weapons were concerned, against a foe which was greatly superior in number. Also, there is no doubt that the natives derived an advantage from the fact that their weapons were made from stone and bone: if they lost their weapons in the course of a battle it did not mean very much since they could quickly make new ones. If necessary, the Norsemen could also make use of bone in the making of arrow-heads and spear-tips, but the making of swords, axes, and knives involved a slow and demanding smelting process. They could not afford to lose their best weapons.

But there is another alternative: the immigrants may in the course of time have intermingled with the natives. Many Eskimo and Indian women are very attractive. If a small Norse settlement had managed to maintain fairly peaceful relations with the North American natives over a long period, the mixing of the races could hardly have been avoided. After the lines of communication with other Norse peoples had been broken, the culture of a much more numerous people would have prevailed.

No other indisputable traces of Norsemen have been discovered in North America, but some time in the future it may very well happen that a find will be made which will throw additional light on events of long ago.

In the earliest accounts of Newfoundland there are some pieces of information which ought to be mentioned. These concern the skin colour of the natives, characterized as white or light, and their hair colour, which is described as black, brown, or yellow. Erroneous information is not hard to find in old accounts, and I would not have mentioned this matter were it not for the fact that these characteristics stubbornly persist in quite a few of the oldest accounts. Most of them were written down a short time after the rediscovery, when any appreciable new racial mixture would be improbable. Besides, we know that the Beotuk Indians, as a result of the inconsiderate encroachments of the white newcomers, very soon assumed a warlike attitude and isolated themselves from the intruders.

It is dangerous to draw conclusions based on such information, and I must emphasize that I am not doing so; nevertheless, this information is so curious that it ought to be mentioned all the same, not least for the reason that it concerns Newfoundland – the very island on which the Norse sites were found.

On October 17th, 1501, Albert Cantino[1] wrote from Lisbon to the Duke of Ferrara and mentioned in his letter Gaspar Cortereal's expedition, which had just returned from Newfoundland with fifty-seven captured natives. Of them he wrote: 'The women have small breasts and the most beautiful bodies, and quite attractive faces. The colour of their skin must be said to be more white than anything else, while the men are considerably darker.'

Around the year 1500 the Portuguese Damiano Goes also wrote in his work *Chronica do felicissimo Rey Dom Emanuel* about the natives that the expedition of Gaspar Cortereal had encountered: 'The people in that country are very barbaric and uncivilized, about the same as the natives in Santa Cruz, except that they are white, and they are so affected by the cold that the white colour is lost when they become older, and they then become a good deal darker.'

With reference to John Cabot's discoveries, Richard Eden wrote in his work *Gatherings from Writers of the New World* (1555): 'Jacobus Bastaldus wryteth thus: The Newe land of baccalaos is a coulde region, whose inhabytauntes are idlatours, and praye to the Soone and moone and dyvers idol. They are whyte people and very rustical, for they eate flesshe and fysshe and all other things rawe.'

Hakluyt[2] states, following Robert Fabyan's Chronicle, that in the seventeenth year of the reign of Henry VII (i.e. August 22nd, 1501, to August 21st, 1502)

> were brought unto the king three men, taken in the new founde Iland, that before I [Fabyan?] spake of in William Purchas time, being Maior. These were clothed in beastes skinnes, and ate rawe fleshe, and spake such speech that no man coulde understand them, and in their demeanour like to bruite beastes, whom the king kept a time after. Of the which vpon two yeeres past after I saw two apparelled after the maner of Englishmen, in Westminster pallace, which at that time I coulde not discerne from Englishemen, till I was learned what they were. But as for speech, I heard none of them vtter one worde.

Also according to Hakluyt, Johan Alphonse wrote as follows about the natives: 'They are a people of goodly stature, and well made, they are very white, but they are all naked and if they were apparelled, as the French are, they would be as white and fair.'[3]

On a map of Terra Nova in Ptolemy's world atlas, published in Venice in 1547-8 by Pietro Andrea Mattioli, is inscribed: 'Terra Nova, of the Codfish, is a cold place. The inhabitants are idolaters, some worship the sun, others the moon, and many other kinds of idols. It is a fair (*blanche*) race, but savage (*rustique*).'

John Guy[4] wrote about his encounter in 1612 with the Beotuk Indians, who at that time seem to have been at a very primitive stage. He said that the colour of their skin was dark, but added: ' … their hair colour varied, some had black hair, some had brown, and others again yellow … '

In this connection, mention should also be made of the broken sword which Gaspar Cortereal's expedition of 1501 found among the natives in Newfoundland (see pages 91–2).

We shall never know exactly what they were like, the people who lived a thousand years ago in the houses at L'Anse aux Meadows. They must have been a strong race, used to hard work, handy as well as knowledgeable about a lot of things, quick and agile—as sailors are apt to become because of the necessity of acting instantaneously with sail and rudder—cool and calculating in the moment of danger. At times they may also have been abrupt and inconsiderate, especially when their own honour or that of the family was involved—in an age of action there was less opportunity to cultivate more refined feelings. And it is probable that the common man in such an aristocratic society had to put up with quite a lot. But everyday life in the Viking Age no doubt contained many other things besides sword-play and fighting, the features written about by the saga-writers, who belonged to later generations. The world of the Norsemen was also to a great extent characterized by work, home, women and children, by love, friendship and family traditions. They too had their dreams as we do—and after all, the difference between men in different ages is not as great as we sometimes think.

They bore within them the knowledge that a mighty ocean separated them from family and friends in Greenland, but they very likely tried to suppress these and similar thoughts. And that was not too hard, for they were young people, having the strength and ability to fend for themselves. They were a people with experience gained from dangerous voyages across the ocean, with open minds and a desire for new experiences in new and strange countries; and in Vinland their lust for adventure was given free rein. Wherever they turned, they encountered unknown shores, forests and rivers full of salmon, and caribou grazing up in the hills. It was a land without end.

Uppermost in their minds was the need to wrest a living from the land; their problem was the same as that of Stone-Age man. Their life in Greenland had made them expert hunters, trappers, and fishermen, but in the new land they encountered new problems. Over what routes did the caribou migrate? What might be the best spots between the islands to harpoon seals? And the hunting of wild animals in big forests was something entirely new for people coming from an Arctic island.

And what about the women? It is worthy of note that the women of the

Viking Age would often accompany their men on their hazardous voyages across the great oceans. They must have been strong women, not least in mind. Women went on Karlsefni's Vinland expedition, and their work in the wilds must have been as significant as that of the Eskimo and Indian women. Eirik the Red's Saga, in telling about the Karlsefni expedition, relates that the men began to fight over the women. I am willing to believe that few passages in the sagas have greater authenticity.

One day in Vinland, a woman gave birth to a child. She was Gudrid, the beautiful wife of Thorfinn Karlsefni. The baby was a boy whom they called Snorri, and he was the first European known to have been born in North America. Was he born in one of the houses at L'Anse aux Meadows?

But a shadow fell across the little settlement in Vinland. On their scouting and hunting trips the men had discovered traces of natives, they had found stone implements, they had seen a fast canoe disappear among the islands. There were other people living in the country. What were they like? They had to be alert, to carry their weapons always, there was no knowing what might happen next. If, in addition, the hunting and fishing turned out to be poor, it is probable that the people living in that strange and distant land would feel discouraged at times.

At L'Anse aux Meadows, then, day followed day and everyone was occupied with his work. In time, men and women would adjust themselves to conditions in the new land. The hunters, armed with bows and spears, would set off into the forests and over the hills in search of the caribou. And they would return bowed down with a heavy load of bleeding meat. Others would go out in small boats to fish or to harpoon a seal. The women would stay in the houses, sewing, preparing skins or cooking, while from time to time some would go out to look for the hunters. From the other side of the river one could hear the beat of a hammer—it was the smith at work.

During the evening they would sit by the long fire, the flames flickering and the smoke slowly rising up through the smoke-hole. And the people would talk about their work and the new and strange land to which they had come, and about their homeland far to the north.

It was my last day at L'Anse aux Meadows. Going for a walk around the site, I took a last look at the excavations—the result of our work during the past years.

I jumped from stone to stone across Black Duck Brook and walked up to the smithy at the top of the terrace. I let my hand slide over the anvil, a smooth stone, one end of which had been broken off. I stood for a while at the pit near by where they made charcoal. I picked up a piece and looked at the very fine annual rings in the wood. I then walked over to the sites where the people lived a thousand years ago, to the hearths, the small ember pits that had been constructed with such great care, and the cooking pit, in which meat had been placed on top of the hot stones and then covered. If only one of these objects could speak!

Right at that spot, on the earthen benches, people used to sit and talk about everything within their ken. Then, when darkness lowered over the ocean, islands, and forests, one after the other would pull his fur blanket round him and lie down for the night. The last one went about it more slowly; with a wooden stick he would carefully scrape all the embers into the little stone chamber and cover them with a layer of ashes.

An old Norwegian verse comes to mind:

> I bury my fire
> late in the evening
> when day is done.
> God grant that my fire
> may never go out.

A stiff breeze came in from the sea, but the air was clear, and the setting sun bathed the green meadow in a soft light. There was a wide view across to the islands and over the ocean. To the north, Belle Isle with its steep shores hovered above the sea like a fairy castle, and in the far distance I could make out the blue coast of Labrador, the coast which the Vinland voyagers had followed southward about a thousand years ago.

My thoughts reverted once more to those bold Norsemen who set out to sea in open ships, sometimes taking women with them, but a compass never, and with only some simple tools with which to fight for existence.

In them there was a thirst for adventure, but I believe that foremost in their thoughts was the hope of finding a new and good land, where their families could settle and live.

Thus it was that young sailors once stood under a square sail, gazing wonderingly across the water to where a strange shore rose above the sea— a New World.

Notes

I THE WAY TO THE WEST

1. *Meddelelser om Grønland*, 88, I (1934).

2. That Greenland had the status of a free state is the prevailing opinion among
   scholars today. Among those who have subscribed to this opinion are Bjørn
   Magnússon Olsen, Finnur Jónsson, Einar Arnórsson, Olafur Lárusson and Knut
   Robberstad.
   See also Johan Schreiner, 'Leiv Eiriksson og Vinland', *Aftenposten* (Oslo: November 5th, 1964); and Helge Ingstad, *Land Under the Pole Star* (Cape, London, 1966),
   p. 225.

3. *Bergsbók* (Parchment Folio No. 1, in the Royal Library, Stockholm), ed. Gustaf
   Lindblad. *Early Icelandic Manuscripts in Facsimile*, V (Copenhagen 1963).

4. *Íslendinga sögur*, 26 (Fosterbrothers' Saga: Reykjavik 1899).

5. *Grønlands historiske Mindesmaerker*, II (1838), p. 681.

6. Saga Hákon Hákonarsonar (Codex Frisianus), MS. No. 45, Fol. Arnamagnaean
   Collection, University Library, Copenhagen. *Corpus codicum Island medii aevi*, 4
   (Copenhagen 1932).

7. *Medd. om Grønl.*, 67 (1924).

8. Fr C. C. Hansen: *Anthropologia medico-historica Groenlandiae antiqua: Herjolfsnes,
   Medd. om Grønl.*, 67 (1924), No. 3.

9. K. Fischer-Møller: *Medd. om Grønl.*, 89 (1942), No. 2. See also Ingstad, op. cit.,
   pp. 306–9.

10. Ibid., pp. 325–32.

II OLD MANUSCRIPTS TELL OF VINLAND THE GOOD

1. *Grønl. Hist. Mindes.*, III (1845), pp. 242–3.

2. Adam of Bremen: *Adami Gesta Hammaburgensis (Descriptio insularum aquilonis)*. A
   Norwegian translation by Halvdan Koht appears in *Historia Norvegiae: Den eldste
   Noregshistoria* (2nd edn, Oslo 1950), p. 88.

3. *Ísl. sögur*, I (Reykjavik 1953), pp. 1–20.

4. *Ísl. sögur*, I, pp. 96–7.

Notes

5. *Studies on the Vineland Voyages* (Copenhagen 1889), pp. 61–3.
6. *Ísl. sögur*, I, pp. 267–8.
7. *Íslenzk fornrit*, 4 (Reykjavik 1935), p. 135.
8. *Ísl. sögur*, VI (Reykjavik 1953), pp. 31 and 98,
9. *Íslandske Annaler indtil 1578* (Christiania 1888), p. 112.
10. *Grønl. Hist. Mindes.*, III, pp. 218–22.
11. *Norges Indskrifter med de yngre runer*. *Hønen-Runerne fra Ringerike* (Christiania 1902). Cf. *Norges Indskrifter indtil Reformationen* (Oslo 1951), pp. 23–68.
12. *Ísl. sögur*, I, pp. 361–90.
13. Ibid., pp. 323–59.
14. *Kungl. Vitterhets- Historie- och Antikvitetsakad. Handlingar*. D. 60:1 (1948).
15. *The Norse Discoverers of America* (Oxford 1921), p. 139.

VI SAILING INFORMATION AND TOPOGRAPHICAL DESCRIPTIONS IN THE SAGAS

1. *Location of Helluland, Markland and Vinland from the Icelandic Sagas* (St John's 1914).
2. *De gamla nordbornas Helluland, Markland och Vinland* (Åbo 1941), No. 1.
3. *Norse Discoverers.*

VII GRAPES AND SKRAELINGS

1. *Nord i Tåkeheimen* (Christiania 1911), pp. 238–304.
2. St Brendan, Abbot of Clonfert. *La 'Navigatio Sancti Brendani' in antico veneziano. Edita ed illustrata da Francesco Novati* (from MS. Ambrosianum D 158) (Bergamo 1892).
3. William Alexander, Earl of Stirling: *An Encouragement to Colonies* (London 1624).
4. Nicolas Denys: *The Description and Natural History of the Coasts of North American Acadia*, tr. by W. F. Ganong (Toronto 1908). Orig. edn *Description géographique et historique des costes de l'Amérique septentrionale. Avec l'histoire naturelle du pais* (Paris 1672).
5. 'Brev fra pave Gregor IX til erkebispen i Nidaros 11. mai 1237', *Diplomatarium Norvegicum*, 1 (1847), No. 16.
6. Sven Söderberg, 'Vinland. Föredrag i Filologiska sällskapet i Lund, mai 1898': reference in *Sydsvenska Dagbladet Snällposten*, 295, Malmö, October 30th, 1910.
7. *Instituttet for sammenlignende kulturforskning* (Oslo 1928), Series A.9, pp. 190–230.
8. *Rhodora*, 12 (1910), pp. 1–38.
9. Gustav Storm: 'Om Betydningen af "Eyktarstadr" i Flatbøgens Beretning om Vinlandsreiserne', *Arkiv for Nordisk Filologi*, 3 (Christiania 1886), pp. 121–31.
10. *Hvor lå Vinland?* (Oslo 1954).
11. *Grønl. Hist. Mindes.*, III (1845), pp. 238–43.
12. *Historical and Statistical Information* ... (Philadelphia 1851–3).

VIII OLD MAPS AND OTHER PRE-COLUMBIAN VOYAGES

1. The copy of the Skálholt map is in the Royal Library, Copenhagen (Gl. kgl. saml. No. 2881). See also N. E. Nørlund: *Islands Kortlaegning* (Copenhagen 1944).

2. *Studies on the Vineland Voyages.*

3. *Vestervejen* (Copenhagen 1954).

4. The Resen map of 1605 is in the Royal Library, Copenhagen. See also Nørlund, op. cit.

5. *The Kensington Stone* (Ephraim, Wisconsin, 1932).

6. Johannes Brøndsted: 'Norsemen in North America before Columbus' (Washington 1953).

7. The letter was first published in Montalboddo Fracan: *Paesi novamente retrovati, et Novo Mondo da Alberico Vesputio Fiorentino intitulato* (Vicentia 1507: facsimile edn, Princeton 1916), pp. 145–7.

8. *Medd. om Grønl.*, 88 (1936), pp. 34–5.

9. *Naturens Verden* (Copenhagen 1961), pp. 353–84.

10. Gisle Oddson: 'Annalium in Islandia farrago' and 'De mirabilibus Islandiae', ed. Halldór Hermansson, *Islandica*, 10 (1917), pp. 2–84.

11. *Det Norske Folks Historie*, V, 1, pp. 314–15.

12. *Det gamle Grønlands Beskrivelse*, ed. Finnur Jónsson (Copenhagen 1930), pp. 29–30.

13. *Grønl. Hist. Mindes.*, III (1845), pp. 120–3.

14. Ibid., pp. 482–4.

15. *Historisk-Topografiske Skrifter om Norge og norske Landsdele, forfattede i Norge i 16. Aarhundrede*, publ. for Det Norske Kildeskriftfond by Gustav Storm (Christiania 1895), p. 85.

16. Asgaut Steinnes: 'Ein Nordpolsekspedisjon år 1360', *Syn og Segn*, 64 (1952), pp. 32–67.

17. Nansen, op. cit., pp. 385–6.

18. Francisco Lopez de Gómara: *La historia general de las Indias* (Anvers 1554), Part I, p. 31. Orig. edn *La Istoria de las Indias y Conquista de Mexico* (Zaragoza 1552).

IX ALONG THE COAST OF NORTH AMERICA

1. *Location of Helluland ...*

2. *Lost America* (Washington 1951).

3. *Naturens Verden* (1961), pp. 353–84.

4. *American Anthropologist*, 57 (1955), pp. 35–43.

5. *Studies on the Vineland Voyages.*

Notes

XI FIRST FLIGHT OVER LABRADOR

1. V. Tanner: 'Outlines of the geography, life and customs of Newfoundland-Labrador', *Acta Geographica Fenniae*, 8 (Helsinki 1944), p. 622.

XIII L'ANSE AUX MEADOWS: THE EXCAVATIONS BEGIN

1. *Medd. om Grønl.*, 89, I (1941), pp. 244–5.
2. Ingstad: *Land Under the Pole Star*, p. 95.

XIV THE LAND AND THE PEOPLE

1. *Klima-vekslinger i historisk og postglacial tid* (Oslo 1926), and *Klima-vekslinger i Nordens historie* (Oslo 1925).
2. *Norsk geogr. tidsskr.*, XIII (Oslo 1951–2), pp. 56–75; and *Norsk geogr. tidsskr.*, XI (Oslo 1946–7), pp. 290–326.
3. 'Nordboernes Undergang på Grønland i geologisk Belysning', *Det Grønlandske Selskabs Aarsskrift* (Copenhagen 1935), pp. 5–18.
4. 'The Climate of Greenland in the 11th and 16th Centuries.'
5. Henry Percival Biggar: *The Precursors of Jacques Cartier, 1497–1534* (Ottawa 1911), p. 64.
6. Ibid.
7. H. P. Biggar: 'The Voyages of Jacques Cartier: publ. from the originals with translations, note and appendices', *Publ. of the Public Archives of Canada* (Ottawa 1924).
8. William Taylor: 'The Fragments of Eskimo Prehistory', *The Beaver* (Winnipeg: Spring 1965).
9. On this subject, see the following authorities:
   Junius Bird: 'Archaeology of the Hopedale Area, Labrador', *Anthropological Papers of the American Museum of Natural History*, 39 (1945), pp. 125–86.
   Elmer Harp, Jr: *The Cultural Affinities of the Newfoundland Dorset Eskimo* (Ottawa 1964).
   —— 'An Archaeological Reconnaissance in the Strait of Belle Isle Area', *American Antiquarian*, 16 (1951), pp. 203–20.
   Diamond Jennes: 'Note on the Beothuk Indians of Newfoundland', *Canadian Dept of Mines: Annual Report for 1927*. Bulletin 56 (1929), pp. 36–9.
   T. G. B. Lloyd: 'On the Stone Implements of Newfoundland', *Journal of the Royal Anthropological Institute, London*, 5 (1875), pp. 233–48.
   W. J. Wintemberg: 'Eskimo Sites of the Dorset Culture in Newfoundland', *American Antiquarian*, 5 (1939), pp. 83–102.
10. According to information supplied to me by Dr William Taylor, Senior Archaeologist at the National Museum of Canada, Ottawa.
11. Elmer Harp, Jr: *Cultural Affinities*; and 'An Archaeological Reconnaissance', pp. 203–20.

12. Information supplied to me by Dr. R. E. Seary, Memorial University, St John's, Newfoundland.

XV   TO THE 'WONDER BEACHES' OF THE SAGA

  1. *The Voyages of the Norsemen to America* (New York 1914).

XVI   ALONG THE COAST OF LABRADOR

  1. W. G. Gosling: *Labrador: its discovery, exploration and development* (London 1910), pp. 309–12.

XVII   TO NORTHERNMOST LABRADOR

  1. *Vinlandsferdene* (Oslo 1937).
  2. *Studies on the Vineland Voyages.*

XX   THE EXCAVATIONS CONTINUE—A JOURNEY TO WHITE BAY

  1. *Lost America.*

XXII   THE FAR WANDERERS

  1. H. P. Biggar: *The Precursors of Jacques Cartier*, p. 64.
  2. Richard Hakluyt: *Divers Voyages Touching the Discovery of America and the Islands Adjacent* (Hakluyt Society, London, 1850), VII, p. 23. Quoted by Fridtjof Nansen: *In Northern Mist* (London 1911), II, p. 333.
  3. J. P. Howley: *The Beothucs or Red Indians* (Cambridge 1915), p. 11.
  4. Ibid., p. 17.

Bibliography

Adam of Bremen: *Adami Gesta Hammaburgensis ecclesiae pontificum ex recensione Lappenbergii.* Ed. altera (Hannover 1876).

Ahlmann, Hans W.: 'Den nutida klimatfluktuationen och dess utforskande', *Norsk geogr. tidsskr.,* XI (Oslo 1946–7), pp. 290–326.

—— 'Glaciärer och klimat i Norden under de senaste tusentalen år', *Norsk geogr. tidsskr.,* XIII (Oslo 1951–2), pp. 56–75.

—— 'Is och eld', *Polarboken* (Oslo 1957), pp. 50–55.

Andersen, Magnus: *Vikingfaerden: En illustrert beskrivelse af 'Vikings' reise i 1893* (Christiania 1895).

Antiquitates Americanae sive scriptores septentrionales rerum ante-Columbiarum in America. Publ. Societas Regia Antiquariorum Septentrionalium (Hafnia 1837).

Arbman, Holger: *The Vikings.* Translated and edited with an introduction by Allan Binns (London & New York 1961).

Beyer, Absalon Pedersøn: *Om Norgis Rige.* Ed. Harald Beyer (Bergen 1928).

Biggar, Henry Percival: *The Precursors of Jacques Cartier, 1497–1534.* A Collection of Documents Relating to the Early History of the Dominion of Canada (Ottawa 1911).

Bird, Junius B.: 'Archaeology of the Hopedale Area, Labrador', *Anthropological Papers of the American Museum of Natural History,* 39 (1945), pp. 125–86.

Bjørnbo, Axel Anthon: *Carthographia Groenlandica* (Copenhagen 1912). *Medd. om Grønl.,* 48.

Bobé, Louis: *Opdagelsesrejser til Gronland, 1473–1806* (Copenhagen 1936). *Medd. om Grønl.,* 55, No. 1.

Bruun, Daniel: *Arkaeologiske Undersøgelser i Julianehaabs Distrikt* (Copenhagen 1896). *Medd. om Grønl.,* 16, pp. 171–495.

—— *Fortidsminder og nutidshjem paa Island. Ny omarbeidet og forøget udgave med et tillaeg om Nordbogaardene i Grønland* (Copenhagen 1928).

—— *The Icelandic colonization of Greenland, and the finding of Vineland* (Copenhagen 1918). *Medd. om Grønl.,* 57.

—— *Oversigt over Nordoruiner i Godthaab- og Frederikshaab-Distrikter* (Copenhagen 1918). *Medd. om Grønl.,* 56, pp. 55–147.

Brøgger, A. W.: *Den norske bosetningen på Shetland-Orknøyene. Studier og resultater* (Oslo 1930).

—— *Vinlandsferdene* (Oslo 1937).

—— 'Vinlandsferdene', *Norsk geogr. tidsskr.,* 6 (Oslo 1937), pp. 65–85.

Bibliography

Brøgger, A. W., and Haakon Shetelig: *Vikingeskipene. Deres forgjengere og etterfølgere* (Oslo 1950). English edn: *The Viking Ships* (Oslo 1953).

Brøndsted, Johannes: 'Norsemen in North America before Columbus', Smithsonian Institution (Washington 1953), pp. 367–405.

—— *Vikingerne* (Copenhagen 1960). English edn: *The Vikings* (Baltimore 1960; revised 1965).

Bugge, Alexander: 'Skibsfarten fra de ældste tider til omkring aar 1600', *Den norske sjøfarts historie* (Christiania 1923), pp. 8–369.

Bugge, Sophus: *Norges indskrifter med de yngre runer. Hønenrunen fra Ringerike* (Christiania 1904).

Bårdssøn, Ívar: *Det gamle Grønlands beskrivelse. Udg. efter Håndskrifterne af Finnur Jónsson* (Copenhagen 1930).

Collins, Henry B.: *Arctic Area. Indigenous Period* (Mexico 1954).

—— 'Recent development in the Dorset culture area', *Memoirs of the Society for American Archaeology*, 9 (1953), pp. 32–9.

Devold, Finn: 'Klimaforandringer', *Polarårboken* (Oslo 1954), pp. 33–41.

Diplomatarium Norvegicum, XVII (Christiania 1913).

Egede, Hans: *Omstaendelig og udførlig Relation angaaende den Grønlandske Missions Begyndelse og Fortsaettelse* (Copenhagen 1738).

Egede, Poul Hansen: *Continuation af Hans Egedes Relationer fra Grønland* (Copenhagen 1939). *Medd. om Grønl.*, 120.

Fernald, Merritt Lyndon: 'Notes on the Plants of Wineland the Good', *Rhodora*, 12 (Lancaster, Pa., 1910), pp. 1–38.

Fischer, Joseph: *The Discoveries of the Norsemen in America*. Tr. from the German by Basil H. Soulsby (London 1903).

Fischer-Møller, K.: 'The mediaeval Norse settlements in Greenland' (Copenhagen 1942). *Medd. om Grønl.*, 89, No. 2.

Fiske, John: *The Discovery of America* (London 1892).

Fægri, Knut: 'Omkring Grønlandsbygdenes undergang', *Naturen* (Bergen 1957), pp. 432–6.

Gathorne-Hardy, G. M.: *The Norse Discoverers of America*. The Wineland Sagas translated and discussed by G. M. G.-H. (Oxford 1921).

Gjessing, Gutorm: *Fangstfolk, et streiftog gjennom Nord-Norsk førhistorie* (Oslo 1941).

Godfrey, William S.: 'Vikings in America. Theories and Evidence', *American Anthropologist*, 57 (1955), pp. 35–43.

Gosling, W. G.: *Labrador: its discovery, exploration, and development* (London 1910).

Gray, Edward F.: *Leif Eriksson, discoverer of America A.D. 1003* (London 1930).

Grenfell, Wilfred T.: *Labrador, the Country and the People* (New York 1909).

Grønlands Historiske Mindesmaerker, I–III (Copenhagen 1838–45).

Gudmundsson, Valtyr: *Privatboligen paa Island i Sagatiden* (Copenhagen 1889).

Hakluyt, Richard: *Divers Voyages Touching the Discovery of America and the Islands Adjacent*. Ed. with Notes and Introduction by John Winter Jones (Hakluyt Society, London 1850), VII.

Harp, Elmer, Jr: 'An Archaeological Reconnaissance in the Strait of Belle Isle Area', *American Antiquarian*, 16 (1951), pp. 203–20.

Harp, Elmer, Jr: *The Cultural Affinities of the Newfoundland Dorset Eskimo* (Ottawa 1964).

Harisse, Henry: *The Discovery of North America* (London 1892).

Hauge, Torbjørn D.: *Blesterbruk og myrjern. Studier i den gamle jernvinna i det østenfjeldske Norge* (Oslo 1946).

Haugen, Einar (tr.): *Voyages to Vinland* (New York 1942).

Hermansson, Halldór: *The Norsemen in America (982–c. 1500)* (Ithaca, N.Y. 1909). *Islandica*, II.

Hoffman, Bernard G.: *Cabot to Cartier. Sources for a Historical Ethnography of Northeastern North America 1497–1550* (Toronto 1961).

Holand, Hjalmar R.: *Explorations in America before Columbus* (New York 1956).

Holtved, Erik: 'Har Nordboerne været i Thule Distriktet?' *Fra Nationalmuseets Arbejdsmark* (Copenhagen 1945), pp. 79–84.

Hovgaard, William: *The Voyages of the Norsemen to America* (New York 1914).

Howley, James P.: *The Beothucs or Red Indians* (Cambridge 1915.)

Ingstad, Helge: *Landet med de kalde kyster* (Oslo 1948).

—— *Landet under Leidarstjernen. En ferd til Grønlands norrøne bygder* (Oslo 1959).

—— *Land under the Pole Star* (Cape, London 1966) (English edn of the above).

—— *Nunamiut. Blant Alaskas innlands-eskimoer* (Oslo 1951).

—— 'Vinland Ruins Prove Vikings Found the New World', *National Geographic Magazine* (Washington, November 1964).

—— *Øst for den store bre* (Oslo 1935). English edn: *East of the Great Glacier* (New York 1937).

Isachsen, Gunnar: *Grønland og Grønlandsisen* (Oslo 1925).

—— 'Hvor langt mot nord kom de norrøne grønlendinger på sine fangstferder i ubygdene?' *Norsk geogr. tidsskr.*, IV (Oslo 1932), pp. 75–92.

Iversen, Johs: *Moorgeologische Untersuchungen auf Grönland* (Copenhagen 1934). *Medd. fra Dansk geol. Foren.*, 8.

—— 'Nordboernes Undergang på Grønland i geologisk Belysning', *Grønl. Selskabs. Aarskr., 1935* (Copenhagen 1935), pp. 5–18.

Jansson, Sven B. F.: 'Sagorna om Vinland, 1. Handskrifterna till Erik den Rödes saga', *Kungl. Vitterhets- Historie- och Antikvitets akademins Handlingar.* D. 60: 1 (1948).

Jansson, Valter: *Nordiska vin-namn. En ortnamnstyp och dess historia* (Lund, 1951).

Jennes, D.: 'Notes on the Beothuk Indians of Newfoundland', *Canadian Department of Mines: Annual Report for 1927.* Bulletin 56 (1929), pp. 36–9.

Johannesson, Jon: *The Date of the Composition of the Saga of the Greenlanders*. Tr. by Tryggvi J. Oleson. Saga Book XVI, 1963, pp. 54–66.

Johnsen, Oscar Albert: *Noregsveldets undergang. Et utsyn og et oppgjør. Nedgangstiden* (Oslo 1944).

Jones, Gwyn: *The Norse Atlantic Saga* (London 1964).

Jónsson, Finnur: 'Eirik den Rødes Saga og Vinland', *Historisk Tidsskrift* (Christiania 1912), pp. 116–47.

—— 'Grønlands gamle Topografi efter Kilderne. Østerbygden og Vesterbygden' (Copenhagen 1899). *Medd. om Grønl.*, 20, pp. 265–329.

—— 'Opdagelsen af og Rejserne til Vinland', *Aarbøger for nordisk Oldkyndighed og Historie* (1915), pp. 205–21.

Bibliography

Kejlbo, Ib Rønne: 'Claudius Clavus and the Vinland Map', *American-Scandinavian Review*, 54 (1966), pp. 126–31.

Koht, Halvdan: *Den eldste Noregshistoria*. Tr. from Latin (Oslo 1950).

Kongespeilet (Konungs skuggsjá). *Speculum Regale*. De norske håndskrifter i faksimile (Oslo 1947). English edn: *The King's Mirror*, tr. Laurence Marcellus Larson (New York 1917).

Kulturhistorisk Leksikon for nordisk Middelalder fra vikingtid til reformasjonstid (Oslo 1956–).

Landnámabók Islands (Copenhagen 1925).

Larsen, Helge, and Jørgen Meldgaard: 'Paleo-eskimo cultures in Disko Bugt, West Greenland' (Copenhagen 1958). *Medd. om Grønl.*, 161, No. 2.

Lloyd, T. G. B.: 'On the Beothucs, a Tribe of Red Indians', *Journal of the Royal Anthropological Institute*, 4 (London 1874), pp. 21–39.

—— 'A Further Account of the Beothucs of Newfoundland', *Journ. Royal Anthr. Inst.*, 5 (London 1875), pp. 222–30.

Løberg, Leif: 'Norrøne Amerikaferders utstrekning', *Norsk hist. tidsskr.* (Oslo 1962).

Magnussen, Finn: 'Om de Engelskes Handel og Færd paa Island i det 15de Aarhundrede', *Nordisk Tidsskrift for Oldkyndighed*, 2 (Copenhagen 1833), pp. 112–69.

Magnusson, M., and Hermann Pálsson (tr. and ed.): *The Vinland Sagas* (Baltimore 1965).

Mallery, Arlington H.: *Lost America. The Story of Iron-Age Civilization Prior to Columbus* (Washington 1951).

Mathiassen, Th.: 'Eskimoernes Sammentræf med nordboerne i Grønland', *Grønland* (Copenhagen 1953), pp. 139–42.

—— *Inugsuk. A mediaeval Eskimo settlement in Upernivik District, West Greenland* (Copenhagen 1931). *Medd. om Grønl.*, 77, pp. 145–339.

—— *The Sermermiut excavations, 1955* (Copenhagen 1958). *Medd. om Grønl.*, 161, No. 3.

Mathiassen, Th., in collaboration with Erik Holtved: 'The Eskimo archaeology of Julianehaab District. With a brief summary of the prehistory of the Greenlanders' (Copenhagen 1936). *Medd. om Grønl.*, 118, No. 1.

Meldgaard, Jørgen: 'Fra Brattalid til Vinland', *Naturens Verden* (Copenhagen 1961), pp. 353–84.

—— 'Om de gamle Nordboere og deres skæbne. Betragtninger over Helge Ingstads bog *Landet under Polarstjernen*', *Grønland* (Copenhagen 1961), pp. 93–102.

—— 'A Paleo-Eskimo Culture in West Greenland', *American Antiquarian*, 17 (1951–2), pp. 222–30.

Mohn, Henrik: *Vindene i den nordlige del av Nordsjøen og vikingetogene* (Christiania 1914).

Munch, P. A.: *Det Norske Folks Historie* (Christiania 1852–63).

Munn, W. A.: *Wineland Voyages. Location of Helluland, Markland, and Vinland* (St John's 1929).

Næss, Almar: *Hvor lå Vinland?* En studie over solobservasjoner i de norrøne sagaer: with a summary in English (Oslo 1954).

Nansen, Fridtjof: *Klima-vekslinger i historisk og postglacial tid* (Oslo 1926).

—— *Klima-vekslinger i Nordens Historie* (Oslo 1925).

—— *Nord i Tåkeheimen. Utforskningen av jordens nordlige strøk i tidlige tider* (Christiania 1911). English edn: *In Northern Mists. Arctic Exploration in Early Times*, tr. Arthur G. Chater (London 1911).

—— 'The Norsemen in America', *Geographical Journal* (London 1911), pp. 557–80.

Nielsen, Niels: 'Jærnudvindingen paa Island i fordums Tider', *Aarbøger for nordisk Oldkyndighed*, III, 16 (1926), pp. 129–74.

—— *Evidence on the extraction of iron in Greenland by the Norsemen* (Copenhagen 1930). *Medd. om Grønl.*, 76, pp. 195–210.

—— *Evidence of iron extraction at Sandnes, in Greenland's west settlement* (Copenhagen 1936). *Medd. om Grønl.*, 88, No. 4.

'Norges indskrifter med de yngre runer', *Norges indskrifter indtil Reformationen* (Oslo 1951), pp. 23–68.

Nørlund, Poul: *Buried Norsemen at Herjolfsnes* (Copenhagen 1924). *Medd. om Grønl.*, 67, pp. 1–271.

—— *De gamle Nordbobygder ved verdens ende. Skildringer fra Grønlands Middelalder* (Copenhagen 1934).

Nørlund, Poul, in collaboration with Aage Roussell: *Norse Ruins at Gardar, the Episcopal Seat of Mediaeval Greenland* (Copenhagen 1930). *Medd. om Grønl.*, 76, pp. 1–170.

Nørlund, Poul, and Mårten Stenberger: *Brattahlid* (Copenhagen 1934). *Medd. om Grønl.*, 88.

Norsk biografisk leksikon (Oslo 1921–).

Norske folks liv og historie gjennem tidene, Det (Oslo 1929–35), vols. I–III.

Olsen, Magnus: *Farms and fanes of ancient Norway* (Oslo 1928).

—— 'Rúnar er ristu rýnastir menn', *Norsk tidsskrift for sprogvidenskap,* V (1932), pp. 167–88.

—— *Sigtuna-Amuletten. Nogen tolkningsbidrag* (Oslo 1940).

Osterman, H.: *Nordmaend på Grønland 1721–1814*, two vols. (Oslo 1940).

Oxenstierna, Count Eric: *The Norsemen* (Greenwich, Conn. 1965).

Paasche, Fredrik: *Landet med de mørke skibene* (Oslo 1938).

—— *Norges og Islands litteratur indtil utgangen av Middelalderen* (Oslo 1957).

Petersen, Jan: *Vikingetidens redskaper* (Oslo 1951).

Reeves, Arthur Middleton (ed. and trans.): *The Finding of Wineland the Good. The History of the Icelandic Discovery of America* (London 1895).

Reynolds, Hans: *Grønland: Vestre Bygdi* (Oslo 1926).

Robertson, William: *History of America*, two vols. (London 1777).

Rogers, J. D.: *Newfoundland. A historical geography of the British colonies*, vol. V, part iv (Oxford 1911).

Roussell, Aage: *Farms and churches in the mediaeval Norse settlements of Greenland* (Copenhagen 1941). *Medd. om Grønl.*, 89, No. 1.

—— *Sandnes and the neighbouring farms* (Copenhagen 1936). *Medd. om Grønl.*, 88, No. 2.

Rowley, Graham: 'The Dorset culture of the Eastern Arctic', *American Anthropology,* New Series 42 (1940), pp. 490–9.

Schoolcraft, Henry R.: *Historical and Statistical Information Respecting the History, Condition and Prospects of the Indian Tribes of the United States*, three vols. (Philadelphia 1851–3).

Schreiner, Johan: 'Leiv Eiriksson og Vinland' (*Aftenposten*. Oslo: Nov. 5th, 1964).

Shetelig, Haakon: *Vikingeminner i Vest-Europa* (Oslo 1933). *Institutet for sammenlignende kulturforskning*, Ser. A. 16.

Bibliography

Skelton, Raleigh Ashlin: *Explorers' Maps. Chapters in the Cartographic Record of Geographical Discovery* (London 1958).

Snorri Sturluson: *The Prose Edda*, tr. Arthur G. Brodeur (New York 1916).

―― *Heimskringla. History of the Kings of Norway*, tr. Lee M. Hollander 1964).

Soga um Eirik Raude: Gamalnorsk grunntekst og nynorsk umsetjing ved Severin Eskeland: second edn (Oslo 1924).

Solberg, Ole: 'Ivar Bårdssøns Grønlandsbeskrivelse', *Norsk geogr. tidsskr.*, III (Oslo 1931), pp. 314–21.

Speck, Frank G.: *Beothuk and Micmac* (New York 1922).

―― 'Culture Problems in North-eastern North America', *Proceedings of the American Philosophical Society*, 65 (Philadelphia 1926), pp. 272–311.

Spjeldnes, Nils, and Kari E. Henningsmoen: 'Littorina littorea: an indicator of Norse settlement in North America?', *Science*, 141 (1963), pp. 275–6.

Steen, Sverre: 'Fartøier i Norden i Middelalderen', *Nordisk Kultur*, XVI (1934), pp. 282–300.

―― *Ferd og fest. Reiseliv i norsk sagatid og middelalder* (Oslo 1942).

Steensby, H. P.: *The Norsemen's route from Greenland to Wineland* (Copenhagen 1918). *Medd. om Grønl.*, 56, pp. 151–202.

―― 'Uddrag af Prof. dr. phil. H. P. Steensby's Dagbog om Rejsen til "Vinland"' (Copenhagen 1921). *Medd. om Grønl.*, 77, pp. 45–116.

Stefansson, Vilhjalmur: *Greenland* (New York 1942).

―― 'Greenland was a Republic in Leiv's time', *Leiv Eiriksson Review* (Brooklyn 1935).

Steinnes, Asgaut: 'Ein Nordpolsekspedisjon år 1360', *Syn og Segn* (1958), pp. 32–67.

Stenberger, Mårten: 'Island och Grönland som nordisk bygd under vikingetid och medeltid', *Ymer*, 61 (Stockholm 1941), pp. 241–63.

Storm, Gustav: *Islandske Annaler indtil 1578* (Christiania 1888).

―― *Studier over Vinlandsreisene, Vinlands geografi og ethnografi* (Copenhagen 1888).

English edn: *Studies on the Vineland Voyages* (Copenhagen 1889).

―― 'Søfareren Johannes Scolvus og hans reise til Labrador eller Grønland', *Historisk Tidsskr.*, Ser. 2, Vol. 5 (Christiania 1886), pp. 385–400.

Strong, William Duncan: 'A stone culture from northern Labrador and its relation to the Eskimo-like cultures of the North-east', *American Anthropology*, New Series 32 (1930), pp. 126–43.

Söderberg, Sven: 'Vinland.' Föredrag i Filologiska sällskapet i Lund, mai 1898. *Sydsvenska Dagbladet Snällposten*, no. 295, Oct. 30th, 1910 (Malmö).

Sølver, Carl V.: *Vestervejen. Om vikingernes sejlads* (Copenhagen 1954).

Tanner, V.: *De gamla nordbornas Helluland, Markland och Vinland. Ett försök att lokalisera Vinlands-resornas huvudetapper i de isländske sagorna* (Åbo 1941).

―― 'Outlines of the geography, life and customs of Newfoundland-Labrador', *Acta Geographica Fenniae* (Helsinki 1944).

―― 'Ruinerna på Sculpin Island (Kanayotok) i Nain's skärgård, Newfoundland-Labrador', *Geografisk tidskrift*, 44 (Copenhagen 1941), pp. 129–55.

Taylor, William E., Jr: 'Review and Assessment of the Dorset Problem', *Anthropologica*, 1 (Ottawa 1959), pp. 24–46.

Thórdarson, Matthias: *The Vinland Voyages* (New York 1930).

Torfaeus, Tormod: *Historia Vinlandiae Antiqua* (Copenhagen 1705).

Vebæk, Christen L.: 'The climate of Greenland in the 11th and 16th centuries', *Conference on the Climate of the 11th and 16th Centuries* (Aspen, Colorado, June 16th–24th, 1962).

—— 'Inland farms in the Norse East Settlement. Archaeological Investigations in Julianehaab District, Summer 1939' (Copenhagen 1943). *Medd. om Grønl.*, 90, pp. 1–110.

—— 'Nordboforskningen i Grønland. Resultater og fremtidsopgaver', *Geografisk tidsskrift*, 46 (Copenhagen 1943), pp. 101–28.

—— 'Topographical and archaeological investigations in the Norse Settlements in Greenland. A survey of the work of the last 10 years', *Third Viking Congress* (Reykjavik 1958), pp. 107–22.

—— 'Vatnahverfi', *Fra Nationalmuseets Arbejdsmark, 1952* (Copenhagen 1952), pp. 101–114.

Vilmundarson, Tórhallur: 'Reflections on the Vinland Map', *American-Scandinavian Review*, 54 (1966), pp. 20–4.

Vinland Map and the Tartar Relation, The, By R. A. Skelton, Thomas E. Marston and George D. Painter (New Haven and London 1965).

Visted, Kristoffer, and Hilmar Stigum: *Vår gamle hondekultur*, I (Oslo 1951).

Wahlfren, Erik: *The Kensington stone, a mystery solved* (Madison 1958).

Werenskiold, Werner: 'De norske bygders undergang på Grønland', *Norsk geogr. tidsskr.*, X (Oslo 1945), pp. 157–63.

Wintemberg, W. J.: 'Eskimo sites of the Dorset culture in Newfoundland', *American Antiquarian*, 5 (1939), pp. 309–33.

Index

ADAM OF BREMEN, 28–9, 69, 74–5, 76, 159–60
Ahlmann, Hans W., 145
Albert T. Gould (hospital boat), 111
Alexander, Dave, 207
Alexander, William, 72
Alexis Fjord, 172
Algonquin Indians, 80, 126, 148*n*, 188
Alphonse, Johan, 224
Ameralikfjord, 92
Andersen, Magnus, 35
Anderson, Job, 137
Anse aux Meadows, L', 18, 63, 72, 98, 132, 177, 182, 194–5
    author's arrival at, 114–15, 121
    excavation of house-sites, 122, 133–42, 174, 193, 195–207, 210–21
    ember pits, 134, 197, 210
    possible bath-house, 135
    few artifacts, 135–6, 219
    cairns, 140–42
    topography and life of, 143–7, 152–7, 225–7
    driftwood, 144–5
    Indians and Eskimoes and, 151, 169
    origin of name, 152
    large house-site, 174, 195, 204, 210–12, 214
    cooking pits, 197–8, 210
    iron extraction, 198–202
    smithy, 199–200
    Leif Eriksson's possible 'large houses' at, 211–12, 221
    reasons for believing sites Norse and pre-Columbian, 213, 214–21
    Norse spindle-whorl, 214–15, 216, 221
    proof of women's presence, 215, 221
    'long-house' type, 215
Anticosti Island, 127, 130
Archer, Colin, 122
Ari Marsson, 29, 59*n*
Ari Thorgilsson, 29
Arnald, Bishop, 30
arrow-head, quartzite, 93
auks, great, 146, 151
Avaldamon, 59, 80

Baccalieu (coastal vessel), 109
Baffin Island, 21, 28, 60, 63, 65, 69, 132, 150, 177, 178, 179, 220

Bang, Hans Hvide, 179, 182, 186, 193, 204, 207
Bareis, Charles, 204
bath-houses, 135
Battle Harbour, 173
Bauld, Cape, 64, 84, 112
Beardmore (Ontario), 90
Beardsley, Tony, 214
bears:
    polar, 21, 53, 95, 113, 131, 132, 145, 155, 161–2, 208
    black, 117, 154, 165–6, 180, 181
Belle Isle, 63, 66, 115, 133, 158, 173, 227
Belle Isle, Strait of, 66, 84, 90, 103, 106, 107, 122–3, 131–2, 140, 145, 148, 151, 158, 173, 175, 209
beluga, 123, 125
Beotuk Indians, 107, 148–9, 150, 209
Bergen, 21, 23, 95, 96
Bergsland, Kurt, 85–6
berries, wild, 72–3, 76, 140, 144, 147, 155, 173, 174–5, 208, 220
Beyer, Absalon Pedersen, 95
Bianco, B. Andrea, 87
Bird, Dr Junius, 204, 212–13, 214
Bird, Peggy, 214
biafal garment, 53
Bjarmeland, 31
Bjarney, 53, 65
Bjarneyar, 53
Bjarni Herjolfsson, 17, 32, 33, 37, 39–41, 52, 54, 55, 58, 65
    route and topography, 60–62, 69, 112, 163
Black Death, 23
Black Duck Brook, 114, 133, 140, 156, 174, 196–203, 217, 226
    smithy near, 199–203, 205
Black Duck Pond, 140
Blake, Carson, 137
Blake, Sidney, 117
Blanc-Sablon, 131, 148
bog-iron, 20, 136, 198–203
Botten, Harald, 16
Bradore Bay, 131
Bragi the Old, 75
Brattahlid, 16–17, 20, 38, 41, 43, 46, 52, 65, 135, 221
Brendan, St, 71
Brøgger, A. W., 67, 177

Index

Index

Index

Index